The Quality Toolbox

D1637452

Also available from ASQ Quality Press

The Change Agents' Handbook: A Survival Guide for Quality
Improvement Champions
David W. Hutton

Reinventing Communication: A Guide to Using Visual Language for
Planning, Problem Solving, and Reengineering
Larry Raymond

Excellence Is a Habit: How to Avoid Quality Burnout
Thomas J. Barry

Mapping Work Processes
Dianne Galloway

The ASQ Total Quality Management Series

> TQM: *Leadership for the Quality Transformation*
> Richard S. Johnson
>
> TQM: *Management Processes for Quality Operations*
> Richard S. Johnson
>
> TQM: *The Mechanics of Quality Processes*
> Richard S. Johnson and Lawrence E. Kazense
>
> TQM: *Quality Training Practices*
> Richard S. Johnson

To request a complimentary catalog of publications, call 800-248-1946.

The Quality Toolbox

Nancy R. Tague

ASQ Quality Press
Milwaukee, Wisconsin

The Quality Toolbox
Nancy R. Tague

Library of Congress Cataloging-in-Publication Data

Tague, Nancy R., 1955–
    The quality toolbox / Nancy R. Tague.
        p.   cm.
    Includes bibliographical references and index.
    ISBN 0-87389-314-X (alk. paper)
    1. Group problem solving.   2. Self-directed work groups.
    I. Title.
    HD30.28.T33   1994
    658.4'036—dc20   94-33049
                                                      CIP

10 9 8 7 6

ISBN 0-87389-314-X

Acquisitions Editor: Susan Westergard
Project Editor: Jeanne W. Bohn
Production Editor: Annette Wall
Marketing Administrator: Mark Olson
Set in Avant Garde and Sabon by Linda J. Shepherd.
Cover design by Paul Tobias.

ASQ Mission: To facilitate continuous improvement and increase customer satisfaction by identifying, communicating, and promoting the use of quality principles, concepts, and technologies; and thereby be recognized throughout the world as the leading authority on, and champion for, quality.

For a free copy of the ASQ Quality Press Publications Catalog, including ASQ membership information, call 800-248-1946.

Printed in the United States of America

  Printed on acid-free recycled paper

American Society for Quality

Quality Press
611 East Wisconsin Avenue
P.O. Box 3005
Milwaukee, Wisconsin 53201-3005

For my parents
who taught me the most important lessons about quality
and who have always believed in me

Contents

Figures

Tables

Preface

The idea for this book originated when a group of facilitators in my company, well down the road of quality improvement, asked me to teach them new tools to use with their quality teams. They were stuck in a rut of using just a few familiar standards: brainstorming, multivoting, fishbone and Pareto diagrams. Their knowledge of the wide choice of methods and techniques that can be used in quality improvement was limited. Frustrated at being able to teach so few of the available tools in a training session, I decided to create a reference that they could use to locate and learn new tools on their own.

The question they asked after "What tools exist?" was "When do we use them?" The facilitators knew far more tools than they commonly used, but they did not know how to choose and apply tools at appropriate times during the process of quality improvement. So woven through the reference book was guidance on fitting the tools into the quality improvement process.

Since then, the book has been used with groups just getting started with quality improvement. It gives them more confidence with the basic tools and the quality improvement process they have learned. It also gives them a way to continue learning *just-in-time,* as they encounter needs for new methods. Team members, as well as facilitators and team leaders, have copies of the *Toolbox* on their shelves and refer to it between or during meetings.

Sometimes anything labeled "quality" is considered separate from day-to-day activities, but quality improvement extends into many areas that are not labeled "quality." Anyone planning strategy, solving a problem, developing a project plan, seeking ideas or agreement from other people, or trying to understand the customer better can use these tools to produce higher quality outcome more easily. By whatever name we call it, quality improvement should be a significant part of everything that every one of us does.

The Quality Toolbox is a comprehensive reference to a variety of methods and techniques: those most commonly used for quality improvement, many less commonly used, and a half dozen created by the author—not available elsewhere. The reader will find the widely used seven basic quality control tools (for example, fishbone diagram and Pareto chart) as well as some of the newer management and planning tools, sometimes called the seven new QC tools (for example, affinity diagram and arrow diagram). Tools are included for generating and organizing ideas, evaluating ideas, analyzing processes, determining root causes, planning, and basic data-handling and statistics.

Most reference books of statistical techniques do not include other quality improvement tools. Yet, those improving the quality of their work will need both kinds of tools at different times. This is true in both manufacturing and service organizations. In service organizations, and business and support functions of all organizations, people often fear statistical tools. They do not understand when and how to call upon their power. By combining both types of tools and providing guidance for when to use them, this book should open up the wide range of methods available for improvement.

The book is written and organized to be as simple as possible to use so that anyone can find and learn new tools without a teacher. Above all, *The Quality Toolbox* is an instruction book. The reader can learn new tools or, for familiar tools, discover new variations or applications. It also is a reference book. It is organized so that a half-remembered tool can be found and reviewed easily and so that the reader can quickly identify the right tool to solve a particular problem or achieve a specific goal.

With this book close at hand, a quality improvement team becomes capable of more efficient and effective work with less assistance from a trained quality consultant. I hope that quality and training professionals also will find the *Toolbox* a handy reference and quick way to expand their repertoire of tools, techniques, applications, and tricks.

Acknowledgments

The tools of quality improvement have been developed by many people over a long time. Some of the toolmakers are well known, but many of the tools have been talked and written about so often that their origins are lost. I have been able to identify originators of many of the tools and have given credit to their inventiveness in the notes. I am equally grateful to those whose names I do not know. Everyone who has contributed to the body of quality knowledge has helped us all find the satisfaction of learning, improving, and becoming just a bit more excellent.

Creating this book required the guidance and help of many people. My first teachers, mentors, and colleagues in quality improvement were Tom Dominick and Mark Rushing, and I am grateful for the experience of working with both of them. Tom introduced me to quality improvement as a discipline and shared his enthusiasm for the value of quality methods in an organization. He taught me to borrow, adapt, and customize from many sources. Mark's depth of understanding, innovativeness, and integrative thinking make him a source for a wealth of ideas and insight. I have learned much from working beside him and from our conversations about new ideas and applications.

Too many people to name individually have helped me understand the concepts and methods of quality improvement, especially my colleagues in quality. My thanks to each of you who have shared your ideas, successes, and failures with me. I am grateful to all the people of Ethyl and Albemarle Corporations, whom I have taught and learned from, as we labored together to apply these methods to improve our work and organizations.

I am indebted to Dave Zimmerman, who created initial drafts of several tools when this book was first expanded beyond a thin compendium of the most basic ones. He first brought brainwriting and list reduction to my attention. The entertaining example for the importance–performance analysis was devised by Dave.

Finally, my wholehearted gratitude to Dianne Muscarello, without whom this book would never have come together. My thanks for hot meals and clean laundry as deadlines approached, for monotonous checking of lists and comparison of revisions, for computer expertise and a valuable nonexpert perspective on the text, and most of all for unending support and encouragement and believing that I could do it.

1
How to Use This Book

A carpenter with only a hammer, one screwdriver, a pair of pliers, and a straight-blade saw, can build cabinets that are functional, but plain and crude. The carpenter with many different tools at hand will be able to create unique and well-crafted items and solve problem situations.

Like a carpenter's toolbox, *The Quality Toolbox* provides you with a choice of many appropriate tools for the wide variety of situations that occur on the road to continuous improvement. Fifty-one different tools—techniques and methods—plus numerous variations are described with step-by-step instructions.

If the *Toolbox* were only a step-by-step guide to many tools, it would be difficult to use. No one wants to read such a book cover-to-cover. How can you know a tool will be useful if you don't already know the tool? Several aids help guide you to the right tool for the situation.

The Tool Matrix

The Tool Matrix (Table 1.1) lists all the tools in the book and categorizes them in three different ways to help you find the right one. To search for a tool, ask yourself three questions.

1. *What do we want to do with this tool?* A carpenter who wants to cut something will look for some type of saw, not for a screwdriver. Quality improvement tools also can be grouped according to how they are used.

Table 1.1. Tool Matrix.

	Tool	E/F	Mission	Customer requirements	Current state	Opportunities	Root causes	Changes	Do it	Monitor	Standardize	Learnings
Idea Creation Tools	Affinity diagram	E/F	X	X	X	X	X	X			X	X
	Brainstorming	E	X	X	X	X	X	X			X	X
	Brainwriting	E	X	X	X	X	X	X			X	X
	Nominal group technique (NGT)	E	X	X	X	X	X	X			X	X
	Relations diagram	E/F		X		X	X	X		X	X	X
Process Analysis Tools	Cost-of-quality analysis	E			X	X	X					
	Critical-to-quality analysis	E			X	X	X					
	Deployment flowchart	E/F			X	X	X	X	X	X	X	
	Flowchart	E/F		X	X	X	X	X	X	X	X	
	Matrix diagram	F		X	X	X	X	X	X	X	X	
	Relations diagram	E/F		X	X	X	X	X		X	X	X
	Requirements matrix	E		X	X	X				X	X	
	Requirements-and-measures tree	E		X	X	X		X		X	X	
	Storyboard	E	X	X	X	X		X	X	X	X	X
	Top-down flowchart	E/F	X		X	X	X	X	X	X	X	
	Work-flow diagram	E			X	X	X	X	X	X	X	
Cause Analysis Tools	Contingency diagram	E				X	X	X	X		X	
	Fishbone diagram	E				X	X					
	Force field analysis	E				X	X	X	X		X	
	Is-is not matrix	F				X	X					
	Matrix diagram	F		X	X	X	X	X	X	X	X	
	Pareto chart	F				X	X	X		X	X	
	Scatter diagram	F				X	X			X		
	Stratification	F			X		X			X	X	
	Tree diagram	E				X	X	X	X	X	X	
	Why-why diagram	E					X					

Table 1.1. (*continued*)

	Tool	E/F	Mission	Customer requirements	Current state	Opportunities	Root causes	Changes	Do it	Monitor	Standardize	Learnings
Planning Tools	Activity chart	F	X					X	X	X	X	
	Arrow diagram	F	X					X	X	X	X	
	Benefits and barriers exercise	E				X	X	X	X		X	X
	Contingency diagram	E				X	X	X	X		X	
	Deployment flowchart	E/F		X	X	X	X	X	X	X	X	
	Flowchart	E/F	X		X	X	X	X	X	X	X	
	Force field analysis	E				X	X	X	X		X	
	Matrix diagram	F		X	X	X	X	X	X	X	X	
	Mission statement wordsmithing	E/F	X									
	Operational definitions	F	X	X	X	X	X	X	X	X	X	
	Plan–do–check–act cycle	F	X					X	X		X	X
	Relations diagram	E/F		X		X	X	X			X	X
	Storyboard	E	X	X	X	X	X	X	X		X	X
	Top-down flowchart	E/F	X		X	X	X	X	X	X	X	
	Tree diagram	E				X	X	X	X		X	
	Work-flow diagram	E			X	X	X	X	X	X	X	
Evaluation Tools	ACORN test	F	X									
	Continuum of team goals	F	X									X
	Decision matrix	F				X	X	X			X	
	Effective–achievable matrix	F				X	X	X			X	
	List reduction	F		X	X	X	X	X			X	
	Matrix diagram	F		X	X	X	X	X	X	X	X	
	Mission statement checklist	F	X									
	Multivoting	F		X		X	X	X			X	X
	Plan–results matrix	F								X	X	
	PMI	F	X			X	X	X			X	

Table 1.1. *(continued)*

	Tool	E/F	Mission	Customer requirements	Current state	Opportunities	Root causes	Changes	Do it	Monitor	Standardize	Learnings
	Box plot	F			X	X	X			X	X	
	Checksheet	F			X	X	X		X	X	X	
	Control charts	F			X	X	X		X	X	X	
	Graphs	F		X	X	X	X		X	X	X	
	Histogram	F			X	X	X			X	X	
	Importance–performance analysis	F		X	X	X				X	X	
Data Collection and Analysis Tools	Kolmogorov–Smirnov test	F			X	X	X		X	X	X	
	Normal probability plot	F			X	X	X		X	X	X	
	Operational definitions	F	X	X	X	X	X	X	X	X	X	
	Pareto chart	F				X	X	X		X	X	
	Performance index	F			X	X			X	X	X	
	Process capability	F			X	X				X	X	
	Requirements-and-measures tree	E		X	X	X				X	X	
	Run chart	F			X	X	X		X	X	X	
	Scatter diagram	F				X	X			X		
	Stratification	F			X	X	X			X	X	
	Survey	E/F		X	X	X	X	X		X	X	

Idea creation tools: When you want to come up with new ideas, or organize many ideas.

Process analysis tools: When you want to understand a work process or some part of a process. Processes start with inputs coming from suppliers, do something with those inputs, and end with outputs going to customers.

Cause analysis tools: When you want to discover the cause of a problem or situation.

Planning tools: When you want to plan what to do.

Evaluation tools: When you want to narrow a group of choices to the best one, or when you want to evaluate how well you have done something.

Data collection and analysis tools: When you want to collect data or analyze data you have collected.

On the Tool Matrix, the tools are grouped according to these categories. Notice that some tools show up in several categories. These versatile tools can be used in a variety of ways.

2. *Where are we in our quality improvement process?* A carpenter would only use fine sandpaper when the cabinet is almost done. Some tools are useful only at certain steps in the quality improvement process.

If you are not sure what this question means, read chapter 2. It describes 10 steps of a general process for quality improvement. This process, which is used in the author's organization, was deliberately written in ordinary, common-sense language. A translation to standard quality terminology is shown beside it. Your organization's process probably is written differently and has more or fewer steps. However, you should be able to find all the elements of your process in the 10-step process.

On the Tool Matrix, the columns list the 10 steps. Each tool that can be used in that step of the process is marked with an X.

3. *Do we need to expand or to focus our thinking?* The process of quality improvement goes through alternating periods of expanding our thinking to many different ideas and focusing our ideas to specifics. The expanding period is creative and can generate new and innovative ideas. The focusing period is analytical and action oriented. To obtain results you have to stop considering options, decide what to do, and do it!

See Figure 1.1 for an illustration of how the expand–focus sequence works. To choose the most worthwhile problem to attack, first expand your thinking to many different problems: big, small, annoying, and expensive problems. Next, focus your thinking: use a set of criteria to choose one, well-defined problem to solve.

E - X - P - A - N - D
FOCUS

Your thinking

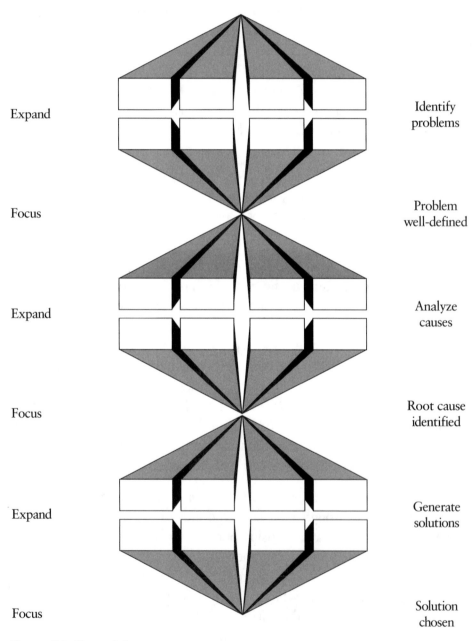

Expand	Identify problems
Focus	Problem well-defined
Expand	Analyze causes
Focus	Root cause identified
Expand	Generate solutions
Focus	Solution chosen

Figure 1.1. Expand–focus sequence.

Now, expand your thinking to many possible causes of the problem. Could it be this? Could it be that? Maybe what's happening is. . . . After getting lots of ideas, use methods such as data collection, analysis, and logical reasoning to narrow all possible causes to the few that really are the culprits.

Finally, expand your thinking once again to many ways to solve the problem. From a variety of solutions, choose the one most likely to work in your unique circumstances.

Some tools are designed specifically to help you expand your thinking. Others are designed solely to help you focus. A few encompass both modes: the first few steps of the tool expand your thinking and the final steps lead you through focusing. Some tools can either expand or focus your thinking, depending on how and when they are used. For example, flowcharts can be used to expand your thinking to all possible problems in a process. Or, they can guide a group to focus on the one way everyone has agreed the process will operate from this time forward.

The third column of the Tool Matrix shows an E for *expansion* and an F for *focusing*. Tools that encompass both modes or that can be used for either purpose are indicated by E/F.

Example

Let's look at an example of the Tool Matrix in use. Suppose your team has tested a solution; it worked and you are ready to install it throughout your organization. Suppose that as you are beginning to plan how to do that, your team wants to consider what might go wrong. How would you find potential tools to help you?

First, you would ask, "What do we want to do with this tool?" You need to plan, so you would look on the Tool Matrix in the group labeled "Planning tools." There are 16 tools in that group.

Then you would ask, "Where are we in our quality improvement process?" You are at step 9: "If it worked, how can we do it every time?" or, in quality jargon, "Standardize." On the Tool Matrix, under the column for that step, you will find 15 tools marked with an X.

Your third question would be, "Do we need to expand or focus our thinking?" By considering everything that might go wrong, you are expanding your thinking, so you would eliminate five tools marked with F. That leaves 10 possible tools.

What next? Now you are ready to turn to the main section of the book and browse through the tools.

The Tools

The tools are listed in alphabetical order, rather than by categories, so that whenever you know the name of the tool, you know exactly where to find it. Six sections describe each tool.

Description: A few short sentences explain what the tool is and what it does.

When to Use: This section describes the situations in which you would want to use this tool. A situation might be a particular stage of the quality improvement process, a certain kind of problem, or after another tool has been used.

Procedure: A step-by-step numbered procedure guides you through using the tool. This section is very basic, so you can always use it as a quick reference.

Example: You are introduced to a situation when that tool was appropriate for a team's situation, and the way the tool was used is explained. Calculations, the thinking behind various steps, and the conclusions that could be drawn also are explained. Some of these examples are fictional; others are based on true situations that have been disguised. Whenever a tool involves a chart or diagram, an example or drawing is shown. Blank forms that can be photocopied often are provided.

Variation 1, 2, 3, and so on: When the tool can be used in several ways, the step-by-step procedure for each variation is written out. Often, examples are provided for the variation.

Considerations: This section includes tips, tricks, and warnings—notes to help you use the tool more easily, avoid problems, or add additional flair or sophistication. Thus, this section adds all the detail and color that were omitted from the basic procedure.

Example

Let's return to the example, with your team ready to spread a solution throughout the organization. What happens after using the Tool Matrix to narrow the list of tools to 10? You would browse through those 10 tools, reading just the "Description" and "When to Use." When you flipped the pages to the contingency diagram, you would read, "The contingency diagram identifies and pictures what might go wrong in a process or plan, and ways to avoid these problems." When do you use this? "When planning implementation of a phase of a project, especially the solution," and

"Especially, before launching a change." That sounds like exactly what you need.

Now you know how to use this book to identify and learn the tools that are most useful in your specific situation. You might be wondering, "How do all these tools fit together to create improvements?" The next section, "The Quality Improvement Process," outlines the process and tools used each step of the way, and "Quality Improvement Stories" tells how four teams actually used the tools to improve their work.

2

The Quality
Improvement Process

A quality improvement process presents a series of steps to think about and work through. These steps help you ask questions, gather information, and take actions effectively and efficiently. Thus, a quality improvement process provides a framework that guides you from the initial improvement challenge to successful completion of the effort.

A quality improvement process provides the most value by preventing you from skipping important steps along the way. Often groups do not think about their customers, or they jump to a solution without understanding root causes. Following a quality improvement process will keep you from making these mistakes. A quality improvement process also helps a group work together and communicate their progress to others. Everyone knows what you are trying to accomplish at any point and where you are headed next.

A quality improvement process can be used in any time frame. It often takes months to work a difficult problem through the entire process, but the process is also useful when improvement ideas must be generated quickly. In an hour or two, the process can guide your thinking through various aspects of a situation to a well-founded plan. Also, a quality improvement process can be used by anyone. While improvement teams most often employ the process, it can be used by any group, from plant site to executive offices, or by any individual.

Figure 2.1 shows a 10-step quality improvement process. This process, used in the author's organization, is written in a generic way. If your organization has an official improvement process, it will be written differently and have a different number of steps. You should, however, be able to find

Common terminology	Quality terminology
1. What do I or we want to accomplish?	Identify mission.
2. Who cares and what do they care about?	Identify customers and requirements.
3. What are we doing now and how well are we doing it?	Assess current state.
4. What can we do better?	Define preferred state, problems, and improvement opportunities.
5. What prevents us from doing better? (What are the underlying problems?)	Identify barriers and root causes.
6. What changes could we make to do better?	Develop improvement solutions, strategies, tactics, and plans.
7. Do it.	Implement plans.
8. How did we do? If it didn't work, try again.	Monitor results; recycle if necessary.
9. If it worked, how can we do it every time?	Standardize.
10. What did we learn? Let's celebrate!	Conclude project.

Figure 2.1. The 10-step quality improvement process.

all the elements of your process in the 10-step process. In this chapter and throughout the book, this generic process will demonstrate how the process of improvement proceeds and how tools are used within the process.

The 10-step process uses ordinary, common-sense language. In Figure 2.1, each step is also rewritten in terminology commonly used in quality programs. Both are included so one or both phrases will communicate clearly to you.

A third way of understanding the quality improvement process is shown in Figure 2.2. This flowchart shows the sequence of working through the steps. Usually the best sequence does not proceed smoothly

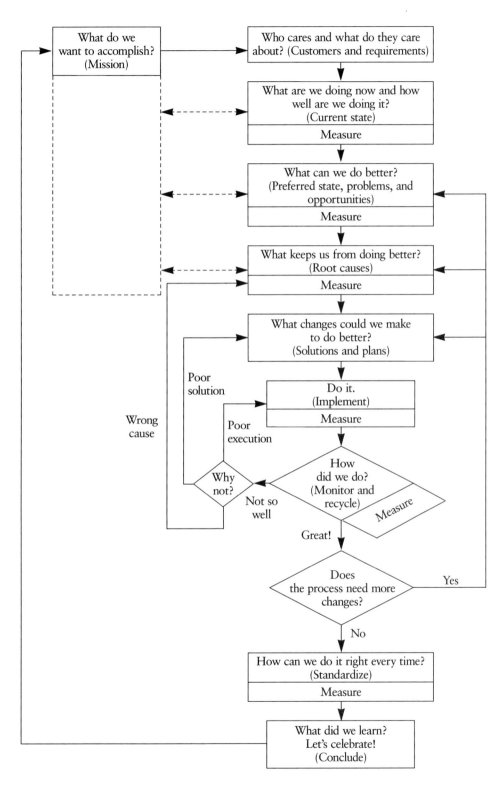

Figure 2.2. Quality improvement process flowchart.

from the first step to the last. One might need to go back and recheck the mission, or go back to an earlier step when a change does not work, or after implementing one change go back to work on a second one. Also, because measurement is significant in any quality improvement process, the flowchart shows which steps of the process have measurement as a key element.

The rest of this chapter discusses each step of the quality improvement process in detail, listing tools that can be used at each step and offering tips to make the quality improvement process itself a powerful tool for improvement.

The Quality Improvement Process

1. **What do we want to accomplish?**
   Identify mission and make initial plans.

   Expanding tools
   > Affinity diagram
   > Brainstorming
   > Brainwriting
   > Mission statement wordsmithing
   > Nominal group technique (NGT)

   Focusing tools
   > ACORN test
   > Affinity diagram
   > Continuum of team goals
   > List reduction
   > Mission statement checklist
   > Mission statement wordsmithing
   > Multivoting
   > Operational definitions
   > PMI

   - The mission statement may be provided by the steering committee when the team is established.

   - It is essential to spend time and effort in group discussions and in communication with the steering committee to make sure that a good mission statement is agreed upon and understood by everyone.

- Agreement among the team members and steering committee about the scope of the mission (how broad or narrow) is important.

- Three components make up a good improvement objective: direction of change (increase, decrease, eliminate); measure of quality (number of defects, efficiency); name of process (answering the phone, preparing budget). String the three together and you have a statement of your objective.

- Well-written objectives should be simple, measurable, agreed, realistic, and time-related (SMART).

- Could you explain the importance of your project to external customers?

- If you started with a fuzzy mission which has been clarified, consider whether the team still has the right members to address the new, focused mission.

Planning tools

      Activity chart
      Arrow diagram
      Flowchart
      Plan–do–check–act (PDCA) cycle
      Quality improvement process
      Storyboard
      Top-down flowchart

- Although you probably don't know much detail yet, lay out a general plan with key milestones on it. See Figure 4.94 for an example of a plan.

- Try setting milestones backward. Do you have a deadline for finishing? When do you want to have a solution ready to put in place? When will you have finished studying how things are now? How much time will you allow for gathering customer input?

- Do you have review points established with management or a steering committee? Such reviews can establish timing for your key milestones.

- Marking key milestones off a timeline will create a feeling of accomplishment for the team and sustain motivation.

- As you move through your quality improvement process, revise and update your plan. You will be able to add more specifics later.

2. **Who cares and what do they care about?**
   Identify customers and requirements.

   Expanding tools
   > Affinity diagram
   > Brainstorming
   > Brainwriting
   > Flowchart
   > Nominal group technique (NGT)
   > Relations diagram
   > Requirements matrix
   > Requirements-and-measures tree
   > Storyboard
   > Survey

   Focusing tools
   > Affinity diagram
   > Graphs
   > Importance–performance analysis
   > List reduction
   > Matrix diagram
   > Multivoting
   > Operational definitions
   > Relations diagram
   > Survey

   - Products and customers can be identified for each output on the flowchart. Supplies and suppliers can be identified for each flowchart input.

   - Talk with each of your key customers and suppliers about what they need.

   - Invite key customers and suppliers to sit on teams or involve them through interviews.

   - Never try to go past this step without getting direct input from real, live customers.

3. **What are we doing now and how well are we doing it?**
   Assess current state.

   Expanding tools

> Affinity diagram
> Brainstorming
> Brainwriting
> Cost-of-quality analysis
> Critical-to-quality analysis
> Deployment flowchart
> Flowchart
> Nominal group technique (NGT)
> Relations diagram
> Requirements matrix
> Requirements-and-measures tree
> Survey
> Storyboard
> Top-down flowchart
> Work-flow diagram

   Focusing tools

> Affinity diagram
> List reduction
> Matrix diagram
> Multivoting
> Operational definitions

- For most situations, you will begin this step by drawing a flowchart.

- Include cost-of-quality steps: inspection, rework, delays, what happens when things go wrong.

- Start with a simple flowchart that shows the big picture, then draw one with more detail. For example, you could start with a top-down flowchart and add detail for critical steps. Convert a detailed flowchart into a deployment flowchart to show who is involved when.

- Need more detail? Pick a key step in your process and draw a flowchart with that step's substeps. Trying to handle both explicit detail and a large scope on your flowchart at the same time could overwhelm your team.

- As much as possible involve people who *do* the process.

- Carefully identify inputs and outputs to capture interfaces and cross-functional activities.

- In some situations, a flowchart isn't applicable. It is still important to understand the current state before you proceed.

- Try considering the current state from your customer's point of view.

- Based on your new knowledge of the process, is the mission statement still valid? Do you have all the right people on the team?

Data collection and analysis tools

> Box plot
> Checksheet
> Control charts
> Graphs
> Histogram
> Importance–performance analysis
> Kolmogorov–Smirnov test
> Normal probability plot
> Operational definitions
> Performance index
> Process capability
> Requirements-and-measures tree
> Run chart
> Stratification
> Survey

- To answer the question, "How well are we doing?" you usually will need to start taking measurements in this step.

- How will you know when you have improved? That is the question you are trying to answer with measurement. Develop measurements that will answer that question for you later.

- Study customer requirements and flowcharts to help determine appropriate elements to measure.

- Consider both process and product measures. Process measures tell how things are running, while they are running. Product measures tell you results, after the process is finished. You need both kinds of indicators.

- When planning data collection, think about how the data will be analyzed and used. This affects what kind of data you want to collect and how you will collect it.

4. **What can we do better?**

   Define preferred state, problems, and improvement opportunities.

   First, expand your thinking and identify many possibilities. What would the *best* look like? What are all the things you could do better?

   Expanding tools
   > Affinity diagram
   > Barriers and benefits exercise
   > Brainstorming
   > Brainwriting
   > Contingency diagram
   > Cost-of-quality analysis
   > Critical-to-quality analysis
   > Deployment flowchart
   > Fishbone diagram
   > Flowchart
   > Force field analysis
   > Nominal group technique (NGT)
   > Relations diagram
   > Requirements matrix
   > Requirements-and-measures tree
   > Storyboard
   > Top-down flowchart
   > Tree diagram
   > Work-flow diagram

   - This is an expansion point; get as many ideas as the group can generate.

   - Many teams have an almost irresistible urge to jump to solutions at this point. Often, solutions are disguised as problems: "We don't have enough people." It is an important role of the facilitator to keep the team focused on problems and causes until both are well understood.

   - Often it helps to draw an ideal flowchart and then determine the gap between what is really happening and the ideal. The ideal should eliminate all rework, checking, approvals, delays, fixing errors—anything that finds or solves problems.

- Think boldly and creatively when envisioning the ideal state. Do not take anything for granted; question all assumptions. The methods of lateral thinking, developed by Edward de Bono, can be very powerful at this step. (See "Recommended Reading" at the end of this book.)

- If there are no problem areas in your flowchart, include more detail.

- The other tools listed can be combined with the flowchart of what is happening today to create the ideal flowchart. Or, those tools alone may make it clear where opportunities for improvement are.

- For processes where time is important, identify how long each step should take and where slowdowns and waits now occur.

- Compare your measurements to customer needs.

After expanding your thinking to lots of improvement opportunities, focus on the most significant.

Data collection and analysis tools
          Box plot
          Checksheet
          Control charts
          Graphs
          Histogram
          Importance–performance analysis
          Kolmogorov–Smirnov test
          Normal probability plot
          Operational definitions
          Pareto chart
          Performance indexing
          Process capability
          Requirements-and-measures tree
          Run chart
          Scatter diagram
          Stratification
          Survey

Other focusing tools
>Affinity diagram
>Decision matrix
>Effective–achievable matrix
>Is–is not matrix
>List reduction
>Matrix diagram
>Multivoting
>PMI
>Relations diagram

- Whenever possible, use data to confirm problems.

- Often, using several data analysis tools gives more insight than just one.

- It is always preferable to prioritize with data, rather than with opinions.

- Use list reduction or multivoting as filters to reduce a long list of ideas to a manageable number.

- Focus on the most significant ways to improve. What will really make a difference to your customers? What will make a long-term difference to your organization?

- Exception to that rule: If your team is new, it is a good idea to go for a quick success with an easier objective in order to learn. Identify a short-term, easily achievable opportunity. These are often called *low-hanging fruit.*

- You can later go back and work on problems not chosen now.

- Set heroic targets for improvement. Heroic targets generate breakthroughs. They challenge people to stretch themselves and to find ways to achieve dramatic improvements.

5. **What prevents us from doing better? (What are the underlying problems?)**
Identify barriers and root causes.

Again, first expand your thinking to many potential causes.

Expanding tools
>Affinity diagram
>Barriers and benefits exercise
>Brainstorming

Brainwriting
Contingency diagram
Cost-of-quality analysis
Critical-to-quality analysis
Deployment flowchart
Fishbone diagram
Flowchart
Force field analysis
Nominal group technique (NGT)
Relations diagram
Top-down flowchart
Tree diagram
Why–why diagram
Work-flow diagram

- The root cause is the fundamental, underlying reason for a problem. The root cause is what causes a problem to happen repeatedly. If you do not identify the root cause, you are just putting a bandage on the problem. It will probably happen again. When you remove the root cause, you have fixed it permanently.

- Explore many ideas before zeroing in on one root cause to solve.

- Thorough probing to root causes will lead you to broad, fundamental issues. Often management policies will be involved—such as training or the design of a system.

- Solving a problem at a deep, fundamental level often will solve other related issues. Remember "inch-wide, mile-deep": choose narrow scopes, but dig deeply into them for best results.

When you have identified many potential causes, focus on the true root cause.

Data collection and analysis tools

Box plot
Checksheet
Control charts
Graphs
Histogram
Kolmogorov–Smirnov test
Normal probability plot
Operational definitions

        Pareto chart
        Run chart
        Scatter diagram
        Stratification

Other focusing tools
        Affinity diagram
        Decision matrix
        Effective–achievable matrix
        Is–is not matrix
        List reduction
        Matrix diagram
        Multivoting
        PMI
        Relations diagram

- Whenever possible, collect data to be sure you have the right cause.

- When planning data collection, think about how the data will be analyzed and used. This affects what kind of data you want to collect and how.

- Some root causes can be verified only by trying out a solution.

- You can return later to work on causes not chosen to be tackled the first time.

6. **What changes could we make to do better?**
Develop improvement solutions, strategies, tactics, and plans.

Once again, generate lots of possible solutions before settling on one.

Expanding tools
        Affinity diagram
        Brainstorming
        Brainwriting
        Contingency diagram
        Deployment flowchart
        Flowchart
        Force field analysis
        Nominal group technique (NGT)
        Relations diagram
        Storyboard

Survey
Top-down flowchart
Tree diagram
Work-flow diagram

- All too often, groups start planning to carry out their first idea. Play with additional ideas and you will probably be able to improve on your first one.

- Get as many solutions as possible, realistic or crazy.

- This is another place where it is important to think boldly and creatively. Lateral thinking methods can help you break out of conventional thinking to original ideas. (See the "Recommended Reading" list.)

- Consider combining two OK solutions into one hybrid *great* solution.

- Ask your customers and suppliers to help develop solutions to problems that affect them.

When you have several workable solutions, evaluate them carefully to focus on the best one.

Focusing tools

Affinity diagram
Decision matrix
Effective–achievable matrix
List reduction
Matrix diagram
Multivoting
Operational definitions
Pareto chart
PMI
Relations diagram

- Ask two types of questions when evaluating potential solutions: How well will this solution achieve the desired results? (effective) How successful will we be in carrying out this solution? (achievable)

- Brainstorm evaluation criteria. What factors need to be considered under the broad headings of "effective" and "achievable"? These become headings of a decision matrix.

- How could a solution be changed to eliminate problems that show up on the decision matrix?

- After a decision matrix has been filled out, summarize with an effective–achievable matrix.

- Discussion about consensus (What does it mean? How can we be sure we have achieved it?) may be important here.

- If possible, involve in the decision process those who will be closely involved in carrying out the solution, including customers and suppliers. You will increase their buy-in.

- Before choosing a solution, the team may need to ask, "Do we have enough information to choose a solution?"

7. **Do it!**

Implement solution.

Planning tools

Activity chart
Arrow diagram
Barriers and benefits exercise
Contingency diagram
Deployment flowchart
Flowchart
Force field analysis
Matrix diagram
Operational definitions
Plan–do–check–act (PDCA) cycle
Storyboard
Top-down flowchart
Tree diagram
Work-flow diagram

Data collection and analysis tools

Checksheet
Control charts
Graphs
Kolmogorov–Smirnov test
Normal probability plot
Operational definitions
Performance index
Run chart

- When a solution is chosen, plan carefully how you will carry it out.

- The more carefully developed your plan, the easier implementation will be.

- A good plan includes what, who, when.

- If possible, it is always a good idea to test the chosen solution on a small scale. Choose a typical area, but avoid one with big or unusual obstacles. Be sure customers are involved. Plan to continue your test long enough to observe problems. If you are successful, in step 9 you can apply your solution elsewhere.

- Be sure to include contingency planning. What can go wrong? Who or what will stand in the way? Identify potential obstacles or barriers and decide how to avoid or overcome them. Think about how you will react when the unexpected happens.

- Have you considered the human elements that will affect your success? Who will feel threatened? What new procedures will be hard to remember?

- Be sure to plan measurement, both to determine the results of the change and to monitor how well your plan was implemented.

- As you unroll your plan, be alert for unexpected observations and problems with data collection.

- Does your solution appear to be creating other problems?

- Be patient.

8. **How did we do? Try again if necessary.**
   Monitor results. Recycle if necessary.

   Tools developed in previous steps
   > Deployment flowchart
   > Flowchart
   > Requirements matrix
   > Requirements-and-measures tree
   > Top-down flowchart
   > Work-flow diagram

   Data collection and analysis tools
   > Box plot
   > Checksheet

Control charts
Graphs
Histogram
Importance–performance analysis
Kolmogorov–Smirnov test
Normal probability plot
Operational definitions
Pareto chart
Performance index
Process capability
Run chart
Scatter diagram
Stratification
Survey

Other focusing tools
Matrix diagram
Plan–results matrix

- Did you accomplish your implementation plan? Did you accomplish your objectives and original mission? The answers to those two questions will indicate whether you need to recycle, and to where.

- If you didn't accomplish what you hoped, three reasons are possible. Your plan may have been poorly executed. You may have developed a poor solution. Or, you may have attacked the wrong cause. You will recycle to step 7 for better execution, to step 6 for a better solution, or to step 5 to find the right cause.

- When you review results, ask whether your targets have been achieved, not just whether there was a change.

- If you plan to test solutions to other root causes or other problems in the same process, it may be better to return to step 4 or 5 now. When all your tests are done, you can put in place all your process changes at once in step 9.

9. **If it worked, how can we do it every time?**
Standardize.

Expanding tools
Affinity diagram
Barriers and benefits exercise

Brainstorming
Brainwriting
Contingency diagram
Deployment flowchart
Flowchart
Force field analysis
Nominal group technique (NGT)
Relations diagram
Requirements matrix
Requirements-and-measures tree
Storyboard
Top-down flowchart
Tree diagram
Work-flow diagram

Data collection and analysis tools

Box plot
Checksheet
Control charts
Graphs
Histogram
Importance–performance analysis
Kolmogorov–Smirnov test
Normal probability plot
Operational definitions
Pareto diagram
Performance index
Process capability
Run chart
Stratification
Survey

Other focusing tools

Activity chart
Affinity diagram
Arrow diagram
Decision matrix
Deployment flowchart
Effective–achievable matrix
Flowchart

  List reduction
  Matrix diagram
  Multivoting
  Plan–do–check–act (PDCA) cycle
  Plan–results matrix
  PMI
  Relations diagram
  Top-down flowchart

- In this step, you introduce to everyone changes that you tested on a trial basis. Also, you make sure that whatever changes have been made become routine. You prevent any slipping back into the same old problems. This is called *standardizing*.

- There are several aspects to standardizing an improved process.

- First, "new and improved" won't do much good unless it is used consistently throughout the organization. Plan to expand your test solution to everywhere it applies.

- Second, everyone involved in the new process must know what to do. Formal and informal training are essential to spread a new process throughout the organization.

- Document new procedures. This will make training easier. Flowcharts and checksheets are great ways to document procedures.

- Putting documentation and checksheets in the workplace also error-proofs the new process.

- Third, humans don't like change. Dramatizing the transition from the old to the new process helps the organization make the change.

- Fourth, plan for problems. Ask, "What is most likely to go wrong?"

- Set up indicators that will flag a problem about to occur. Also try to set up indicators that things are running well.

- Consider all elements of the new process: people, methods, machines, materials, measurement. Have they all been standardized?

- Finally, it is critical to identify who owns the improved process, including responsibility for continued tracking of metrics. A process owner will hold the gain this team has made and set new targets for continuous improvement.

- Your standardization plan also should have a way to monitor customers' changing needs.

10. **What did we learn? Let's celebrate!**
   Conclude project.

   Expanding tools
   > Affinity diagram
   > Barriers and benefits exercise
   > Brainstorming
   > Brainwriting
   > Nominal group technique (NGT)
   > Quality improvement process
   > Relations diagram
   > Storyboard

   Focusing tools
   > Affinity diagram
   > Continuum of team goals
   > List reduction
   > Multivoting
   > Plan–do–check–act (PDCA) cycle
   > Relations diagram

   - Don't quit yet! Take some time to reflect, learn, and feel good about what you have accomplished.

   - Use your mission statement, implementation plans, and team minutes to remind you of the process your team has followed.

   - Identify and record what you have learned: teamwork, improvements, the improvement process you followed, gathering data, your organization. What went well? What would you do differently next time?

   - Use your organization's structure (steering committee, quality advisors, newsletters, conferences, and so on) to share your learning. Use this project's successes and missteps to improve how other teams function.

   - You have worked, struggled, learned, and improved together; that is important to recognize. Plan a party or other event to celebrate the completion of your project.

- Endings often cause painful feelings; this may affect your last few meetings. Be aware of this and acknowledge it if it occurs. Planning your celebration can help deal with this.

- If yours is a permanent team, celebrate the end of each project before you go on to a new improvement project.

- If your team is scheduled to disband, ask yourselves, "Is there some other aspect of this project, or some other project, that this team is ideally suited to tackle?" Your momentum as a successful team may carry you to even greater improvements.

- Congratulations!

Guidance Questions

A team's management, steering committee, or quality advisor is often not sure how best to provide guidance and support to the team. These questions can be asked to probe what the team is doing and help guide it through the process. Team members also could ask themselves these questions.

Some of the questions are general and can be asked throughout the quality improvement process. Others relate to particular steps of the process. Ask these questions throughout the process.

- What is the purpose?

- How do you know?

- Can you show me your data?

- Where are you in the quality improvement process?

- What step number?

- What will you do next?

- What are your major milestones over the next couple of months?

- What obstacles are you running into?

- What can I or we do to help remove them?

- What people issues have you encountered?

- What have you learned?

These questions are related to steps of the process.

1. What do I or we want to accomplish?

   - Have you revisited your mission statement to see if it is still appropriate?

- Where is your mission statement on the continuum of team goals?

2. Who cares and what do they care about?

- Who are your customers?

- What do your customers need? How do you know?

- How are you involving your customers in your quality improvement process?

3. What are we doing now and how well are we doing it?

- Do you have a current flowchart of your process?

- What have you done to analyze your flowchart for problems?

- How will you measure improvement?

- How will you know you are improving?

4. What can we do better?

- What is your vision of the ideal process?

- In a perfect world, how would this process be done?

- What goal have you set?

5. What prevents us from doing better? What are the underlying problems?

- Why? Why? Why?

- What is the root cause of that problem?

6. What changes can we make to do better?

- Have you evaluated alternative solutions?

- What criteria did you use to choose the best solution?

- What is your implementation plan?

7. Do it.

- What problem is that action trying to address?

- Are things going according to plan?

- How are the changes being received?

- What are you doing to deal with problems you are running into?

8. How did we do? If it didn't work, try again.

- What results did you get?

- What were the gaps between actual results and your goal?

- Did it not work because of the wrong solution or the wrong root cause?

- How do you plan to try again?

9. If it worked, how can we do it every time?

  - What have you done to make sure we don't lose the improvements you have made?

  - Is there someplace else this solution or improvement could be applied?

10. What did we learn? Let's celebrate!

  - What did you learn from this experience with the quality improvement process?

  - How would you like to be recognized for your accomplishments?

3

Quality Improvement Stories

Stories and examples often are the best teachers. This chapter presents a few stories that show how groups can use the tools within the quality improvement process. Since there is a tendency to think of statistical tools just in manufacturing and other kinds of tools just in offices, these stories also illustrate how both kinds of tools have value in both settings.

This section concentrates on showing how the tools are used together to create improvement. To understand how this book can help you find tools that fit a particular need, refer to chapter 1.

Some of these stories are based on real teams, but the truth has been stretched, altered, or disguised to illustrate key points, to fill in details the teams did not disclose, or to protect the innocent. The manufacturing story is a composite of several teams' experiences.

Technical Support Department

The people in the technical support department quickly recognized the value of quality improvement methods to improve the service they provide the organization. They began an effort to incorporate improvement methods into the way the entire department operates.

First, they needed to write a mission statement for the department. (Step 1: What do we want to accomplish?) Using mission statement wordsmithing, a small group drafted a mission, which was confirmed by the entire group.

Next, the department needed to identify its customers and find out what they expected from the department. (Step 2: Who cares and what do they care about?) Using NGT and multivoting, a team identified a list of key customers to survey. (See the multivoting example on page 196.) It used a combination of questionnaires and interviews to gather information. The team also surveyed the entire department with a questionnaire. All the survey information was analyzed and communicated broadly using histograms. A requirements matrix was used to summarize customer requirements.

The surveys collected a lot of information about key processes and products from internal customers and people within the department. In addition, the surveys generated data about current performance. (Step 3: What are we doing now and how well are we doing it?) A small group made a storyboard of the department's processes and products, using the ideas collected from the surveys. The storyboard clarified the department's key activities and relationships.

Based on that work, teams were formed for several key processes, to find opportunities for improvement. Each team, working with the guidance of a trained facilitator, recycled back to step 1 of the quality improvement process and worked through all the steps. In order to conclude and disband, a team had to identify ongoing measures for the process and responsibility for those measures. (Step 9: If it worked, how can we do it every time?) The team also had to make a final presentation to the steering committee, which celebrated and publicized the team's accomplishments. (Step 10: What did we learn? Let's celebrate!) As teams concluded and disbanded, others were formed to address new issues. In fact, several years after this process began, a team was formed to improve the department's quality improvement process.

Survey Report Writing Team

One of the teams formed in the technical support department was asked to improve the process of writing survey reports. Technical staff periodically surveyed each manufacturing unit to provide guidance on good practice, and they wrote summary reports of their findings for the units. Both the department and the manufacturing customers were dissatisfied with the timeliness of feedback.

The team used NGT and mission statement wordsmithing to identify its mission statement and goals. (Step 1: What do we want to accomplish?)

> *Mission Statement:* Improve survey report preparation
> through review of the steps in the process.

Goals:

1. Identify factors that delay the issuance of the report.

2. Recommend ways of minimizing these delays.

3. Identify other quality improvement factors and techniques.

The team needed to find out what its customers wanted. (Step 2: Who cares and what do they care about?) Team members used interviews to gather information from several key customers and summarized the results in the format of the requirements matrix, showing both external customers (plant management) and internal customers (department management). All sets of customers required that formal feedback be received within 30 days.

The team needed to understand what happened between the end of the plant visit and issuing the report. (Step 3: What are we doing now and how well are we doing it?) The team drew a flowchart of the process. It was rather complicated: 13 steps, three decision boxes and, if samples needed to be analyzed, another subprocess of nine steps and one decision box. The team also compiled historical data on the time required to issue the report, going back two and one-half years. A control chart showed an average time of 29.9 days—which means that half the time the reports took longer than the customers' requirement of 30 days. (See the chart of individuals control chart example on page 100.) With an upper control limit (UCL) of 85.0, the process performance index (Pp_k) was 0.0018. Clearly the process needed a lot of improvement. (Step 4: What can we do better?)

The team began to identify what was going wrong. (Step 5: What prevents us from doing better?) Using a Pareto chart, team members analyzed data on time required by each step of the process. By far the two longest bars were "Days out of office" and "Days unavailable for writing report," followed by "Days between receiving analysis and writing report" and "Time to analyze samples." Using a fishbone diagram, the team identified the elements that contributed to "Days out of office."

These elements were analyzed to identify changes that would reduce the impact of travel on the reports. (Step 6: What changes could we make to do better?) Suggestions for improvement were brainstormed and evaluated using a decision matrix. The entire staff helped to implement the suggestions. (Step 7: Do it.) One solution was to set triggers in the process to identify problems before the 30-day deadline. For another solution, writers were helped to make schedules (activity diagrams) to ensure they had time to write the report.

The team continued monitoring the control chart for total time. (Step 8: How did we do? If it didn't work, try again.) The process was in control. The average was reduced to 22.1 days, and the UCL to 55.2 days. Although this improvement was significant, it still was not enough to meet the customers' needs. The Cp_k was 0.24. (See the chart of individuals example on page 100.)

The team recycled back to step 5 to study other problems. The Pareto chart of time in each process step showed the longest one was still "Days out of office" (although it was less than one-fourth its previous size). The second most important cause was now "Time to analyze samples." Addressing that step, the team analyzed the time required by different laboratories, using control charts, and found which labs took longer. Three solutions were devised: (1) the team recommended using the quicker labs whenever possible; (2) it put triggers in the process to provide early warning of problems at the labs; and (3) it established a tracking system for samples submitted for analysis. (Step 6: What changes could we make to do better; step 7: Do it.)

We will stop this story here, with the team continuing in a recycle loop. Despite good improvements, the process still does not meet customer requirements. The average is down to 16.8, the UCL to 47.7, and Cp_k is 0.43. (Step 8: How did we do? If it didn't work, try again.) Incremental improvement is not getting the department where it needs to be. The team should consider recycling to an earlier step of the quality improvement process and think about major redesign of the process. (Step 4: What can we do better?) Maybe it could redraw the flowchart, starting with a blank piece of paper. Maybe it could devise a way to fill the customers' need for formal feedback without a written report. Maybe technology could help out: tape recorders, video, electronic communication, artificial intelligence, and so forth. Maybe . . . We'll let you write the story's happy ending.

ZZ-400 Manufacturing Unit

When members of this chemical manufacturing team began their quality improvement process, they already had the following sign on the wall displaying their pride.

Best-Run Unit in the World
Making the Best ZZ-400 in the World!

So, when they began talking about a mission statement, they quickly realized that they had had one for a long time. (Step 1: What do we want to accomplish?)

They also thought they were in good shape in terms of understanding their customers. (Step 2: Who cares and what do they care about?) After all, they had monthly customer audits and visits. But when they started pulling together all the customer specification sheets to keep in one place, they realized that many were several years old and some of the specifications were unfamiliar. So the team spent some time learning about its customers. The team arranged for one or two team members to visit each customer's plant to find out exactly how ZZ-400 was handled and used. For these visits they developed a checksheet of questions to be asked and information to be given. From this information, a task team developed an L-shaped matrix that showed each external customer's product specifications and choice of packaging and delivery options. (See the L-shaped matrix example on page 186.)

While Fred was flipping through the quality training manual during the graveyard shift, it occurred to him that the team was so close to the external customer that everyone forgot about the internal customers: maintenance, shipping, and especially the business groups that really called the shots. Fred headed up a task team that used interviews to learn the needs of the business groups. That information was summarized on a second matrix. The unit also invited maintenance and QC lab people to join its quality improvement team.

Then the team began to focus on its processes. (Step 3: What are we doing now and how well are we doing it?) A flowchart of the manufacturing process was already a daily tool. To decide which process variables to monitor, everyone reviewed the newly collected customer specifications as well as their own expert knowledge of the most sensitive variables in the process. Collecting all this input, another task team set up control charts with historical data used to establish control limits. (See the $\bar{X}$ and R control chart example on page 93.) The entire unit began monitoring its manufacturing process with the control charts.

The team decided to define just what it meant to be "the best-run unit making the best ZZ-400." (Step 4: What can we do better?) Team members brainstormed a list of over 30 indicators. To make some sense out of all these ideas, the team decided to use an affinity diagram, modifying the procedure slightly to allow for the fact that the entire team was on shift-work and members could not meet together. On a rarely used door in the control room members set up Post-It™ notes with the brainstormed ideas on them and left instructions for everyone to work with the notes whenever they had time. After several days, a natural grouping and some headings had emerged. (See the affinity diagram example on page 50.)

The affinity diagram defined five broad areas of performance—product quality, equipment maintenance, manufacturing cost, volume, and safety and environmental. The team used list reduction to select one overall measure for each area. (See the list reduction example on page 182.) Those five measures became the basis for a performance index. (See the performance index example on page 216.)

To complete the performance index, the team had to establish current performance, goals for high performance, and minimum levels of performance. Current performance was quickly measured, but many drafts of the performance index were on the bulletin board for shift review before the team reached consensus on goals and minimums.

At the same time, a subteam was determining process capability for the key production processes, based on the ongoing control charts. To begin improving the quality score of the performance index (measured by percentage of rework) this subteam addressed the lowest Cp_k, product purity. The process was just barely capable, with a Cp_k of only 1.04. One of the ideas volunteered about purity was a traditional but unproven belief around the unit that overall purity dropped whenever traces of iron showed up. The subteam decided to test this belief. (Step 5: What prevents us from doing better?)

A scatter diagram of purity and iron content showed no relationship between the two variables. (See the scatter diagram example on page 250.) Then a mechanic reminded everyone that there were three reactors. Maybe the reactors were different enough that their data should not be combined. The subteam modified the scatter diagram, this time using stratification to separate the three reactors' data. Sure enough, for two of the reactors, increased iron was related to decreased purity. (See the stratification example on page 256.)

All the members of the unit worked on a time-delay fishbone, trying to figure out the source of the iron. (See the fishbone diagram example on page 132.) The flowchart was examined to determine what was different about Reactor 1, which did not show increased iron. They examined control charts and logsheets to try to understand what else was happening when the problem occurred. An is–is not diagram was used to bring together everything they knew about the situation. (See the is–is not diagram example on page 174.) The cause of the problem turned out to be a spare pump that had been installed during a midnight emergency and never replaced. The pump was made of the wrong material. Replacing the pump eliminated the problem. (Step 6: What changes could we make to do better? Step 7: Do it.)

The team members decided that if the problem happened once, it could happen again. So they set out to inform themselves about material-of-construction standards. (Step 9: If it worked, how can we do it every time?) Engineering and maintenance provided information, and the subteam constructed a T-shaped matrix showing material of construction related both to equipment numbers and to the various liquids that were handled in the unit.

Team members also realized that other units might have the same problem, so they publicized their work in the plant newsletter. (Step 10: What did we learn? Let's celebrate!) Then they went on to identify and tackle other opportunities to make the ZZ-400 unit the best.

Safety Subteam

Another subteam was looking for ideas to improve safety and environmental performance. (Step 4: What can we do better?) Along with quality, this area was the most heavily weighted on the performance index. One day Chris told the subteam about the safety approach her neighbor's company used, which involved shift safety circles where individuals could confront co-workers' unsafe behavior. (Step 6: What changes could we make to do better?) The immediate reaction was skeptical, but George suggested that they evaluate the idea before discarding it. Using PMI, subteam members explored various aspects of the concept. (See the PMI example on page 224.) At the end of the exercise, they decided they wanted the safety coordinator at the neighbor's company to talk with them about the approach.

They also spent one meeting building a relations diagram to help them understand the causes of safety incidents and attitudes. (Step 5: What prevents us from doing better?) One key issue was peer pressure. When their guest spoke with them, he confirmed that peer pressure was one of the factors the approach addressed.

The subteam liked the approach, but decided that the way the other company used it would not work for this unit. The subteam used a force field analysis to identify factors that would help the new approach to work and factors that would work against it. Then the subteam developed a roll-out plan, using input from other members of the unit. (Step 7: Do it.)

To explain the new approach to the unit, the subteam made a storyboard on the control room bulletin board. (See the storyboard example on page 253.) During the two weeks it was there, the subteam answered numerous questions. Then the subteam arranged for each shift to do a benefits and barriers exercise. The first shift was not able to see the other groups' ideas until later, but the remaining shifts had the opportunity to compare their ideas with ideas from the groups that had already done the exercise. After the exercise, most of the unit was enthusiastic about trying the approach. Using the barriers identified during the exercise, the subteam modified and launched its plan.

After a few weeks the subteam plans to survey the entire unit to learn how the new approach is perceived. If necessary, the approach will be modified. (Step 8: How did we do? If it didn't work, try again.) The subteam also will continue to monitor the safety score on the performance index. If the approach works, the subteam has ideas about applying it to environmental performance as well. (Step 10: What did we learn?)

4

The Tools

ACORN Test

Description
The ACORN test[1] is a check on a mission statement, to determine whether the mission is well-defined.

When to Use
- While drafting a mission statement, to guide its development
- When the mission statement has been completed, as a check on its quality
- When writing the mission of either an organization or a project team
- When writing subgoals

Procedure
Ask the following questions about the mission:

A—Accomplishment: Does the mission describe results rather than behaviors? Could the mission be verified if the people responsible for it were not there?

C—Control: Do the group's actions determine whether the mission is accomplished? Or, does it depend on actions of others?

O—Only Objective: If this and only this were accomplished, would it be enough? If something else also is required, then subgoals have been identified, not the true mission. (Subgoals do not have to pass the *O* part of the test.)

R—Reconciliation: If this mission is accomplished, will it prevent another group within the organization from accomplishing its mission? Or, does another group share the same mission? Two groups should not be addressing either the same mission or conflicting missions. (Subgoals do not have to pass the *R* part of the test.)

N—Numbers: Can the mission be measured? It must be possible to generate practical, cost-effective data to measure the mission. Measurement will indicate whether or not the mission has been achieved.

Examples

The Engineering Department has drafted this mission statement.

> The Engineering Department serves the business units, manufacturing department, and our customers by being the best at designing and constructing safe, environmentally responsible, easily maintained and operated facilities—better, faster, and at lower total cost than anyone else.

The department checks it against the ACORN test.

A—Engineering has a tangible *accomplishment* when the mission is fulfilled: the steel and concrete of a manufacturing plant.

C—Engineering has broad *control* over its projects, although R&D, manufacturing, and business units provide input and have veto power.

O—Engineering's *only* function is designing and managing the construction of new facilities.

R—As no one else has this function, the mission is *reconcilable.*

N—*Numbers* are routinely available for project schedule and cost as well as safety, environmental, and operational performance. The group decided it needed to develop an operational definition and measures for "better," which everyone intuitively understands to mean best technology and methods.

The customer satisfaction team at the Parisian Experience Restaurant wrote this charter statement as it began its work.

> The PERCS team will improve the customer satisfaction ratings of our restaurant by 20%.

When the team applied the ACORN test to the charter, it failed. The team members realized that they do not have control over the customer satisfaction ratings: every waiter, chef, cashier, and manager plays a part. So they tried again with the following statement:

> The PERCS team will direct and support the continuing improvement of customer satisfaction with our restaurant.

That statement failed the ACORN test, too. This time, the statement described behaviors ("direct and support"), not accomplishments. What is the team really going to do? Back to the drawing board for draft number three, which passed the test.

> The PERCS team will identify opportunities to improve customer satisfaction with our restaurant, and will develop and recommend plans that transform those opportunities into value for our customers and our business.

Considerations

- If a mission does not pass the ACORN test, it may actually be in conflict with the goals of the entire company or institution.

- An overall mission statement must pass all five parts of the ACORN test. A subgoal will never pass the O (only objective) part of the test. It may not pass the R (reconcilable) part either, if this goal needs to be balanced against another. But it must pass the A (accomplishment), C (control), and N (numbers) tests.

  Example: Two subgoals of the Engineering Department, to build plants quickly and to build them so they are easily maintained, may not be completely reconcilable with each other. It may add time to the design phase of a project to obtain input from maintenance. These two subgoals must be balanced in order for the department to achieve its mission.

- When the mission of an organization is well-defined according to the ACORN test, one can proceed to evaluate performance against that mission in a meaningful way.

Activity Chart

Gantt Chart, Milestones Chart

Description

An activity chart lays out the tasks of a project in sequential order and shows when each must take place.

When to Use

- When planning a project
- Only when the steps of the project or process, their sequence, and their duration are known
- When monitoring the progress of a project

Basic Procedure

Construction

1. Identify the tasks that need to be done to complete the project. This may be done by brainstorming a list or by drawing a flowchart, storyboard, or arrow diagram for the project. Identify the time required for each task. Finally, identify the sequence. Which tasks must be finished before a following task can begin, and which can happen simultaneously?

2. Draw a horizontal time axis along the top of a page. Mark it off in an appropriate scale for the length of the project (for example, days, weeks).

3. Down the left side of the page, write each task of the project in order. For events that happen at a point in time (such as a presentation), draw a diamond under the time the event must happen. For activities that occur over a period of time (such as developing a plan or holding a series of interviews), draw a bar under the appropriate time on the timeline. Align the left end of the bar with the time the activity begins, and align the right end with the time the activity concludes. Draw just the outlines of the bars and diamonds; don't fill them in.

4. Check that every task of the project is on the activity chart as a bar.

Using the Chart

5. As events and activities take place, fill in the diamonds and bars to show completion. For activities in progress, estimate how far along you are and fill in that much of the bar.

6. Place a vertical marker to show where you are on the timeline. If the chart is posted on the wall, an easy way to show the current time is with a heavy dark string and two thumbtacks.[2]

Example

Figure 4.1 shows an activity chart used to plan a benchmarking study. Twelve weeks are indicated on the timeline. There are two events, getting approvals for the project and for the new process developed in the study. The rest of the tasks are activities stretching over a period of time.

The chart shows the status at Tuesday of the sixth week. The team has finished seven tasks, down through identifying key practices, measures, and documentation. This is the most hectic part of the project, with three time-consuming activities that must happen simultaneously.

The team estimates it is one-fourth finished with identifying benchmark partners and scheduling visits; one-fourth of that bar is filled. Team members have not yet begun to identify the current state. They are behind schedule for those two tasks. They are halfway through collecting public data, which puts them slightly ahead of schedule for that task. Perhaps they need to reallocate their workforce to be able to cover those three activities simultaneously.

There is a fourth activity that could be happening now (develop benchmark questions), but it is not urgent yet. Eventually the team will have to allocate resources to cover it too, before visits can begin.

Compare this chart with the arrow diagram example (Figure 4.7). Both show the same project. Relationships and dependencies between tasks are clearer on the arrow diagram, but the activity chart makes it easier to visualize progress.

Variation

This version is similar to a deployment chart in that it shows responsibilities for tasks.

Complete steps 1 and 2 as described in the basic procedure.

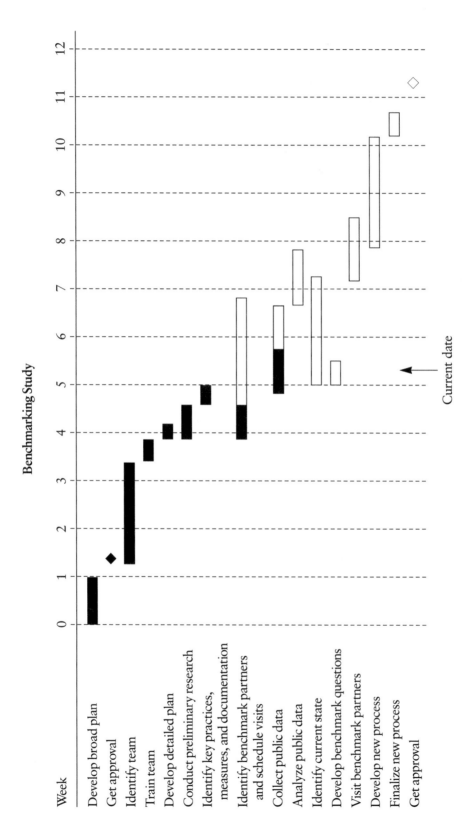

Figure 4.1. Activity chart example.

3. Down the left side of the page, list the people or groups who will have direct responsibility for the project tasks.

4. Transfer from the flowchart, storyboard, or arrow diagram each task of the project. Represent it as a bar opposite the person or group responsible. Align the end tail of the bar with the date that activity begins, and align the right end with the date that activity concludes. Write the task above the bar.

5. Check that every task is on the activity chart as a bar. Review the chart with everyone named on it for their agreement.

Use the chart as described in the basic procedure.

Considerations

- The process of constructing the chart forces group members to think clearly about what must be done to accomplish their goal. Keeping it updated as the project proceeds helps manage the project and head off schedule problems.

- Posting the chart in a visible place helps keep everyone informed and motivated.

- This chart fills some of the same functions as the arrow diagram. This one is easier to construct, can be understood at a glance, and can be used to monitor progress. However, the arrow diagram analyzes the project's schedule more thoroughly, revealing bottlenecks and tasks that are dependent on other tasks.

- It can be useful to indicate the critical path on the chart with bold or colored outlines of the bars for the steps on the critical path. (See "Arrow Diagram" on page 53 for a discussion of critical path.)

Affinity Diagram

Description
The affinity diagram organizes large numbers of ideas into their natural relationships. This method taps the team's creativity and intuition.

When to Use

- Facts or thoughts are in chaos; issues seem too large and complex to grasp

- A breakthrough to new ideas is desired
- Group consensus is necessary
- Often useful following a brainstorming exercise

Procedure

1. Record each idea with marking pens on a separate Post-It™ note or card. (Brainstorm directly onto Post-It™ notes or cards if you suspect you will be following the brainstorm with an affinity diagram.) Randomly spread notes on table, floor, or wall so all are visible to everyone.

The entire team gathers around the cards and participates in the next steps.

2. *It is very important that no one talk during this step.* Look for ideas that seem to be related in some way. Place them side by side. Repeat until all cards are grouped. It's okay to have "loners" that don't seem to fit a group. It's all right to move a card someone else has already moved. If a card seems to belong in two groups, make a second card.

3. *You can talk now.* When ideas are grouped, select a heading for each group. Look for a card in each grouping that captures the meaning of the group. Place it at the top of the group. If there is no such card, write one. Often it is useful to write or highlight this card in a different color.

4. Combine groups into supergroups if appropriate.

Example

The ZZ-400 manufacturing team used an affinity diagram to organize its list of potential performance indicators. Figure 4.2 shows the list team members brainstormed. Because the team works a shift schedule and members could not meet to do the affinity diagram together, they modified the procedure.

They wrote each idea on a Post-It™ note and put all the notes randomly on a rarely used door. Over several days, everyone reviewed the notes in their spare time and moved the notes into related groups. Some people

Possible Performance Measures	
% purity	# of OSHA recordables
% trace metals	# of customer returns
Maintenance costs	Customer complaints
# of emergency jobs	Overtime/total hours worked
lbs. produced	$/lb. produced
Environmental accidents	Raw material utilization
Material costs	Yield
Overtime costs	Utility cost
# of pump seal failures	ppm water
Viscosity	Color
Cp_k values	Service factor
Safety	Time between turnarounds
Days since last lost-time	Hours worked/employee
% rework or reject	lb. waste
Hours downtime	Housekeeping score
% uptime	% capacity filled

Figure 4.2. Brainstorming for affinity diagram example.

reviewed the evolving pattern several times. After a few days, the natural grouping shown in Figure 4.3 had emerged.

Notice that one of the notes, "Safety," has become part of the heading for its group. The rest of the headings were added after the grouping emerged. Five broad areas of performance were identified: product quality, equipment maintenance, manufacturing cost, production volume, and safety and environmental.

Considerations

- The affinity diagram process lets a group move beyond its habitual thinking and preconceived categories. This technique accesses the great knowledge and understanding residing untapped in our intuition.

- Every group that has used this technique has been amazed at how powerful and valuable a tool it is. Try it once with an open mind and you will be another convert.

- Use marking pens. With regular pens, it is hard to read ideas from any distance.

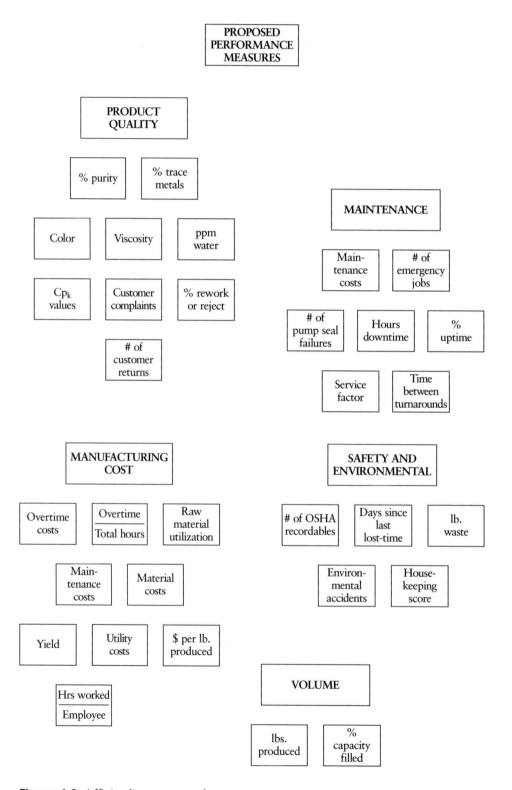

Figure 4.3. Affinity diagram example.

Arrow Diagram

Activity Network Diagram, CPM, CPS, PERT

Description

The arrow diagram is used to plan and show the required order of tasks in a project or process, the best schedule for the entire project, and potential scheduling and resource problems and their solutions. The arrow diagram, lets you calculate the *critical path* of the project. This is the flow of critical steps where delays will affect the timing of the entire project, and where addition of resources can speed up the project.

When to Use

- When planning a complex project or process with interrelated tasks and resources

- When analyzing the timing of a project; this analysis can happen before, during, or after the project

- When allocating resources (such as people, money, and time) to a project

- When monitoring the progress of a project

- When replanning a project in progress, due to changes in conditions or resources

- Only when you know the steps of the project or process, their sequence, and how long each step takes

Procedure

Planning

1. List all the necessary tasks in the project or process. One convenient method is to write each task on the top half of a card or Post-It™ note. Across the middle of the card, draw a horizontal arrow pointing right.

2. Determine the correct sequence of the tasks. Do this by asking three questions for each task.

    - Which tasks must happen before this one can begin?
    - Which tasks can be done at the same time as this one?
    - Which tasks should happen immediately after this one?

It can be useful to create a table with four columns—prior tasks, this task, simultaneous tasks, following tasks.

3. Diagram the network of tasks. If you are using notes or cards, arrange them in sequence on a large piece of paper. Time should flow from left to right and concurrent tasks should be vertically aligned. Leave space between the cards.

4. Between each two tasks, draw circles for events. An *event* marks the beginning or end of a task, a milestone for the project. Thus, events are nodes that separate tasks.

5. Look for three common problem situations and redraw them using dummies or extra events. A *dummy* is an arrow drawn with dotted lines to separate tasks that would otherwise start and stop with the same events, or to show logical sequence of tasks. Dummies are not real tasks.

Problem situations:

- Two simultaneous tasks that start and end at the same events. *Solution:* Use a dummy to separate them.

- Task C cannot start until tasks A and B are complete; a fourth task, D, cannot start until A is complete, but need not wait for B. (See Figure 4.4.) *Solution:* Use a dummy between the end of task A and the beginning of task C.

- A second task can be started before part of a first task is done. *Solution:* Add an extra event where the second task can begin and use multiple arrows to break the first task into two subtasks. In Figure 4.5, instead of the branch shown on the left, draw the arrangement shown on the right.

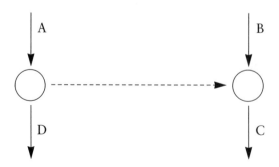

Figure 4.4. Arrow diagram: Dummy showing sequence.

Figure 4.5. Arrow diagram: Subtasks.

6. When the network is correct, label all events in sequence with event numbers in the circle. It can be useful to label all tasks in sequence, using letters.

Scheduling

7. Determine the task times. The *task time* is the best estimate of the time that each task should require. Use one consistent measuring unit (hours, days, weeks). Write the time on each task's arrow.

8. Determine the critical path. The *critical path* is the longest path from the beginning to the end of the project. Mark the critical path with a heavy line or color. Calculate the length of the critical path: the sum of all the task times on the path.

9. Calculate the earliest times each task can start and finish, based on how long preceding tasks take. Start with the first task, where the earliest start is zero, and work forward.

    Earliest start (ES) = the largest earliest finish of the tasks leading into this one

    Earliest finish (EF) = earliest start + task time

10. Calculate the latest times each task can start and finish without upsetting the project schedule, based on how long later tasks will take. Start from the last task, where the latest finish is the project deadline, and work backwards.

    Latest finish (LF) = the smallest latest start of all the tasks leading out of this one

    Latest start (LS) = latest finish – task time

11. Write all four times—*ES, EF, LS, LF*—beside the task arrow. One common way to show them is in four boxes arranged as follows:[3]

Earliest start	Earliest finish
Latest start	Latest finish

12. Calculate slack times for each task and for the entire project.[4] *Total slack* is the time a job could be postponed without delaying the project schedule.

     Total slack = $LS - ES$

Free slack is the time a task could be postponed without affecting the slack of any job following it.

     Free slack = the earliest *ES* of all the tasks leading out of this one – *EF*

Figure 4.6 shows a schematic way to remember which numbers to subtract.

Example

Tasks: Figure 4.7 shows an arrow diagram for a benchmarking project. There are 14 tasks, shown by the solid arrows. The number on the arrow is the task time in days, based on the experience and judgment of the group planning the project.

Events: There are 15 events, represented by the circled numbers. The events mark the beginning and ending times for the tasks. They will serve as milestones for monitoring progress throughout the project.

$$TS = LS - ES$$
$$\text{or } LF - EF$$

$$FS = \text{smallest } ES - EF$$

Figure 4.6. Arrow diagram: Remembering slack calculations.

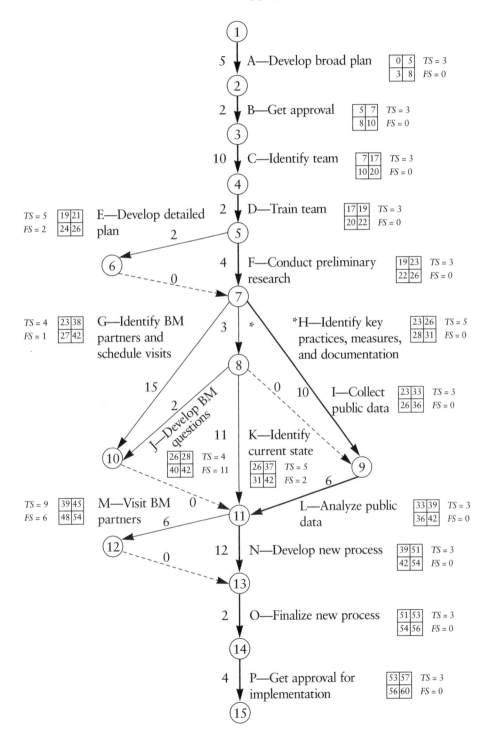

Figure 4.7. Arrow diagram example.

Dummies: Tasks E and F show the first kind of problem situation, where two tasks can occur simultaneously. Developing a detailed plan and conducting preliminary research can be done at the same time. Dummy 6–7 separates them. Task 10–11 is also a dummy to separate the simultaneous tasks J (develop questions) and K (identify current state).

The second kind of problem situation is illustrated around tasks H, I, J, K, and L. Task L (analyzing public data) cannot start until both tasks H (identifying key practices and measures) and I (collecting public data) are done. Task J (develop questions) and task K (identify current state), can start as soon as task H is complete. Task 8–9 is a dummy to separate the starting time of tasks J and K from that of task L.

The third kind of problem situation is illustrated around tasks M, N, and O. Originally, tasks N and O were one task—develop new process. Task M (visiting benchmark partners) can begin at the same time, but the visits need to be completed before final decisions can be made about the new process. To show this, a subtask was created: finalize new process. Now the network shows that the visits must be completed before the process can be finalized. (A dummy is needed because tasks M and N are simultaneous.)

Critical Path: The longest path, marked in bold, is the critical path. Its tasks and their times are:

A	B	C	D	F	I	L	N	O	P
5	2	10	2	4	10	6	12	2	4 = 57

The team was surprised that the external visits, which members assumed would be a scheduling bottleneck, are not on the critical path, if they can schedule visits with a three week lead time, as they assumed. The entire project will require 57 days if all tasks on the critical path proceed as scheduled.

Earliest and Latest Start and Finish Times: The earliest times are calculated forward from the start, using as the earliest start (*ES*) the largest earliest finish (*EF*) of the tasks before the one being calculated. The *ES* for the first task is 0.

Task	*ES*	+	Task time	=	*EF*
A	0		5		5
B	5		2		7
C	7		10		17

Task	ES	+	Task time	=	EF	
D	17		2		19	
E	19		2		21	
F	19		4		23	
G	23		15		38	and so on

The latest times are calculated backward from the end, using as the latest finish (*LF*) the smallest latest start (*LS*) of the tasks following the one being calculated. The project has a 12-week deadline, or 60 working days, so 60 is used as the *LF* for the last task.

Task	LF	–	Task time	=	LS	
P	60		4		56	
O	56		2		54	
N	54		12		42	
M	54		6		48	
L	42		6		36	and so on

These times are shown beside each task, in the four-box grid.

Slack Times: The slack times for each task are shown beside each grid. Because 60 days have been allotted for the project and the critical path adds up to 57 days, there is slack time for all the tasks. For each of the tasks on the critical path, the total slack is 3, the slack time for the entire project. The tasks not on the critical path have up to nine days total slack.

Surprisingly to the team, there is free slack of six days for visiting the benchmark partners, so six days of scheduling problems with the partners can be tolerated without delaying later tasks. There is total slack of nine days for the visits, so if the project is on schedule up to that task, nine days' delay in making visits will not affect the project completion date.

Compare this diagram with the activity chart example (Figure 4.1). Both show the same project. Relationships and dependencies between tasks are clearer on the arrow diagram, but the activity chart makes it easier to visualize progress.

Variation: Program Evaluation and Review Technique (PERT)[5]

This variation allows for uncertain time estimates for individual tasks. Complete steps 1 through 6 (pages 53–55) as in the basic procedure. Then follow with

    7. Make three estimates of the time required for each task.

        • Minimum *(a)*—if everything went right

- Most likely *(m)*—the normal time required; an average of the times if the task were done repeatedly
- Maximum *(b)*—if everything went wrong

Show all three times on the diagram, separated by dashes: 3–5–8. Next calculate the expected time (t_E) and the variance (σ^2) for each task.

$$t_E = \frac{a + 4m + b}{6} \qquad \sigma^2 = \left(\frac{b - a}{6}\right)^2$$

Use the expected time for calculating critical path, earliest and latest start and finish times, and slack times in the basic procedure.

Go on to steps 8 through 12 (pages 55–56). Then

13. Determine the probability (P) that the project will be finished by its deadline, T_D. Calculate three numbers.

T_E = total expected time = the sum of the expected times t_E for all the critical path tasks

$\sigma^2 (T_E)$ = total variance = the sum of the variances for all the critical path tasks

$$Z = \frac{T_S - T_E}{\sqrt{\sigma^2 (T_E)}}$$

Look up the value for Z on the table of area under the normal curve (Table A.1). P is the probability that the project will be finished by its deadline.

Example

To demonstrate these calculations, we will use a critical path with only four tasks. Table 4.1 shows the minimum, most likely, and maximum time estimates $(a, m,$ and $b)$, the expected time (t_E) and the variance (σ^2). If the deadline for the project is 25 days, then $Z = 0.75$. Looking up 0.75 on Table A.1 shows that $P = 0.77$. The probability of completing the project in 25 days or less is 77%.

It may seem surprising that there is a 23% chance of not meeting the deadline, since the total expected time (T_E) for the project is 23.3 days, less than the deadline. Remember, however, that each task's time estimate had a worst case. If everything went wrong and all the worst-case estimates came true, the project would require 36 days.

Table 4.1. PERT example.

Task	$a - m - b$	t_E	σ^2
A	$2 - 5 - 10$	$\dfrac{2 + 20 + 10}{6} = 5.3$	$\left(\dfrac{10 - 2}{6}\right)^2 = 1.8$
B	$5 - 8 - 12$	$\dfrac{5 + 32 + 12}{6} = 8.2$	$\left(\dfrac{12 - 5}{6}\right)^2 = 2.3$
C	$3 - 6 - 8$	$\dfrac{3 + 24 + 8}{6} = 5.8$	$\left(\dfrac{8 - 3}{6}\right)^2 = 0.7$
D	$2 - 4 - 6$	$\dfrac{2 + 16 + 6}{6} = 4.0$	$\left(\dfrac{6 - 2}{6}\right)^2 = 0.4$
		$T_E = 23.3$	$\sigma^2 (T_E) = 5.2$

$$T_D = 25$$

$$Z = \frac{25 - 23.3}{\sqrt{5.2}} = 0.75$$

$$P = 0.77$$

Considerations

- If any task on the critical path is delayed, all tasks on the critical path will be pushed back. If there is no slack in the overall project, the project will be delayed.

- The timing of tasks with some free slack can be left to the judgment of those handling the task, as long as they do not delay the task more than the amount of free slack.[6]

  Example: The team making benchmark visits can spread its schedule over 12 days instead of the planned six days without consulting with the rest of the project team.

- When tasks without free slack are delayed, the times and slack for all following jobs must be recalculated.

- Slack time can be negative.

  Example: If the time allotted for the benchmarking project was less than 57 days, or if the critical path tasks become delayed by more than three days, the slack time would become negative, and ways to make up that time would have to be found.

- To speed up a project schedule, find ways to increase resources or reduce scope only for those tasks on the critical path. Speeding up tasks not on the critical path will have no effect on the overall project time. It may be possible to move resources from noncritical tasks to critical ones.

  Example: To complete the benchmarking project in 10 weeks instead of 12, ways might be found to identify the team faster (task C), to get public data more quickly (task I), to get faster approvals (tasks B and P), or to speed up any of the other six tasks on the critical path. Collapsing the visit schedule (tasks G or M) will not complete the project sooner.

- However, when critical path tasks are shortened, the entire network must be recalculated. New tasks may now be on the critical path, and they can be examined for opportunities to shorten the schedule.

  Example: In the benchmark project, if a way were found to collect public data (task I) in five days instead of 10, scheduling visits (task G) would now lie on the critical path.

- Another way to shorten the project time is to rethink the sequence of tasks on the critical path. If some of them can be done simultaneously, total project time can be reduced.

- In the arrow diagram process, involve a team of people who have broad knowledge about the project or process.

- The easiest way to construct the diagram when first laying out the sequence is to find the path with the most tasks. Lay out that path first, then add other parallel paths.

- No loops are allowed in the network of tasks. A loop would be a sequence where task A is followed by task B, followed by task C, followed by task A.

- Be aware that the length of an arrow is not related to the amount of time the task takes. Arrow lengths depend simply on the way you have chosen to depict the network of tasks.

- A common notation labels tasks with their starting and ending events. A task that starts at event 4 and ends at event 7 would be labeled task 4–7.

- For very complex networks of tasks, computer programs that do the calculations for you are available.

- This chart fills some of the same functions as the activity chart. It analyzes the project's schedule more thoroughly, revealing the critical path and dependencies between tasks. However, the activity chart is easier to construct, can be understood at a glance, and can be used for monitoring progress.

- Many project planners are familiar with this type of planning tool under the names Program Evaluation and Review Technique (PERT) and Critical Path Method (CPM). These methods were developed in the late 1950s by the U.S. Navy and the DuPont Company, respectively. Arrow diagram and activity network diagram are terms used for this tool in various descriptions of the set of seven new QC tools.

Benefits and Barriers Exercise

Description
The benefits and barriers exercise[7] helps individuals see both personal and organizational benefits of a proposed change. It also clarifies perceived obstacles to accomplishing the change. Most important, it generates individual and group buy-in to the change.

When to Use
- When trying to decide whether to proceed with a change

- When trying to generate buy-in and support for a change

- After the concept has been developed, but before detailed design of a plan, to identify obstacles that need to be considered in the design

- Especially for major changes, such as launching a quality effort or implementing a recognition program

Procedure
Materials needed: flipchart paper, marking pen, and masking tape for each group of five to seven people; paper and pen or pencil for each individual.

1. Explain the purpose of the exercise and how it will be done. Emphasize that everyone's active involvement is important. Divide

the participants into groups of five to seven each and assign break-out rooms and leaders, who have been coached in advance on their role.

2. Do benefits first. Show the group this statement, written on flip-chart paper and posted where all can see.

> Assume that it is now two years in the future and we have been successful in implementing [name of concept or change]. What benefits do you see for yourself as an individual, for your work group, and for the company as a whole?[8]

3. Each group brainstorms benefits using the NGT method. (See "Nominal Group Technique" [NGT] on page 201 for details on this structured brainstorming method.) Collect ideas by category in either of two ways.

   - Conduct three separate NGT sessions, first collecting benefits for the individual, then for the work group, then for the company.

   - Or, conduct one NGT, and mark each idea when collected with a code (such as I, W, C) indicating who benefits.

4. Each group uses multivoting to choose the top three benefits in each of the three categories. (See "Multivoting" on page 195 for more detail on this prioritization method.) Let each participant vote for his or her top five in each category. Each group should select a spokesperson. Allow 1 to 1½ hours for steps 3 and 4.

5. Reassemble the entire group. Each spokesperson should report on

   - How the exercise went: the extent of participation, how much agreement there was, and so forth

   - The top three benefits in each category (a total of nine benefits)

6. Follow with barriers. Show the group this statement.

> What are the barriers that we as an organization are going to have to overcome in order to make [name of concept or change] a success and thereby achieve the benefits?[9]

7. Each group brainstorms barriers using the NGT method. Do not separate individual, work group, and company barriers.

8. Each group identifies the top three barriers, again using multivoting. A different spokesperson should be selected. This breakout session should last 45 minutes to an hour.

9. Reassemble the entire group. Each spokesperson reports the group's top three barriers.

10. After the meeting, transcribe the flipchart pages from all the groups and send them to the participants with the meeting notes.

Variation: Small Group

When the group is too small to form several breakout groups, spokespersons are not needed. At step 5, the facilitator should ask the group to discuss briefly how the process went. Step 9, of course, is omitted.

Considerations

- When the proposed change is major and involves a lot of emotion and potential resistance, it becomes valuable to do this exercise with enough people to form several breakout groups. Fifteen to 28 individuals are ideal. Hearing other groups generate similar ideas validates each individual's ideas and feelings and reinforces each individual's commitment.

- An outside facilitator can be valuable with a significant change and high-ranking participants.

- Individuals must be familiar with the proposed change before the exercise can be done.

- During the report-backs, the facilitator should listen for and comment on similarities between the groups' ideas.

- All perceived barriers must be taken seriously and addressed in the design of the plan.

Conducting the NGT

- Avoid discussing ideas until after the lists are completed. Also avoid responding to barriers until the end.

- The brainstorming rule of "no criticism, no censoring" applies.

- Whoever is writing the ideas should write what the speaker says as closely as possible. If the idea must be shortened, ask the speaker if the summary captures the idea accurately.

- Write large enough that everyone can read the ideas. Generally, that means letters about two inches high.

• As a page is filled, tear it off and tape it to the wall where it can be seen by the entire group.

Box Plot

Box-and-Whisker Plot

Description

The box plot is a graph that summarizes groups of data for easy understanding and comparison.

When to Use

• When analyzing or communicating the overall pattern of data, rather than the detail

• When comparing two sets of data

• When there is not enough data for a histogram

• To summarize the data represented by another graph, such as a control chart or run chart

Procedure

1. List all the data values in order from smallest to largest. We will refer to the total number of values, the count, as *n*. We will refer to the numbers in order like this: X_1 is the smallest number; X_2 is the next smallest number; up to X_n which is the largest number.

2. *Medians:* Cut the data in half. Find the median—the point where half the values are larger and half are smaller.

   • If the total number of values (*n*) is odd: The median is the middle one. Count $(n + 1)/2$ from either end.

   $$\text{median} = X_{(n + 1)/2}$$

   • If the total number of values (*n*) is even: The median is the average of the two middle ones. Count $n/2$ and $n/2 + 1$ from either end. Average those two numbers:

   $$\text{median} = \frac{X_{n/2} + X_{n/2 + 1}}{2}$$

3. *Hinges:* Cut the data in quarters. Find the hinges—the medians of each half.

 • If the total number of values is even, the median was the average of $X_{n/2}$ and $X_{n/2 + 1}$. Take the values from 1 to $X_{n/2}$ and find their median just as in step 2. This is the lower hinge.

 • If the total number of values is odd, the median was $X_{(n + 1)/2}$. Take the values from 1 to the median and find their median, just as in step 2. This is the lower hinge.

 Do the same with the values at the upper end to find the upper hinge.

4. *H-spread:* Calculate the distance between the hinges, or H-spread:

$$\text{H-spread} = \text{upper hinge} - \text{lower hinge}$$

5. *Inner fences:* These are values separating data that are outside the distribution from data that are probably a predictable part of the distribution. Inner fences are located beyond each hinge at 1½ times the H-spread.

$$\text{upper inner fence} = \text{upper hinge} + 1.5 \times \text{H-spread}$$

$$\text{lower inner fence} = \text{lower hinge} - 1.5 \times \text{H-spread}$$

6. *Outer fences:* Data beyond these values are far outside the distribution and deserving of special attention. Outer fences are located beyond the inner fences 1½ times the H-spread.

$$\text{upper outer fence} = \text{upper inner fence} + 1.5 \times \text{H-spread}$$

$$\text{lower outer fence} = \text{lower inner fence} - 1.5 \times \text{H-spread}$$

7. Draw the box plot. Scale the axis appropriately for the range of data. Draw a box with ends at the hinge values. Draw a line across the middle of the box at the median value. Draw a line at each inner fence value. Draw dashed lines from the ends of the box to the first value inside the inner fences. (This is called an *adjacent value.*) Place a dashed crossbar at that value. Draw small circles representing any outlying data points occurring beyond the inner fences. Draw double circles to represent data points outside the outer fences.

8. If you are comparing several data sets, repeat the procedure for each set of data.

9. Analyze the plot. Look for

- Location of the median
- Spread of the data: how far the hinges and fences are from the median
- Symmetry of the distribution
- Existence of outside points

Example

Suppose two bowling teams, the Avengers and the Bulldogs, have the scores shown in Figure 4.8. Which team is better?

1. The scores are already in order from smallest to largest. There are 14 scores for each team. So $n = 14$.

2. *Median:* There is an even number of scores, so the median is the average of the two middle ones. We must count $n/2$ and $n/2 + 1$ from one end.

$$n/2 = 14/2 = 7 \text{ and } n/2 + 1 = 8$$

Count to the seventh and eighth scores in each group and average them.

$$\text{Median A} = \frac{149 + 150}{2} = 149.5$$

$$\text{Median B} = \frac{155 + 159}{2} = 157$$

Bowling scores

The Avengers

126   134   137   142   145   148   149   150   155   157   160   165   170   198

The Bulldogs

103   139   147   152   153   154   155   159   161   163   163   165   176   183

                  ↑   ↑   ↑

              hinge   median   hinge

Figure 4.8. Data for box plot example.

3. *Hinges:* We must find two medians, first of values 1 through 7 and then of values 8 through 14. There are 7 values in each half, an odd number, so we count $(7 + 1)/2 = 4$ from either end. Count up four from the lowest score and down four from the highest score.

   upper hinge A = 160   lower hinge A = 142

   upper hinge B = 163   lower hinge B = 152

4. *H-Spread:* The distance between hinges is

H-spread	= upper hinge	– lower hinge		
H-spread A =	160	–	142	=	18
H-spread B =	163	–	152	=	11

5. *Inner fences:*

   upper inner fence   = upper hinge + 1.5 × H-spread

upper inner fence A =	160	+ 1.5 ×	18		
	=	160	+	27	= 187
upper inner fence B =	163	+ 1.5 ×	11		
	=	163	+	16.5	= 179.5

   lower inner fence   = lower hinge – 1.5 × H-spread

lower inner fence A =	142	–	27	= 115
lower inner fence B =	152	–	16.5	= 135.5

6. *Outer fences:*

   upper

   upper outer fence   = inner fence + 1.5 × H-spread

upper outer fence A =	187	+	27	= 214
upper outer fence B =	179.5	+	16.5	= 196

   lower

   lower outer fence   = inner fence – 1.5 × H-spread

lower outer fence A =	115	–	27	= 88
lower outer fence B =	135.5	–	16.5	= 119

Figure 4.9 is the box plot of the two teams' scores. While the Avengers have a star and the Bulldogs have a poor player, overall the Bulldogs tend to score higher and more consistently than the Avengers.

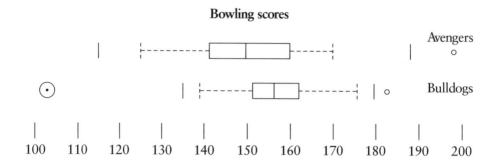

Figure 4.9. Box plot example.

Variations

The box plot originally was created by John W. Tukey.[10] Many variations have been proposed for calculating, drawing, and using box plots. Whenever you use a variation on the basic box plot, draw solid lines beyond the hinges to indicate you are not conforming to Tukey's rules. Some variations follow:[11]

- *Simple box plot:* Instead of calculating and drawing fences and outliers, draw lines from the ends of the box (hinge values) to the highest and lowest data values.

- *Modified box plot:* Calculate the arithmetic average of all the data values and represent that value with a dot on the box plot. The closer the average is to the median, the more symmetrical the distribution.

- *Modified-width box plot:* When using two or more box plots to compare several data sets, the widths of the boxes can be drawn proportional to the sample size of the data sets.

- Parentheses can be drawn on the plot to represent 95% confidence limits.

- *Ghost box plot* or *box-plot control chart:* A box plot can be drawn with dotted lines directly on a control chart or other graph of individual data points to show a summary of the data. This variation is especially useful if several plots represent sequential subgroups of the data. For example, one ghost box plot in the middle of a set of 15 data points prior to a process change and another in the middle of the next set of 15 data points after the change.

Considerations

- The box plot is a powerful tool because it is simple to construct yet yields a lot of information.

- Use a box plot to summarize data when there are not enough values to draw a histogram.

- Use a box plot instead of a histogram or stem-and-leaf display when you are comparing several sets of data.

Brainstorming

Description

Brainstorming is used to generate a large number of ideas in a short period of time.

When to Use

- When a broad range of options is desired

- When creative, original ideas are desired

- When participation of the entire group is desired

Procedure

1. Review the topic or problem to be discussed. Often it is best phrased as a *why, how,* or *what* question. Make sure the entire team understands the subject of the brainstorm.

2. Allow a minute or two of silence for everyone to think about the question.

3. Invite team members to call out their ideas. Record all ideas on a flipchart, in words as close as possible to those used by the contributor. No discussion or evaluation of any kind is permitted.

4. Continue to generate and record ideas until several minutes' silence produces no more.

Variations

- There are many versions of brainstorming. This is the most basic. See also "Nominal Group Technique," "Brainwriting," "Affinity Diagram," and "Fishbone Diagram" for more structured brainstorming techniques.

- Variation one: For five to 10 minutes, ask each team member to make a list of ideas on a piece of paper. Then go around the group and have each person read aloud one idea.

- Variation two: First allow only minimal or partial solutions. Then allow only outrageous and unrealistic solutions. Try to combine the ideas into reasonable alternatives.

Considerations

- *No criticism!* Laughter and groans are criticism. When there is criticism, people begin to evaluate their ideas before stating them. Fewer ideas are generated and creative ideas are lost.

- Try to avoid any evaluation, including positive comments such as "Great idea!" That implies that another idea that did not receive praise was mediocre. Judgment and creativity are two functions that cannot occur simultaneously.

- The more the better. Studies have shown that there is a direct relationship between the total number of ideas and the number of good, creative ideas.

- The crazier the better. Be unconventional in your thinking. Try the opposite of someone else's idea. Don't hold back any ideas. Crazy ideas are creative. They often come from a different perspective. Crazy ideas often lead to unique solutions, through modification or sparking someone else's imagination.

- Hitchhike. Build on someone else's idea.

- Encourage people to rapidly speak whatever ideas pop into their heads. The recording of ideas must not slow down the idea-generation process. If necessary, have several people recording ideas.

- Keep all ideas visible. When ideas overflow to additional flipchart pages, post previous pages around the room so the ideas are still visible to everyone.

Brainwriting

Description

Brainwriting is a nonverbal form of brainstorming.[12] Team members write ideas on sheets of paper, and then exchange the papers and write more ideas.

When to Use

- To generate a list of ideas when a topic is too controversial or emotionally charged for a verbal brainstorming session
- To encourage equal participation, when verbal brainstorming sessions are typically dominated by a few members

Procedure

1. Team members sit around a table. The facilitator poses a question or problem to the group.

2. Each team member writes ideas on a sheet of paper. When an individual has written four ideas, he or she places the sheet in the center of the table and selects another sheet. New ideas (up to four) are added to the previous list. That sheet goes back in the center, and another sheet is chosen.

3. The exercise ends after 10 to 15 minutes or after no one is generating more ideas. The sheets are collected for consolidation and discussion.

Variation: Method 6–3–5

1. Six people sit around a table. (That is the 6.) The facilitator poses a question or problem.

2. Each person writes down three ideas. (That is the 3.)

3. After five minutes, sheets are passed to the left. (That is the 5.)

4. Continue the process in five-minute blocks until all have their own sheets back.

Considerations

- Use a nonverbal tool when the team needs quiet time or when quieter members might not contribute fully.

- Passing sheets allows team members to build on each other's ideas without crushing them in the process.

- Method 6–3–5 works well for developing one or a few ideas. The emphasis can be placed on adding to the existing ideas on the page, rather than creating a list of scattered ideas.

Checksheet

Description

A checksheet is a structured, prepared form for collecting and analyzing data. It also can be used to confirm and record that steps of a process were done.

When to Use

- When collecting data on the frequency or patterns of events, problems, defects, defect location, defect causes, and so forth

- When collecting data from a production process

- When data can be observed and collected repeatedly by the same person or at the same location

- When standardizing a long list of actions, such as multiple preventive maintenance checks on a piece of equipment

- Data collection can occur at any step of the project

Procedure

1. Decide what will be observed. Develop operational definitions.

2. Decide when data will be collected and for how long.

3. Design the form. Set it up so that data can be recorded simply by making check marks or Xs or similar symbols and so that data does not have to be recopied for analysis.

4. Label all spaces on the form.

5. Test the checksheet for a short trial period to be sure it collects the appropriate data and is easy to use.

6. Each time an observation occurs, record data on the checksheet.

Telephone interruptions

Reason	Day					
	Mon	Tues	Wed	Thurs	Fri	Total
Wrong number	卌	||			卌	卌 ||	20
Info request	||	||	||	||	||	10
Boss	卌	||	卌 ||			||||	19
Total	12	6	10	8	13	49

Figure 4.10. Checksheet example.

Example

Figure 4.10 shows a checksheet used to collect data on telephone interruptions. The tick marks were added as data was collected over several weeks' time. What days are worst for interruptions? Which interruptions are most frequent?

Variation: Confirmation Checksheet

This kind of checksheet is used to confirm that steps of a process are carried out completely.

1. Decide what actions must be done. If sequence is important, decide on the order.

2. Design the form. Set it up so that actions can be confirmed simply by making check marks, Xs, initials, or similar symbols and so that data does not have to be recopied for analysis.

3. Label all spaces on the form. Include places for identifying information such as names, dates, lot numbers, and so on.

4. Test the checksheet for a short trial period to be sure the steps and sequence are correct, that appropriate data is recorded, and that the checksheet is easy to use.

5. Each time the process is carried out, use the checksheet to confirm the steps and record that they were performed.

Considerations

- A common way to lay out a checksheet is to list what you are observing (events, problems, types of errors, and so on) in a column down the left side. Divide the remainder of the page into columns for easy data collection. The columns might represent dates, times, locations of defects, or any other category that you wish to use to analyze the data later.

- When designing your form, use illustrations whenever possible. This makes the checksheet easier to use and can reveal patterns during your later analysis. For example, to collect data on damaged packages, include a sketch of the package and have data collectors put an X where they see the damage. If you are studying where errors occur on a report, put check marks on a sample of the report.

- Think about how data is received or how you will want to analyze it later, and consider keeping separate sheets for different aspects of the collection or analysis. For example, use separate checksheets for international and domestic shipment errors, if different people handle international and domestic shipments.

- Keep the checksheet near the point where the data to be recorded will occur. For example, if you are monitoring types of telephone interruptions, keep the checksheet next to your telephone. This will help you collect the data consistently.

- If observations occur frequently, you may choose to record samples rather than every observation. In step 2, decide when an observation will be recorded. You may decide to use a time interval (every 30 minutes) or a frequency (every fifth phone call).

Contingency Diagram

Description

The contingency diagram identifies and pictures what might go wrong in a process or plan, and ways to avoid these problems.

When to Use

- When identifying causes
- When planning implementation of a phase of a project, especially the solution
- Especially, before launching a change

Procedure

1. Phrase the situation (problem or action) and write it in the center of a flipchart page, inside an oval.

2. Brainstorm actions that cause things to go wrong. Here are some questions to spark your thinking.

   For a problem

   - How could you make the problem happen?
   - What makes the problem continue or worsen?

   For a plan or action

   - What would thwart the team's planned action?
   - What assumptions are we making that might be wrong?

   Draw arrows pointing toward the circle and write each idea on an arrow.

3. For each action, describe actions that would prevent it. Write these beside or under the problem actions, in a different color.

Example

Figure 4.11 shows a contingency diagram used to expand ideas about a problem in the office: secretaries having to retype documents frequently. One possible cause is "Author changes mind" for which a prevention is "More author preplanning." "Poor communications" is a cause that can be prevented by "Author/typist discussion." "Rushed preparation" could be prevented by "Establish requirements earlier." Six causes and preventions are shown on the diagram. Obviously, more could be identified by people involved with the problem.

Considerations

- Try combining this tool with the rules and techniques of brainstorming.
- First generate many possibilities of things that could go wrong until the group runs out of ideas. Then go back and identify possible preventions. By sequencing the ideas this way, the brain is functioning in one mode at a time.
- If several possible preventions are thought of, write them all down.

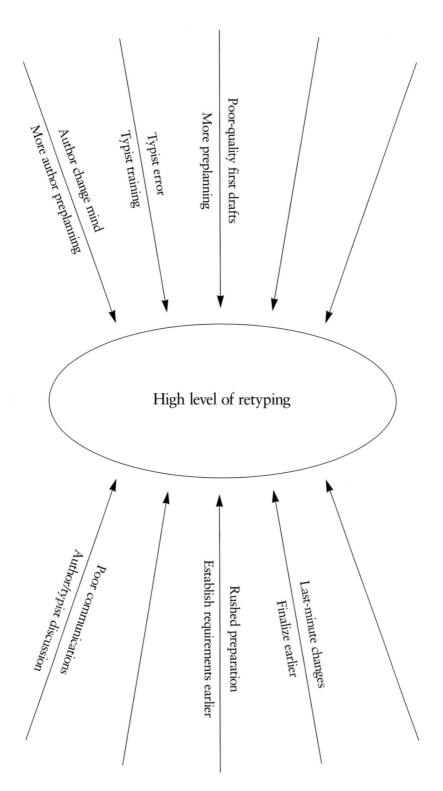

Figure 4.11. Contingency diagram example.

Continuum of Team Goals

Description

The continuum of team goals evaluates how general or specific a goal or mission statement is. It helps people clarify their understanding of the team's goals.

When to Use

- To stimulate and structure discussion about a team's goal or mission statement; especially

- In a steering committee or other management group, to clarify the scope of a task assigned to a project team

- At the beginning of a project, when team members may have different ideas about the scope of the team's assignment

- In a meeting between the team and management to achieve common understanding of the project scope, either at the beginning of the project or when it has stalled

- When writing or improving a project goal or mission statement

Procedure

1. If a goal or mission statement already exists, write it on a flipchart or overhead transparency so that all participants can see it.

2. Draw a continuum scale (Figure 4.12) on a flipchart or overhead transparency so that all participants can see it. Have each participant decide where he or she would place the assignment of the group along the continuum scale, based on his or her view of what is expected of the project team. This can be done orally or in writing. If a goal or mission statement already exists, each participant also should decide where the statement falls along the continuum.

3. Record all participants' marks. Use the group chart as a basis for discussion leading to consensus on the project scope. Be sure to consider whether this scope is appropriate.

4. If necessary, rewrite the goal or mission statement to reflect the consensus understanding of the project scope.

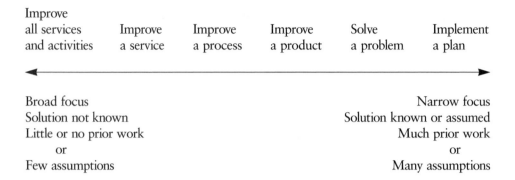

Figure 4.12. Continuum of team goals.

Examples

The following mission belongs at the far left of the continuum, "Improve all services and activities," because it includes all aspects of the department.

> The Engineering Department serves the business units, manufacturing department, and our customers by being the best at designing and constructing safe, environmentally responsible, easily maintained and operated facilities—better, faster and at lower total cost than anyone else.

Any mission statement written to describe an organization's purpose should be at the far left.

Here is the mission of the Parisian Experience Restaurant's customer satisfaction team.

> The PERCS team will identify opportunities to improve customer satisfaction with our restaurant, and will develop and recommend plans that transform those opportunities into value for our customers and our business.

This statement is located between "Improve all services and activities" and "Improve a service." (Since the scale is continuous, goals may fall between the tick marks.) While many services will be examined by the team (for example, providing gourmet food and providing an experience of luxury), some activities of the restaurant, such as buying ingredients or hiring employees, will not be considered because they do not directly affect customer satisfaction.

Some examples follow of goals for other restaurant teams that one can imagine. None are right or wrong. The best goal depends on what the group needs to accomplish and the prior work that has been done by this group or others.

Improve a service: "Enable quick, convenient and unobtrusive payment." It may seem odd that "enabling payment" is a service, but helping that necessary exchange to happen painlessly is indeed a service. This goal focuses the team on improving that service by whatever means it can create. The team is free to improve the current process or to devise a completely new one, such as restaurant membership and monthly billing.

Improve a process: "Improve the process of presenting the bill and collecting payment." This time, the team members are restricted to making a current process for payment better. They do not have the freedom to devise a totally new method for the customer to pay.

Improve a product: "Improve the layout of the bill." This mission is even more focused, and the team even more restricted, not just to a current process but to a current product: the piece of paper that functions as a bill. Although the team may completely change the format, its solution should still involve a piece of paper functioning as a bill. Note that no particular problem is defined in this statement.

Solve a problem: "Make the bill format easier for customers to read." This time a problem is implied: the current bill format is hard for customers to read. The team is not asked to make any other changes to the bill, such as better overall appearance.

Implement a plan: "Train the staff on how to use the new bill." This mission is the most focused of all. The team is not asked to create any changes or improvements, merely to carry out a task identified by others.

An example of an unclear statement is "Improve the mail service at a lower cost."

Two missions—improve a service (mail service) and solve a problem (cost) are mixed here. Is the focus on generally improving the mail service, with cost being a limitation the team must work within? Or is the focus on reducing cost? The answer is not clear, so there should be discussion to clarify the intent, and the statement should be rewritten. There can be two separate goals at different points on the continuum, as long as they are separate and both are clear to everyone: "Improve the mail service; as part of that improvement, reduce the net cost of mail service." This statement says that the basic goal is "improve a service," but there is a specific problem which everyone recognizes and wants to solve.

The following final example is the statement that spawned the idea of the continuum:

> Improve report preparation through review of the steps in
> the process.

This seems to be a clear example of "improve the process." After several months, the team members thought their work was done. They had made clear improvements to the process. Management said it was too early to disband, and the team did not understand why.

The conflict was traced to the beginning of the project and different understandings of the team's mission. An early status report gives a clue: "The team was formed to recommend changes to the IHS report writing process that will reduce the time to issue a survey report." This sounds like "solve a problem," not "improve a process." Despite significant improvements, the team had not reduced the time as much as management expected.

When the team and the steering committee discussed where on the continuum the team's mission belonged, different expectations became visible to everyone. Early discussion of expectations, using the continuum, would have avoided the conflict and provided better focus for the effort.

Considerations

- If the continuum is new to participants, the facilitator of the meeting should start by explaining the continuum, using an example such as the restaurant one.

- If different people place the project in different places on the continuum, the issue is not "Who is right?" but "What is right?" The appropriate scope needs to be determined, then clarified, so everyone understands it the same way, and the project statement needs to be rewritten so it conveys to everyone what is expected of the team.

- Where a mission statement belongs along the continuum depends not on the results of accomplishing the mission, but on the freedom or constraints the mission gives the team. For example, the statement, "Install new software XYZ on all PCs" may have the result of improving computer service. However, this statement does not allow the team to consider and choose how best to improve service; the team is asked to implement a specific plan.

- To facilitate discussion, try having each person describe which words in the mission statement caused the placement of his or her mark.

- Unless its assigned goal logically follows from work that already has been done, a team should consider whether its scope should be expanded to a point farther left on the continuum. Think more broadly than the immediate problem at hand or the current way of doing things to creative alternatives that eliminate problems instead of just fixing them, that add value rather than just adding efficiency.

Example: A team planning to make the bill easier to read (solve a problem) should consider the benefits of improving the overall format and appearance of the bill (improve a product) or even studying alternative ways of requesting payment (improve a service).

- When determining whether the scope is appropriate, consider such things as the makeup of the team, budget constraints, and timing expectations.

- The team's and management's scopes must match, so that the team's efforts will support the organization's overall strategy and solutions will be readily accepted and supported.

Control Charts

Description

The control chart is a graph used to analyze variation from a process. By comparing current data to historically determined lines, one can make conclusions about whether the process is stable or is being affected by special causes of variation. There are many types of control charts. Each is designed for a specific kind of process or data.

When to Use

- When you want to predict the expected range of outcomes from a process

- When determining whether or not a process is stable (in statistical control)

- When analyzing patterns of process variation from special causes (nonroutine events) or common causes (built into the process)

- When determining how to proceed with a quality improvement project—to prevent specific problems, or to make fundamental changes to the process

- When you want to control ongoing processes by finding and fixing problems as they occur

When to Use $\bar{\text{X}}$ and R Chart

- Only when the process data to be analyzed are measured on a continuous scale

- When the process data are not normally distributed
- When you want to detect small process changes
- Only when data are generated frequently

When to Use Chart of Individuals

- Only when the process data to be analyzed are measured on a continuous scale (for example, temperature, weight, time)
- Only when the distribution of data from the process is normal (see "Histogram" for a discussion of normal distribution and see "Normal Probability Plot" and "Kolmogorov–Smirnov Test" for two ways to determine whether it is normal)
- When each data point is already a natural subgroup (such as one batch) or data are gathered infrequently

When to Use Moving Average–Moving Range Chart

- Only when the process data to be analyzed are measured on a continuous scale
- When the process data are not normally distributed, but data are not available frequently enough to use an $\bar{X}$ and R chart, such as batch processes that make only one or two batches per day
- When you want to detect small process changes, but data are not available frequently enough to use an $\bar{X}$ and R chart

When to Use Attribute Charts

- Only when data are counted rather than measured on a continuous scale.
- When monitoring defects or other observations that have only two states: present or not present. For example, an item can have 2 defects or 3 defects, but not 2.6 defects.

Basic Procedure

1. Choose the appropriate control chart for your data.
2. Determine the appropriate time period for collecting and plotting data.

3. Follow the procedure for that control chart to construct your chart and analyze data on it.

4. When you see an out-of-control signal on the control chart, investigate the cause. Write on the control chart how you investigated and what you found. Write the cause and how it was corrected.

5. Continue to plot data as they are generated. As each new data point is plotted, check for new out-of-control signals.

6. When you start a new control chart, the process may be out of control. If so, the control limits calculated from the first 20 points are conditional limits. When you have at least 20 sequential points from a period when the process is operating in control, recalculate control limits.

Considerations

- Common out-of-control tests include

Single point outside: One point outside the control limits. In Figure 4.13, the eleventh point is above the UCL.

Run: Too many consecutive points on one side of the average. The run can be 7 points in a row, 10 points on one side out of 11 points in a row, or 12 points on one side out of 14 in a row. In Figure 4.13, points 2 through 15 show an out-of-control pattern of 12 out of 14 points below the average.

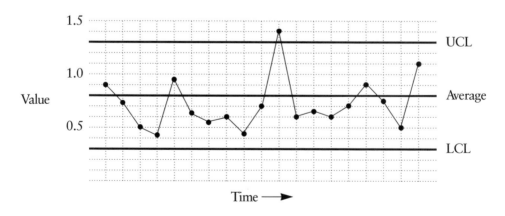

Figure 4.13. Control chart.

Trend: A series of points heading up or down. Use the method described in the scatter plot example on page 250 to divide the chart into four quadrants and count points in opposite quadrants. Use the trend test table (Table 4.11) to decide if the number of points indicates a trend.

Number of runs: The average line is crossed too few or too many times. Use the number of runs table (Table 4.2) for this test. Count the total number of points, skipping any points lying directly on the average line. Determine number of runs by counting the number of times the line between data points crosses the average line. If the data

Table 4.2. Number of runs table.

Total number of points	OK if number of runs is between
Less than 10	Too small to tell
10–11	3–8
12–13	3–10
14–15	4–11
16–17	5–12
18–19	5–14
20–21	6–15
22–23	7–16
24–25	8–17
26–27	8–19
28–29	9–20
30–31	10–21
32–33	11–22
34–35	11–25
36–37	12–25
38–39	13–26
40–41	14–27
42–43	15–28
44–45	15–30
46–47	16–31
48–49	17–32
50–59	18–33
60–69	22–39
70–79	26–45
80–89	31–50
90–99	35–56
100–109	39–62
110–119	44–67
120–129	48–73

line touches the average line and then returns to the same side, do not count it as crossing. In Figure 4.13, there are eight runs. Looking up 19 points on the table, the chart could have 5 to 14 runs, so 8 is acceptable.

- Some control charts have special requirements for their out-of-control tests. Check the analysis section of your particular control chart.

- These tests for patterns are based on statistics. They test whether the data are truly statistically random. If not, an underlying pattern must be identified.

- The tests do not judge whether patterns are desirable or undesirable. For example, a trend may be toward better performance or toward worse performance. It is just as important to do something to understand and keep good performance as it is to eliminate bad performance.

- Using too many tests for out-of-control conditions can cause a false positive—a problem signalled when one doesn't really exist. Every condition just listed has a small probability of occurring from random chance. When many tests are used simultaneously, those small chances multiply. Use no more than four or five tests, or you will be looking constantly for problems that don't exist. For most processes, just a few tests will reveal many improvement opportunities.

- The time period chosen for collecting and plotting data is based on how fast variation occurs in the process. The process should have time to change between samples.

- *Autocorrelation* is the problem that occurs if you take data too frequently. For example, suppose liquid is continually flowing both into and out of a tank so that the contents are completely replaced every three hours. If you are monitoring temperature, you should not plot it more often than every three hours. Data taken more frequently will be autocorrelated.

- Control limits should be recalculated only when the process has experienced a permanent change that you understand. You should not recalculate limits after each 20 points or after each page of the chart.

- Choose numerical scales that include the values for the control limits plus a little extra.

- For controlling an ongoing process, control charts are most useful when plotted as soon as the data is generated by the people who are working with the process. Collecting lots of data on a checksheet and plotting them by computer later will create charts that are prettier but of limited use.

- When data come from a nonnormal distribution (such as a skewed distribution), control limits of a chart of individuals will not represent the process accurately. Depending on the situation, those limits will result in many more or many less out-of-control signals than are actually occurring. Use an $\bar{X}$ and R chart instead.

- Blank control chart forms and worksheets are provided for each type of chart. Permission is granted to copy these charts for individual use.

- Control charts are easy and powerful to use, but they are often applied incorrectly. The more knowledgeably they are used, the more they can improve your processes. This summary contains only the basics of control charts, intended as a reference. Take a class, study some books, or obtain expert help to get the most value out of control charts in your processes.

- Two excellent books about control charts are *Understanding Statistical Process Control* by Wheeler and Chambers and *Statistical Methods for the Process Industries* by McNeese and Klein. (See the "Recommended Reading" section at the back of this book.) They contain more information about these and other control charts, including examples of their construction and use.

$\bar{X}$ (X-Bar) and R Chart
See "Control Charts" on page 84 for more information.

Description
The $\bar{X}$ (X-bar) and R chart is a control chart used to study variable data, especially data that does not form a normal distribution.

When to Use

- When the process data to be analyzed are measured on a continuous scale (for example, temperature, weight, time)

- When the process data are not normally distributed
- When you want to detect small process changes
- When data are generated frequently
- In discrete manufacturing, where a sample of four or five pieces may be used to represent production of several hundred or thousand pieces

Procedure

Construction

1. Determine the appropriate time period for collecting and plotting data. Determine the number of data points per subgroup (*n*). Collect at least 3*n* data points to start the chart. For example, with subgroup size of three, 60 data points will be needed to create 20 subgroups.

2. If the raw data do not form a normal distribution, check whether the averages of the subgroups form a normal distribution. (The normal probability plot or the Kolmogorov–Smirnov test can be used to do this.) If not, increase the subgroup size.

3. Calculate $\bar{\bar{X}}$ (X-double bar), $\bar{R}$ (R-bar) and the control limits using the $\bar{X}$ and R chart or moving average–moving range chart worksheet, (Figure 4.14) and the $\bar{X}$ and R chart or moving average–moving range chart (Figure 4.15).

4. On the "Average" part of the chart, mark the numerical scale, plot the subgroup averages, and draw lines for the average of the averages and for the control limits for $\bar{X}$. On the "Range" part of the chart, mark the numerical scale, plot the ranges, and draw lines for the average range and for the control limits for R.

5. Analyze the chart for out-of-control signals.

6. When you see an out-of-control signal on the control chart, investigate the cause. Write on the control chart how you investigated and what you found. Write the cause and how it was corrected.

7. Continue to plot the control chart as data are generated. As each data point is plotted, check for new out-of-control signals.

8. When you start a new control chart, the process may be out of control. If so, the control limits calculated from the first 20 points are conditional limits. When you have at least 20 sequential points from a period when the process is operating in control, recalculate control limits.

Process: _____

Data dates: _____

Calculated by: _____

Date: _____

Step 1. Calculate average $\bar{X}$ and range R (the difference between the highest and lowest values) for each subgroup. Record on chart.

Number of values in each subgroup = n = _____

Number of subgroups to be used = N = _____

Step 2. Look up control limit factors.

n	$A2$	$D3$	$D4$	
2	1.880	—	3.267	$A2$ = _____
3	1.023	—	2.574	
4	0.729	—	2.282	$D3$ = _____
5	0.577	—	2.114	
6	0.483	—	2.004	$D4$ = _____
7	0.419	0.076	1.924	

Step 3. Calculate averages ($\bar{\bar{X}}$ and $\bar{R}$).

Sum of the averages = $\Sigma\bar{X}$ = _____

Average of the averages = $\bar{\bar{X}}$ = $\Sigma\bar{X}$ ÷ N

= _____ ÷ _____ = _____

Sum of the ranges = ΣR = _____

Average of the ranges = $\bar{R}$ = ΣR ÷ N

= _____ ÷ _____ = _____

Step 4. Calculate control limits.

$3\hat{\sigma}$ estimate for $\bar{X}$ chart = $3\hat{\sigma}_{\bar{X}}$ = $A2$ × $\bar{R}$

= _____ × _____ = _____

Upper control limit for $\bar{X}$ chart = $UCL_{\bar{X}}$ = $\bar{\bar{X}}$ + $3\hat{\sigma}_{\bar{X}}$

= _____ + _____ = _____

Lower control limit for $\bar{X}$ chart = $LCL_{\bar{X}}$ = $\bar{\bar{X}}$ − $3\hat{\sigma}_{\bar{X}}$

= _____ − _____ = _____

Upper control limit for R chart = UCL_R = $D4$ × $\bar{R}$

= _____ × _____ = _____

Lower control limit for R chart = LCL_R = $D3$ × $\bar{R}$

= _____ × _____ = _____

Figure 4.14. $\bar{X}$ and R chart or moving average–moving range chart worksheet.

Process:	Variable:	Units:	Limits set by:	Date:
	$UCL_{\bar{X}}$:	$LCL_{\bar{X}}$:	$\bar{\bar{X}}$:	UCL_R:	$\bar{R}$:

Date																														
#1																														
#2																														
#3																														
#4																														
#5																														
#6																														
Sum																														
Avg																														
Range																														

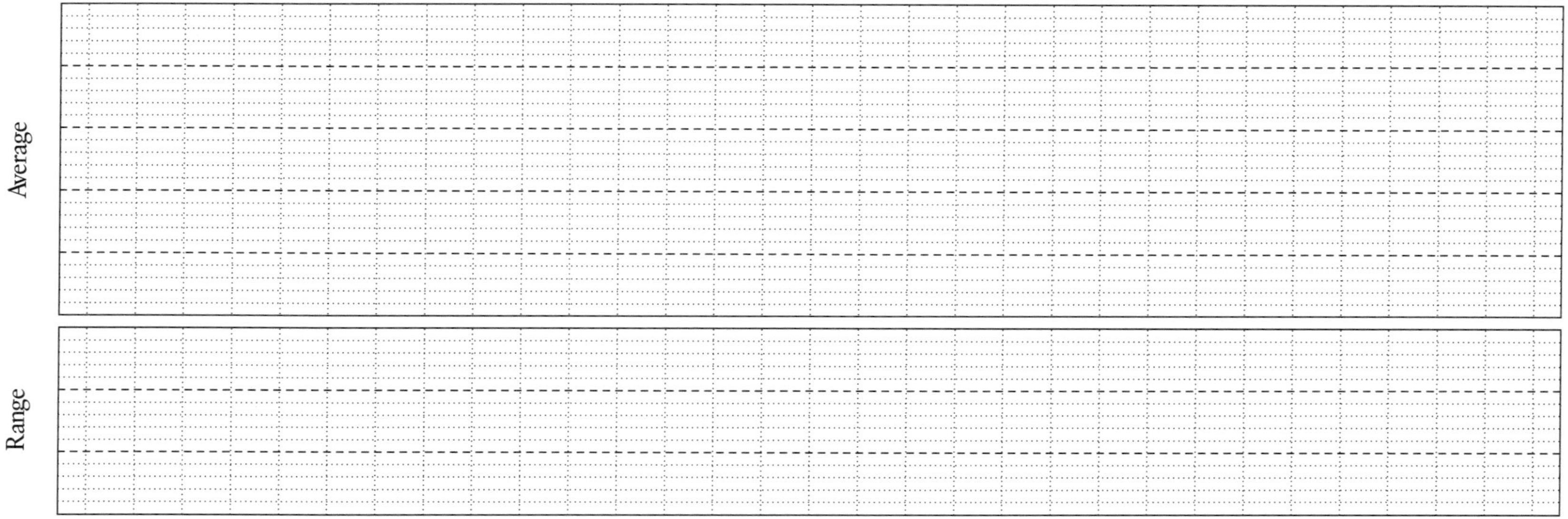

Average

Range

Figure 4.15. $\bar{X}$ and R chart or moving average–moving range chart.

Analysis

1. Check the *R* chart for out-of-control signals. All the tests listed in the considerations section (page 86) can be used.

2. If the *R* chart is in control, check the $\bar{X}$ chart for out-of-control signals. All the tests listed in the control chart considerations section can be used.

Example

The ZZ-400 team collected a set of 40 values, arranged in time sequence, for product purity. The histogram in Figure 4.16 gives an indication that the data are slightly skewed, as data that are being pushed toward 100% or 0% often are. The team will try subgrouping the data by twos. Figure 4.17 shows the data.

The first subgroup contains values one and two: 99.7 and 99.6. Their average is 99.65 and their range is 0.1. The second subgroup contains values three and four: 99.7 and 99.4. Their average is 99.55 and their range is 0.3. The calculations are continued for all the data, as shown (see Figure 4.17). At this point, the team checks the distribution of subgroup averages with a normal probability plot. The distribution is approximately normal, so subgroup size of two is acceptable.

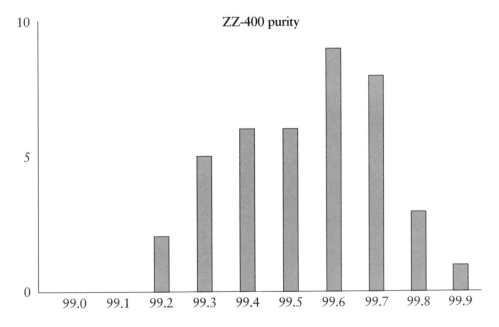

Figure 4.16. Histogram of $\bar{X}$ and *R* chart example.

Now, using the worksheet, averages and control limits can be calculated. See the completed worksheet (Figure 4.18) for the calculations.

The subgroup averages and ranges are plotted, and the averages and control limit lines are drawn on the chart. Figure 4.17 shows the control chart. There are no out-of-control signals.

Considerations

- This is the most commonly used type of control chart.

- For most nonnormal distributions, a subgroup size of two or three will be adequate. If the data are highly nonnormal, a subgroup size of four or five might be needed.

- The subgroup size and sampling method should be chosen to minimize the chance of variations occurring within the subgroup and to maximize the chance of variations occurring between the subgroups.

- For subgroup sizes smaller than seven, LCL_R will be 0. Therefore, there will be no out-of-control signals below LCL_R.

- An out-of-control signal on the R chart indicates that the overall variation of the process has changed, although the process averages (the $\overline{X}$ values) may show no unusual variation.

- When the chart is first drawn, if the R chart is out of control, the control limits calculated for the $\overline{X}$ chart will not be valid. Find and eliminate the source of variation in the R chart and start over to establish new control limits.

- Choose numerical scales that include the values for the control limits plus a little extra.

Chart of Individuals

XmR Chart

See "Control Charts" on page 84 for more information.

Description

The chart of individuals is a control chart used to study variable data that form a normal distribution.

X̄-R or Moving Average–Moving Range Chart

Process:				ZZ-400				Variable: $Purity$				Units: %		Limits set by: PW		Date: 8/29/93
								$UCL_{\bar{X}}$: 99.88	$LCL_{\bar{X}}$: 99.20	$\bar{\bar{X}}$: 99.54				UCL_R: 0.59	$\bar{R}$: 0.18	

Date	8/4	8/5	8/6	8/7	8/8	8/9	8/10	8/11	8/12	8/13	8/14	8/15	8/16	8/17	8/18	8/19	8/20	8/21	8/22	8/23
#1	99.7	99.7	99.4	99.5	99.7	99.6	99.3	99.6	99.5	99.7	99.6	99.5	99.7	99.7	99.4	99.6	99.2	99.7	99.4	99.5
#2	99.6	99.4	99.3	99.8	99.4	99.9	99.2	99.3	99.6	99.6	99.8	99.4	99.8	99.3	99.5	99.7	99.5	99.6	99.3	99.6
#3																				
#4																				
#5																				
#6																				
Sum																				
Avg	99.65	99.55	99.35	99.65	99.55	99.75	99.25	99.45	99.55	99.65	99.70	99.45	99.75	99.50	99.45	99.65	99.35	99.65	99.35	99.55
Range	0.1	0.3	0.1	0.3	0.3	0.3	0.1	0.3	0.1	0.1	0.2	0.1	0.1	0.4	0.1	0.1	0.3	0.1	0.1	0.1

Figure 4.17. X̄ and R chart example.

Process: _____ZZ-400 Purity_____

Data dates: _____8/4 – 8/23/93_____

Calculated by: _____PW_____

Date: _____8/29/93_____

Step 1. Calculate average $\bar{X}$ and range R (the difference between the highest and lowest values) for each subgroup. Record on chart.

Number of values in each subgroup = n = __2__

Number of subgroups to be used   = N = __20__

Step 2. Look up control limit factors.

n	A2	D3	D4		
2	1.880	—	3.267	A2 =	_1.880_
3	1.023	—	2.574		
4	0.729	—	2.282	D3 =	_____
5	0.577	—	2.114		
6	0.483	—	2.004	D4 =	_3.267_
7	0.419	0.076	1.924		

Step 3. Calculate averages ($\bar{\bar{X}}$ and $\bar{R}$).

Sum of the averages   = $\Sigma\bar{X}$ = _1991_

Average of the averages   = $\bar{\bar{X}}$ = $\Sigma\bar{X}$ ÷ N

                                = _1991_ ÷ _20_ = _99.54_

Sum of the ranges   = ΣR = _3.6_

Average of the ranges   = $\bar{R}$ = ΣR ÷ N

                                = _3.6_ ÷ _20_ = _0.18_

Step 4. Calculate control limits.

$3\hat{\sigma}$ estimate for $\bar{X}$ chart   = $3\hat{\sigma}_{\bar{x}}$ = A2 × $\bar{R}$

                            = _1.880_ × _0.18_ = _.34_

Upper control limit for $\bar{X}$ chart = $UCL_{\bar{x}}$ = $\bar{\bar{X}}$ + $3\hat{\sigma}_{\bar{x}}$

                            = _99.54_ + _.34_ = _99.88_

Lower control limit for $\bar{X}$ chart = $LCL_{\bar{x}}$ = $\bar{\bar{X}}$ − $3\hat{\sigma}_{\bar{x}}$

                            = _99.54_ − _.34_ = _99.20_

Upper control limit for R chart = UCL_R = D4 × $\bar{R}$

                            = _3.267_ × _0.18_ = _0.59_

Lower control limit for R chart = LCL_R = D3 × $\bar{R}$

                            = _____ × _____ = _____

Figure 4.18. $\bar{X}$ and R chart example worksheet.

When to Use

- Only when the process data to be analyzed are measured on a continuous scale (for example, temperature, weight, time)

- Only when the distribution of data from the process is normal. (See "Histogram" for a discussion of normal distribution and see "Normal Probability Plot" or "Kolmogorov–Smirnov Test" for ways to determine whether it is normal.)

- When each data point is already a natural subgroup, such as one batch, or data are gathered infrequently

Procedure

Construction

1. Determine the appropriate time period for collecting and plotting data. Collect at least 20 data points, arranged in time order, from the process to be studied.

2. Determine if the distribution of the data is normal. The normal probability plot or Kolmogorov–Smirnov test can be used to test the data for normality.

3. Calculate the average, called $\bar{X}$ (X-bar), and the control limits using the chart of individuals worksheet (Figure 4.19) and the chart of individuals form (Figure 4.20).

4. On the "Value" part of the chart, mark the numerical scale, plot the individual values, and draw lines for the average and the control limits for X. On the "Range" part of the chart, mark the numerical scale, plot the ranges, and draw lines for the average moving range and the UCL_R.

5. Analyze the chart for out-of-control signals.

6. When you see an out-of-control signal on the control chart, investigate the cause. Write on the control chart how you investigated and what you found. Write the cause and how it was corrected.

7. Continue to plot data as they are generated. As each new data point is plotted, check for new out-of-control signals.

8. When you start a new control chart, the process may be out of control. If so, the control limits calculated from the first 20 points are conditional limits. When you have at least 20 sequential points from a period when the process is operating in control, recalculate control limits.

Process: _____

Data dates: _____

Calculated by: _____

Date: _____

Step 1. Calculate $\bar{X}$.

Number of values	=	n	=	_____		
Sum of the values	=	ΣX	=	_____		
Average	=	$\bar{X}$	=	ΣX	$\div$	n
			=	_____ $\div$ _____ = _____		

Step 2. Calculate $\overline{MR}$.

Calculate the ranges (the difference between two consecutive data points) and record on the form. Ignore negative signs.

Number of moving ranges	=	$n - 1$	=	_____		
Sum of the moving ranges	=	ΣMR	=	_____		
Average moving range	=	$\overline{MR}$	=	ΣMR	$\div$	$(n - 1)$
			=	_____ $\div$ _____ = _____		

Step 3. Calculate control limits.

Estimate 3 standard deviations	=	$3\hat{\sigma}_X$	=	2.66	$\times$	$\overline{MR}$
			=	2.66	$\times$	_____ = _____
Upper control limit for X chart	=	UCL_X	=	$\bar{X}$	$+$	$3\hat{\sigma}_X$
			=	_____	$+$	_____ = _____
Lower control limit for X chart	=	LCL_X	=	$\bar{X}$	$-$	$3\hat{\sigma}_X$
			=	_____	$-$	_____ = _____
Upper control limit for R chart	=	UCL_R	=	3.267	$\times$	$\overline{MR}$
			=	3.267	$\times$	_____ = _____

Figure 4.19. Chart of individuals worksheet.

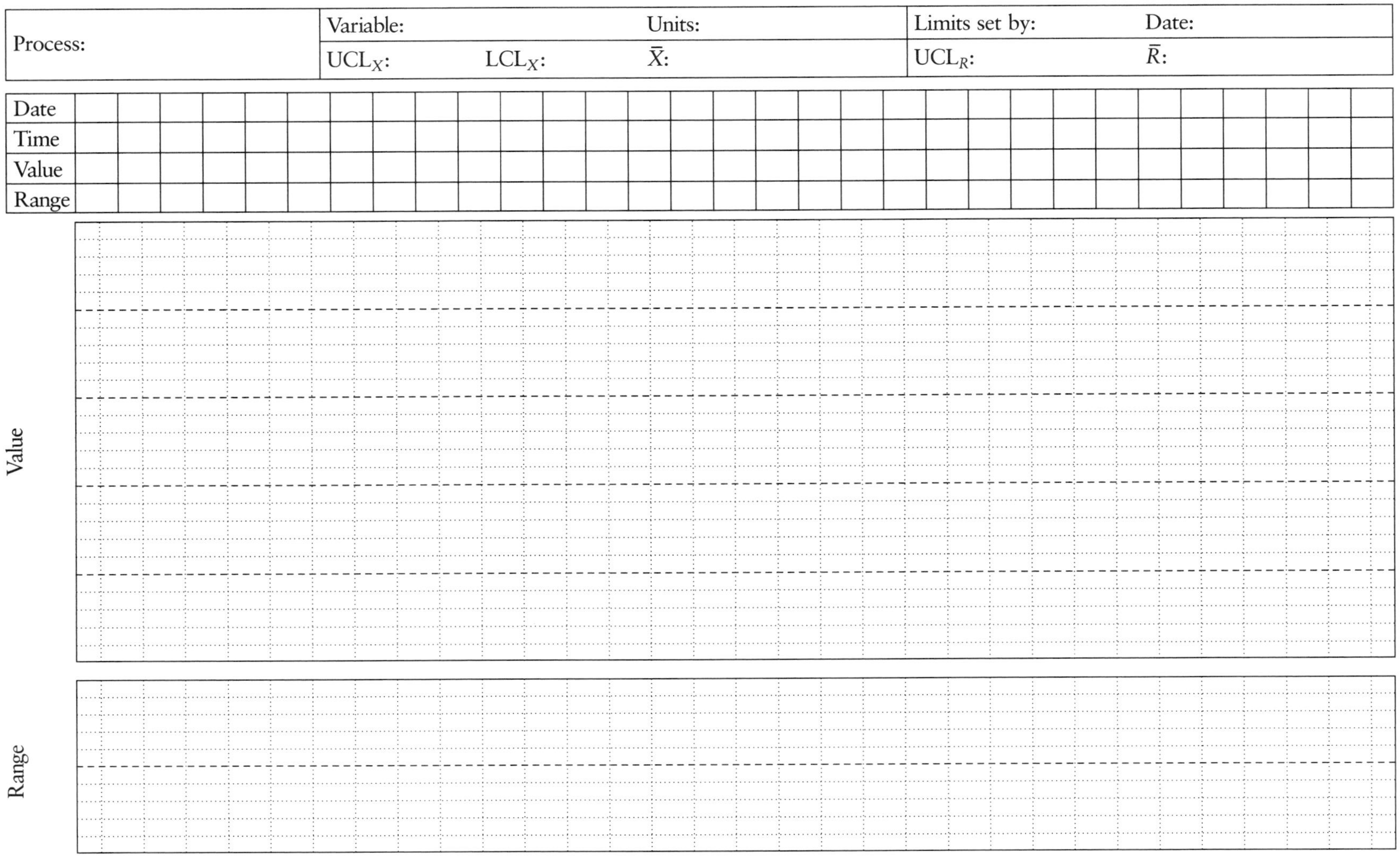

Figure 4.20. Chart of individuals.

Analysis

1. Check the *R* chart for out-of-control signals. All the tests listed in the control chart considerations section (page 86) can be used.

2. If the *R* chart is in control, check the *X* chart for out-of-control signals. All the tests listed in the control chart considerations can be used.

Example

Figure 4.21 shows the "value" portion of the chart of individuals drawn by the survey report writing team. The team had over two years of historical data for the time between end of survey and issuing report. The initial control limits are calculated from data taken the first year. This chart shows the second half of the data.

There is an out-of-control signal around points 70 to 76: seven points in a row below the average. If the team had been keeping a control chart at the time, it should have investigated what was different then about the process. Notice the period between reports 95 and 117 when the process went wildly out of control. The team identified a special cause: new people in the group.

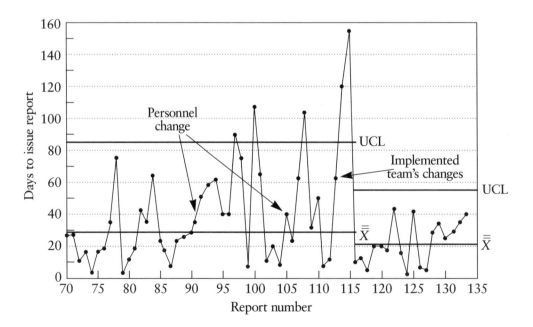

Figure 4.21. Chart of individuals example.

Immediately after that period, the team implemented its first improvements. Notice the drop in both the average and the UCL.

Considerations

- Choose numerical scales that include the values for the control limits plus a little extra.

Moving Average–Moving Range Chart

See "Control Charts" on page 84 for more information.

Description

The moving average–moving range (MA–MR) chart is a control chart used to study variable data that are generated slowly, especially data that do not form a normal distribution.

When to Use

- When the process data to be analyzed are measured on a continuous scale (for example, temperature, weight, time)

- When the process data are not normally distributed, but data are not available frequently enough to use an $\bar{X}$ and R chart

- When you want to detect small process changes, but data are not available frequently enough to use an $\bar{X}$ and R chart

- When monitoring batch processes that make only one or two batches per day

Procedure

Construction

1. Determine the appropriate time period for collecting and plotting data. Determine the number of data points per subgroup (n). Collect at least $20 + n - 1$ data points to start the chart. For example, with subgroup size of three, you will need 22 data points.

2. Calculate subgroup averages and ranges. Subgroup averages and ranges are calculated differently for the *MA–MR* chart than for the $\overline{X}$ and *R* chart.

    a. Record the first *n* individual values in the first column on the moving average chart (Figure 4.15). These values form the first subgroup.

    b. Drop the oldest value from the subgroup and record the remaining values in the second column, starting at the top. Write the next value in the bottom position to complete the second subgroup.

    c. Continue the process for all the data. You should finish with $n - 1$ fewer subgroups than there are individual values.

    d. Calculate the average (*MA*) and range (*MR*) for each subgroup. See the example for a sample calculation.

3. If the raw data do not form a normal distribution, check whether the averages of the subgroups do. (The normal probability plot or Kolmogorov–Smirnov test can be used to do this.) If not, increase the subgroup size.

4. Calculate $\overline{MA}$ (MA-bar), $\overline{MR}$ (MR-bar), and the control limits using the $\overline{X}$ and *R* chart or moving average–moving range chart worksheet (Figure 4.14).

5. On the "Average" part of the chart, mark the numerical scale, plot the subgroup averages, and draw lines for the average of the averages and for the averages' control limits. On the "Range" part of the chart, mark the numerical scale, plot the ranges, and draw lines for the average range and the range control limits.

6. Analyze the chart for out-of-control signals.

7. When you see an out-of-control signal on either part of the control chart, investigate the cause. Write on the control chart how you investigated and what you found. Write the cause and how it was corrected.

8. As each new data point is collected, continue to form a new subgroup, calculate the subgroup average and range, and plot the control chart. As each data point is plotted, check for new out-of-control signals.

9. When you start a new control chart, the process may be out of control. If so, the control limits calculated from the first 20 points are

conditional limits. When you have at least 20 sequential subgroups from a period when the process is operating in control, recalculate control limits.

Analysis

1. Check the moving range chart for out-of-control signals. "Points outside the control limits" is the only valid test. Do *not* check for runs or trends. These tests are not valid because the same individual values are included in more than one subgroup.

2. If the moving range chart is in control, check the moving average chart for out-of-control signals. Again, looking for points outside the control limits is the only valid test.

Example

Individual values, in time order, are 3, 5, 6, 1, 2, 5. Table 4.3 shows columns of subgroups and the calculations for the averages and ranges.

Considerations

- For subgroup sizes smaller than seven, LCL_R will be 0. Therefore, there will be no out-of-control signals below LCL_R.

- An out-of-control signal on the moving range chart indicates that the overall variation of the process has changed, although the subgroup averages (the MA values) may show no unusual variation.

Table 4.3. *MA–MR* chart example calculation.

	Subgroup #			
	1	2	3	4
Value #1	3	5	6	1
Value #2	5	6	1	2
Value #3	6	1	2	5
Sum	14	12	9	8
Average (*MA*)	4.7	4.0	3.0	2.7
High	6	6	6	5
Low	3	1	6	1
Range (*MR*)	3	5	5	4

- When the chart is first drawn, if the *MR* chart is out of control, the control limits calculated for the *MA* chart will not be valid. Find and eliminate the source of variation in the *MR* chart and start over to establish new control limits.

- Choose numerical scales that include the values for the control limits plus a little extra.

Attribute Charts

See "Control Charts" on page 84 for more information.

Description

Attribute charts are control charts used to study data about the number of defects in a group.

When to Use

- When data are counted (attribute data) rather than measured on a continuous scale

- When monitoring defects or other observations that have only two states: present or not present. For example, an item can have 2 defects or 3 defects, but not 2.6 defects.

Four control charts analyze variation in attribute data: the *p* chart; the *np* chart; the *c* chart; and the *u* chart. They are all based on examining *lots*, groups of items, for defects. Table 4.4 shows the differences between the four types of attribute charts.

Procedure: p *Chart*

Construction

1. Gather the data.

   a. Determine the definition of a lot. The lot should be large enough to contain several defects and should not vary more than 25%.

   b. Determine the number of lots (*N*) to collect before calculating control limits. Collect data from at least 20 lots.

Table 4.4. Types of attribute charts.

Type of chart	Lot size	How are defects counted?	Example
p	Can vary	Item good or no good	Number of accurate invoices per day. The number of invoices per day can vary.
np	Constant	Item good or no good	Number of defective drums per lot. The lot size is always 60.
u	Can vary	Many defects possible per item	Number of changes to engineering drawings each week. The number of drawings per week can vary.
c	Constant	Many defects possible per item	Number of black specks in 1 gram of product.

    c. For each lot, count the total number of items (n) and the number of defective items (X). Calculate the proportion nonconforming, $p = X/n$.

    d. Record the values of X, n, and p on the attribute chart (Figure 4.22).

2. Plot the data on the chart.

    a. Scale the chart. Leave plenty of room above the highest point and below the lowest point (unless lowest is 0).

    b. Plot the values of p on the chart. Connect consecutive points.

3. Calculate the average proportion defective $\bar{p}$ and the control limits. If lots sizes are within 20% of each other, use the np chart worksheet (Figure 4.23). For n, use an average lot size $\bar{n}$:

$$\bar{n} = \frac{n_1 + n_2 + n_3 + \ldots + n_k}{N}$$

where N is the number of lots.

Note: Theoretically, control limits should be calculated for each different lot size. Practically, this is not necessary as long as the lot sizes do not vary by more than 20%. See the alternate procedure that follows for a more exact determination of control limits.

Process:	Data being counted:		Limits set by:		Date:
	UCL:	LCL:	Average:		

Date																							
Time or lot #																							
Number nonconforming																							
Lot size																							
Proportion nonconforming																							

Proportion nonconforming, p or np
or Defects, c or u

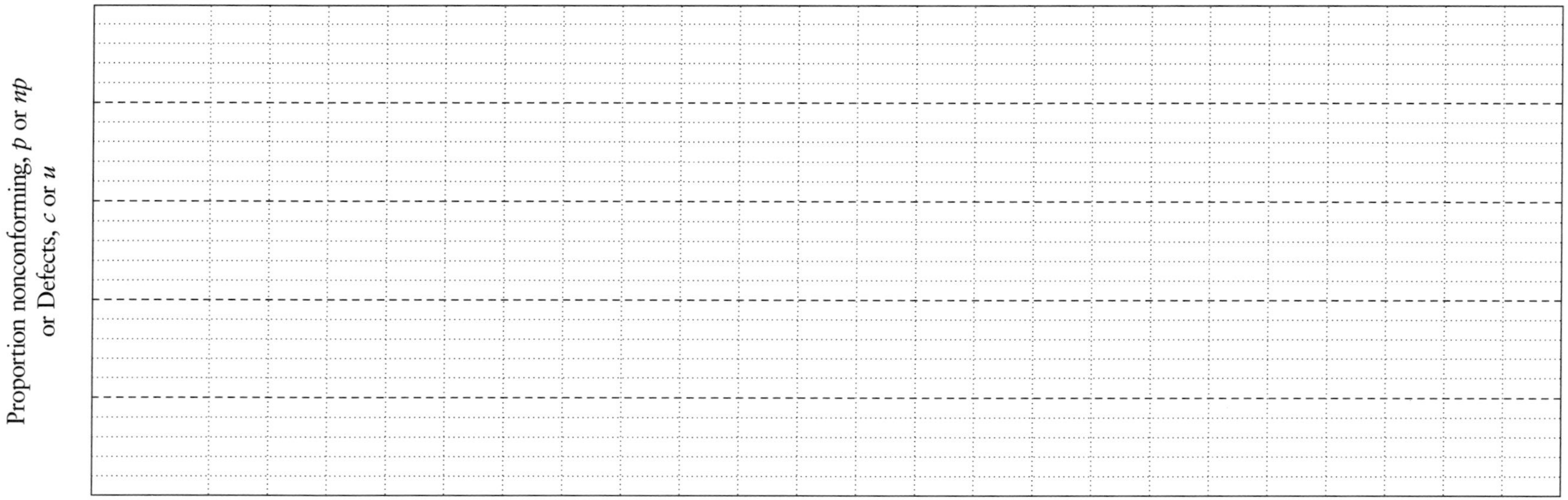

Figure 4.22. Attribute chart.

Process: _____

Data dates: _____

Calculated by: _____

Date: _____

Step 1. Calculate average.

Lot size	=	n	=	_____		
Number of lots	=	N	=	_____		
Sum of the total number defects	=	Σx_i	=	_____		
Average	=	$n\bar{p}$	=	Σx_i	÷	N
			=	_____	÷	_____
			=	_____		

Step 2. Calculate $3\hat{\sigma}$.

Calculate $1 - \bar{p}$ $\quad = \quad 1 \quad - \quad$ _____ $\quad = \quad$ _____

$n\bar{p}\ (1 - \bar{p})$ $\quad = \quad$ _____ $\times$ _____ $\quad = \quad$ _____

$\sqrt{n\bar{p}\ (1 - \bar{p})}$ $\quad = \quad \sqrt{\rule{1cm}{0pt}}$ $\quad = \quad$ _____

$3\hat{\sigma}_p$ $\quad = 3\sqrt{n\bar{p}\ (1 - \bar{p})}$

$\quad = 3 \ \times$ _____ $\quad = \quad$ _____

Step 3. Calculate control limits.

Upper control limit $\quad = \ \text{UCL}_p \ = \ n\bar{p} \ + \ 3\hat{\sigma}_p$

$\quad = \quad$ _____ $+$ _____ $=$ _____

Lower control limit $\quad = \ \text{LCL}_p \ = \ n\bar{p} \ - \ 3\hat{\sigma}_p$

$\quad = \quad$ _____ $-$ _____ $=$ _____

Figure 4.23. np chart worksheet (where lot size is constant).

4. Draw lines for $\bar{p}$ and the control limits on the chart and label them.

5. Analyze the chart for out-of-control signals.

6. When you see an out-of-control signal on the chart, investigate the cause. Write on the chart how you investigated and what you found. Write the cause and how it was corrected.

7. Continue to plot data as they are generated. As each new data point is plotted, check for new out-of-control signals.

8. When you start a new chart, the process may be out of control. If so, the control limits calculated from the first 20 points are conditional limits. When you have at least 20 sequential points from a period when the process is operating in control, recalculate control limits.

Analysis
Check the chart for out-of-control signals. All the tests listed in the control chart considerations on page 86 can be used.

Considerations

- For a p chart, a lot should be a group of items. The number of items per group can vary. If all the groups have the same number of items, use the np chart.

- Each item in the lot is either good or bad. Do not count several defects per item. If you wish to count multiple defects per item, use a c chart or u chart.

Alternate Procedure: p Chart
This procedure gives instructions for a more exact determination of control limits. This procedure must be used if lot size varies more than 20%.

1. Gather the data as in the basic procedure. Lot size can vary more than 20 percent.

2. Plot the data on the attribute chart as in the basic procedure.

3. Calculate the average proportion defective $\bar{p}$ and the control limits, using the p chart worksheet (where lot size is not constant) (Figure 4.24). There will be four control limits: inner and outer upper control limits and inner and outer lower control limits.

4. Draw lines for $\bar{p}$ and the control limits on the chart and label them.

5. Continue with steps 5 through 8 of the p chart procedure on this page.

Process: _____

Data dates: _____

Calculated by: _____

Date: _____

Step 1. Calculate average.

Smallest lot size $= n_S =$ _____   Largest lot size $n_L =$ _____

$\sqrt{n_S} =$ _____ $\sqrt{n_L} =$ _____

Sum of the total number defects $= \Sigma x_i =$ _____

Sum of the total number examined $= \Sigma n_i =$ _____

Average $= \bar{p} = \Sigma x_i \div \Sigma n_i$

$=$ _____ $\div$ _____ $=$ _____

Step 2. Estimate 3σ.

Calculate $1 - \bar{p} = 1 -$ _____ $=$ _____

$\bar{p}(1 - \bar{p}) =$ _____ $\times$ _____ $=$ _____

$\sqrt{\bar{p}(1 - \bar{p})} =$ $\sqrt{\text{\_\_\_\_}} =$ _____

$3 \times \sqrt{\bar{p}(1 - \bar{p})} = 3 \times$ _____ $=$ _____

$3\hat{\sigma}_{po} = 3\sqrt{\bar{p}(1 - \bar{p})} \div \sqrt{n_S}$

$=$ _____ $\div$ _____ $=$ _____

$3\hat{\sigma}_{pi} = 3\sqrt{\bar{p}(1 - \bar{p})} \div \sqrt{n_L}$

$=$ _____ $\div$ _____ $=$ _____

Step 3. Calculate control limits.

Outer limits   Inner limits

Upper control limit $= \text{UCL}_{po}$ Upper control limit $= \text{UCL}_{pi}$

$= \bar{p} + 3\hat{\sigma}_{po}$ $= \bar{p} + 3\hat{\sigma}_{pi}$

$=$ ___ $+$ ___ $=$ ___ $=$ ___ $+$ ___ $=$ ___

Lower control limit $= \text{LCL}_{po}$ Lower control limit $= \text{LCL}_{pi}$

$= \bar{p} - 3\hat{\sigma}_{po}$ $= \bar{p} - 3\hat{\sigma}_{pi}$

$=$ ___ $-$ ___ $=$ ___ $=$ ___ $-$ ___ $=$ ___

Figure 4.24. p chart worksheet (where lot size is not constant).

Analysis

Check the chart for out-of-control signals. The tests listed in control chart considerations on page 86 can be used, except for this change to the "single point outside" test:

- If a point falls between the inner and outer limits, calculate exact control limits for that point, using the actual lot size, n, for that point.

$$\text{UCL}_p = \bar{p} + 3 \sqrt{\frac{\bar{p}\,(1 - \bar{p})}{n}} \qquad \text{LCL}_p = \bar{p} - 3 \sqrt{\frac{\bar{p}\,(1 - \bar{p})}{n}}$$

The process is out of control if the point falls outside these control limits.

Procedure: np *Chart*

Construction

1. Gather the data.

    a. Determine the definition of a lot. The lot should be large enough to have several defects occur. The lot size must be constant. Determine the lot size n.

    b. Determine the number of lots to collect before calculating control limits. Collect data from at least 20 lots.

    c. For each lot, count the number of nonconforming items found (X). Calculate the proportion nonconforming, $np = X/n$.

    d. Record the values of X, n, and np on the attribute chart (Figure 4.22).

2. Plot the data for np on the chart.

    a. Scale the chart. Leave plenty of room above the highest point and below the lowest point (unless lowest is 0).

    b. Plot the values of np on the chart. Connect consecutive points.

3. Calculate the average proportion defective $\overline{np}$ and the control limits, using the np chart worksheet (Figure 4.23).

4. Draw lines for $\overline{np}$ and the control limits on the chart and label them.

5. Analyze the chart for out-of-control signals.

6. When you see an out-of-control signal on the chart, investigate the cause. Write on the chart how you investigated and what you found. Write the cause and how it was corrected.

7. Continue to plot data as they are generated. As each new data point is plotted, check for new out-of-control signals.

8. When you start a new chart, the process may be out of control. If so, the control limits calculated from the first 20 points are conditional limits. When you have at least 20 sequential points from a period when the process is operating in control, recalculate control limits.

Analysis
Check the chart for out-of-control signals. All the tests listed in the control chart considerations on page 86 can be used.

Considerations

- For an *np* chart, a lot should be a group of items. All lots must have the same number of items. If the number of items in a lot varies, use the *p* chart.

- Each item in the lot is either good or bad. Do not count several defects per item. If you wish to count multiple defects per item, use a *c* chart or *u* chart.

Procedure: c *Chart*

Construction

1. Gather the data.
    a. Determine the definition of a lot. The lot should be large enough that defects have a chance to occur. The lot size must be constant.
    b. Select the number of lots to be collected before calculating control limits. Collect data from at least 20 lots.
    c. For each lot, count the number of defects (c).
    d. Record the values of c on the attribute chart (Figure 4.22). Ignore the rows for lot size and proportion nonconforming.

2. Plot the data on the chart.
    a. Scale the chart. Leave plenty of room above the highest point and below the lowest point (unless lowest is 0).
    b. Plot the values of c on the chart. Connect consecutive points.

3. Calculate the average number of defects $\bar{c}$ and the control limits, using the c chart worksheet (Figure 4.25).

Process: _____

Data dates: _____

Calculated by: _____

Date: _____

Step 1. Calculate average.

Number of lots	=	N	= _____
Sum of the counts	=	Σc	= _____
Average count	=	$\bar{c}$	= Σc ÷ N
			= _____ ÷ _____
			= _____

Step 2. Calculate control limits.

Calculate = 3 × $\sqrt{\bar{c}}$

= 3 × $\sqrt{\underline{\hspace{1cm}}}$ = _____

Upper control limit

UCL_c = $\bar{c}$ + $3\sqrt{\bar{c}}$

= _____ + _____ = _____

Lower control limit

LCL_c = $\bar{c}$ − $3\sqrt{\bar{c}}$

= _____ − _____ = _____

Figure 4.25. c chart worksheet.

4. Draw $\bar{c}$ and the control limits on the chart and label them.

5. Analyze the chart for out-of-control signals.

6. When you see an out-of-control signal on the chart, investigate the cause. Write on the chart how you investigated and what you found. Write the cause and how it was corrected.

7. Continue to plot data as they are generated. As each new data point is plotted, check for new out-of-control signals.

8. When you start a new chart, the process may be out of control. If so, the control limits calculated from the first 20 points are conditional limits. When you have at least 20 sequential points from a period when the process is operating in control, recalculate control limits.

Analysis
Check the chart for out-of-control signals. All the tests listed in the control chart considerations on page 86 can be used.

Considerations

- The lot can be one item (such as an invoice) or one area (1 square foot), or it can be multiple items (such as 100 invoices) or larger areas (10 square feet).
- For a *c* chart, more than one defect can be counted per item or area.

Procedure: u *Chart*

Construction

1. Gather the data.

   a. Determine the definition of one lot. The lot should be large enough so that defects have a chance to occur. The number of items in a lot can change from one lot to another. However, it should not vary by more than 25%.

   b. Select the number of lots to be collected before calculating control limits. Collect data from at least 20 lots.

   c. For each lot, count the total number of items (n) and the number of defects (c). Calculate the number of defects per lot, $u = c/n$.

   d. Record the values of c, n, and u on the attribute chart (Figure 4.22).

2. Plot the data on the chart.

    a. Scale the chart. Leave plenty of room above the highest point and below the lowest point (unless lowest is 0).

    b. Plot the values of u on the chart. Connect consecutive points.

3. Calculate the average number of defects per lot $\bar{u}$ and the control limits, using the u chart worksheet (Figure 4.26).

    Note: Theoretically, control limits should be calculated for each different lot size. Practically, this is not necessary as long as the lot sizes do not vary by more than 20%.

4. Draw lines for $\bar{u}$ and the control limits on the chart and label them.

5. Analyze the chart for out-of-control signals.

6. When you see an out-of-control signal on the chart, investigate the cause. Write on the chart how you investigated and what you found. Write the cause and how it was corrected.

7. Continue to plot data as they are generated. As each new data point is plotted, check for new out-of-control signals.

8. When you start a new chart, the process may be out of control. If so, the control limits calculated from the first 20 points are conditional limits. When you have at least 20 sequential points from a period when the process is operating in control, recalculate control limits.

Analysis

Check the chart for out-of-control signals. All the tests listed in the control chart considerations section on page 86 can be used.

Alternate Procedure: u *Chart*

This procedure gives instructions for a more exact determination of control limits. This procedure must be used if lot size varies more than 20%.

1. Gather the data as in the basic procedure. Lot size can vary more than 20%.

2. Plot the data on the attribute chart as in the basic procedure.

3. Modify the u chart worksheet calculations of the average proportion defective $\bar{u}$ and the control limits. Use the shortcut approach detailed for the p chart alternate procedure. Calculate outer limits using the smallest possible lot size and inner limits using the largest possible lot size. Draw all four control limits on the chart.

Process:_____

Data dates:_____

Calculated by:_____

Date:_____

Step 1. Calculate average.

Number of items   = Σn =   _____

Number of defects   = Σc =   _____

Average   = $\bar{u}$ = Σc ÷ Σn

=   _____   ÷   _____   =   _____

If the lot size does not vary more than 25%, calculate the average lot size.

Number of lots   =   N   =   _____

Average lot size   = $\bar{n}$ = Σn ÷   N

=   _____   ÷   _____   =   _____

Step 2. Calculate control limits

Calculate $3\sqrt{\bar{u}/\bar{n}}$

=   3   × $\sqrt{\bar{u}}$ ÷ $\sqrt{\bar{n}}$

=   3   × $\sqrt{}$ ÷ $\sqrt{}$

=   3   ×   _____   ÷   _____   =   _____

Upper control limit

UCL_u = $\bar{u}$ + $3\sqrt{\bar{u}/\bar{n}}$

=   _____   +   _____   =   _____

Lower control limit

LCL_u = $\bar{u}$ − $3\sqrt{\bar{u}/\bar{n}}$

=   _____   −   _____   =   _____

Figure 4.26. u chart worksheet.

5. Continue with the remaining steps of the *u* chart procedure.

6. When you analyze your chart, another calculation is necessary when a point falls within the outer and inner limits. Calculate the exact limits for that point, using the actual lot size, *n*, for that *u* value.

$$\mathrm{UCL}_u = \bar{u} + 3\sqrt{\bar{u}/n}$$

$$\mathrm{LCL}_u = \bar{u} - 3\sqrt{\bar{u}/n}$$

The process is out of control if the point falls outside these control limits.

Considerations

- The lot can be one item (such as an invoice) or one area (1 square foot), or it can be multiple items (such as 100 invoices) or larger areas (10 square feet).

- For a *u* chart, more than one defect can be counted per item or area.

Cost-of-Quality Analysis

(Red and Green Circle Exercise)

Description

A cost-of-quality analysis is a way of studying the flowchart of a process to identify problems. The analysis helps a team look critically at individual steps of a process to find opportunities for improvement.

Cost of quality means those costs incurred because of poor quality, costs that would not be incurred if things were done right the first time and every time. In a cost-of-quality analysis, one looks for activities that incur costs of quality.

When to Use

- When flowcharting a process, to be sure that cost-of-quality activities are included

- After flowcharting a process, to identify problems, potential causes, and areas to concentrate improvement efforts

Procedure

1. Draw a detailed flowchart of the process.

2. Identify all process steps (including recycle loops) that incur costs of quality: inspection, fix, and damage control. (See "Considerations" in this section for definitions of these costs.) Draw a red circle (red for *Stop*) around those steps or recycles.

3. If no or few steps have red circles, ask "What can go wrong? How do we tell if things go wrong? How does the process handle things going wrong?" If necessary, add steps to the flowchart.

4. For each red circle, ask "What process step, done perfectly, would allow us to eliminate this red-circled step?" Draw a green circle (green for *Go*) around each step identified here.

5. The green circles show areas to look for ways to prevent problems and in general to seek improvement. Green circles will contain the root causes of problems identified by the red circles.

Example

Figure 4.27 shows a cost-of-quality analysis for the flowchart for filling an order. (See the flowchart example, Figure 4.33). Unfortunately, this book is printed in black and white, so you will have to imagine red and green.

Imagine the dotted circles are red: inspections, fixes (including rework), and damage control. They were drawn first. Note that on this flowchart, all the decision diamonds are checking, or inspection, steps. Also, the two recycle loops are fix steps.

There are no damage control steps because this flowchart does not show what happens when things go wrong with the external customer. What if a good customer is mistakenly refused credit? Or the customer is unhappy with the delivery date? Or the wrong product is shipped? Or the bill is incorrect? If those possibilities were shown, they would be circled in red.

At the next step in the analysis, preventions for each red (dotted) circle are sought in previous boxes on the flowchart. For the inspection "Is product good?" and the recycle loop flowing from the "No" answer, the prevention is "Make product." If product were made perfectly each time, the question "Is product good?" would be unnecessary. Imagine that the solid circle around "Make product" is green. For "Are materials good?" and the recycle loop flowing from that decision diamond, the preventions are "Order materials" and "Vendor." Notice that although we don't

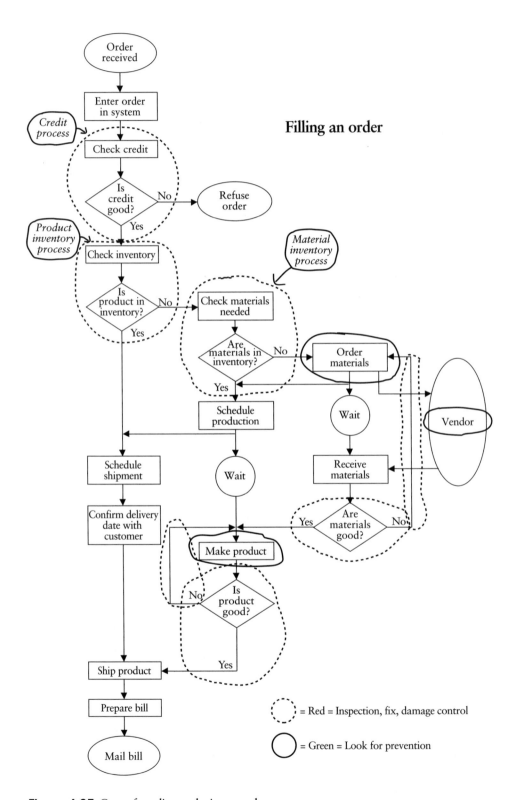

Figure 4.27. Cost-of-quality analysis example.

control what the vendors do, their processes cause us to add an inspection step. That is why it is important to involve suppliers in your quality improvement efforts.

If problems with the external customer had been flowcharted and circled in red, then green circles would be drawn around "Check credit," "Schedule shipment," "Ship product," and "Prepare bill." Doing these right prevents later damage control.

For three red (dotted) circles, no opportunities for prevention can be found on this flowchart. "Are materials in inventory?" depends on the material inventory process; "Is product in inventory?" depends on the product inventory process; "Is credit good?" depends on the credit process (and also on the customer). Names of those processes have been written in and circled with green. The team may decide that to improve the order-filling process, the material inventory process that links with it should be studied.

Considerations

- There are three types of activities that incur costs to be eliminated:

  Inspection: Testing, inspecting, or checking to determine whether a failure or error has occurred. For example, proofreading, counter-signing a document.

  Fix: Correcting, reworking, or disposing of errors or poor output that are identified before the customer is affected. For example, redoing a report when wrong information is discovered in it.

  Damage control: Correcting, reworking, or disposing of errors or poor output that are identified after the customer is affected. Also, handling problems that arise because the customer has been affected. For example, explaining to the customer how we are solving the problem.

- There is a fourth type of cost of quality: *prevention.* It usually is preferable (cheaper and easier) to handle problems through prevention rather than waiting until inspection, fix, or damage control are needed. Quality improvement is based on preventing problems from occurring. Through a cost-of-quality analysis, you can identify process steps that are inspection, fix, or damage control (red circles) in order to determine prevention measures (green circles) that can reduce or even eliminate those steps.

- The process steps circled in red probably will never actually disappear. We are all human, so we will never be perfect. However, thinking about the ideal, perfect world helps us to see where to focus improvement efforts. For example, we may always want to do a final inspection to check whether the product is good. But to improve the process, we should work on getting better at making product, rather than on better checking.

- If a flowchart has few or no red circles, it may have been drawn with very little detail, as a big picture. This analysis can be done only with flowcharts that include enough detail to show the problems and fixes.

- Often, opportunities for improvement will be found beyond the boundaries of your flowchart. A narrow scope may have been the best way to draw the part of the process in which you were interested. However, do not limit yourself to that scope when you identify opportunities for improvement.

Critical-To-Quality Analysis

Description

A critical-to-quality analysis is a way of studying the flowchart of a process to find problems. The analysis studies inputs and outputs and identifies the steps that influence quality of the process and its outputs.

When to Use

- When flowcharting a process, to be sure that steps critical to the process's quality are included

- After flowcharting a process, to identify problems and potential causes

- Whenever looking for opportunities for improvement in a process

Procedure

1. Draw a detailed flowchart of the process.

2. Look at the input side of your flowchart and answer Who, What, When, Where, and How.

   - Who provides the input?

- What is the input? (for example, information, printed form, authorization, raw material)
- When is it received? (time and frequency)
- Where on the flowchart is it received? Used?
- How critical is it? Its timing?

Write the answers to these questions on the flowchart, using whatever symbols your group finds meaningful. Common markings are a box or oval for Who, an arrow for Where, words on the arrow for What, diamonds or circles for When and How.

3. Study at the output side of your flowchart and answer Who, What, When, Where, and How.

- Who receives the output?
- What is the output?
- When is it needed? (time and frequency)
- Where on the flowchart does it come from?
- How critical is it to the receiver? Its timing?

Write the answers to these questions on the flowchart, using your own symbols.

4. For each input, list your needs. (For example, on time? Correct? Complete? Easy to use?) Evaluate whether the input meets your needs.

5. For each output, list your customer's needs. Evaluate whether the output meets those needs.

6. Find critical-to-quality steps.

- Steps where an input determines what happens next in the process
- Steps where you can measure whether inputs or outputs are meeting needs
- Steps where the quality of your output can be hurt or helped

Mark or color these steps so they stand out.

7. Focus on these critical-to-quality steps to find any problems happening with them.

Considerations

- If you have trouble answering any of the questions, your flowchart may not be detailed enough. Do one of two things. You can include more detail on the flowchart, expanding each step into its substeps. Or, if the flowchart covers a broad scope, narrow your focus, choosing just one section of the process and expanding it.

- At step 5, interviewing customers is the best way to answer the questions. Also ask your customers the answers to the When and How questions in step 3.

Decision Matrix

Description

A decision matrix evaluates and prioritizes a list of choices. The team first establishes a list of criteria and then evaluates each choice against those criteria.

When to Use

- When a list of options must be narrowed to the one choice

- After a list of problems has been generated

- After a list of potential solutions has been developed

- After a brainstormed list of choices has been reduced to a manageable number by list reduction or some other wide screening tool

Procedure

1. Brainstorm the evaluation criteria appropriate to the situation. It is useful to get customers involved in this process. Generic criteria that are often used include
   - Effectiveness
   - Feasibility
   - Capability
   - Cost
   - Time required
   - Enthusiasm (of team and of others)

2. Discuss and refine the list of criteria. Identify any "must" or "must not" criteria. Reduce the list of criteria to the five or six that the team believes are most important. Tools such as list reduction and multivoting may be useful here.

3. Assign a relative weight to each criterion, based on how important that criterion is to the situation. Do this by distributing 10 points among the criterion. The assignment can be done by discussion and consensus. Or each member can assign weights and the numbers for each criterion added for a composite team weighting.

4. Draw a matrix. Put the criteria across the top and the list of choices down the left side.

5. Evaluate each choice against the criteria.

   Option 1: Establish a rating scale for each criterion.

   > 1 = slight extent   2 = some extent   3 = great extent
   > or   1 = little to 5 = great
   > or   1 = high   2 = medium   3 = low

   Make sure that your rating scales are consistent. Word your criteria and set the scales so that the high end of the scale (5 or 3) is always the rating that would tend to make you select that choice: most impact on customers, greatest importance, least difficulty, greatest likelihood of success.

   Option 2: For each criterion, rank order all choices according to how well each meets the criterion. Number them with 1 being the choice that is least desirable according to that criterion.

6. Multiply each choice's rating by the weight. Add the points across the row for each choice. The choice with the highest score will not necessarily be the one to choose, but the relative scores can generate meaningful discussion and lead the team toward consensus.

Variation: Problem Matrix

This tool becomes a problem matrix when you use it to answer the question, "Which problem should we work on?" Follow instructions as previously listed. Possible criteria are

- Within control of the team
- Financial payback

- Resources required (for example, money and people)
- Customer pain caused by the problem
- Team interest or buy-in
- Effect on other systems
- Management interest or support
- Difficulty of solving
- Time required to solve

Variation: Solution Matrix

This tool becomes a solution matrix when you use it to answer the question, "Which solution should we implement?" Follow instructions as previously listed. Possible criteria are

- Root causes addressed by this solution
- Cost to implement (for example, money and time)
- Ease of implementation
- Time until solution is fully implemented
- Cost to maintain (for example, money and time)
- Ease of maintenance
- Support or opposition to the solution
- Enthusiasm by team members
- Safety, health, or environmental factors
- Training factors
- Potential effects on other systems
- Potential effects on customers or suppliers
- Potential problems
- Potential negative consequences

Example

Figure 4.28 shows a decision matrix used by the Parisian Experience Restaurant's customer service team to decide which aspect of the overall problem of "long wait time" to tackle first. The problems that have been

Decision matrix: Long wait time

Criteria→ ▼Problems	Customer pain 5	Ease to solve 2	Effect on other systems 1	Speed to solve 2	
Customers wait for host	High—Nothing else for customer to do 3 × 5 = 15	Medium—Involves host and bussers 2 × 2 = 4	High—Gets customer off to bad start 3 × 1 = 3	High—Observations show adequate empty tables 3 × 2 = 6	28
Customers wait for waiter	Medium—Customers can eat breadsticks 2 × 5 = 10	Medium—Involves host and waiters 2 × 2 = 4	Medium—Customer still feels unattended 2 × 1 = 2	Low—Waiters involved in many activities 1 × 2 = 2	18
Customers wait for food	Medium—Ambiance is nice 2 × 5 = 10	Low—Involves waiters and kitchen 1 × 2 = 2	Medium—Might result in extra trips to kitchen for waiter 2 × 1 = 2	Low—Kitchen is design/space limited 1 × 2 = 2	16
Customers wait for check	Low—Customers can relax over coffee, mints 1 × 5 = 5	Medium—Involves waiters and host 2 × 2 = 4	Medium—Customers waiting for tables might notice 2 × 1 = 2	Low—Computerized ticket system is needed 1 × 2 = 2	13

Figure 4.28. Decision matrix example.

identified are "Customers wait for host," "Customers wait for waiter," "Customers wait for food," and "Customers wait for check."

The criteria that have been identified are "Customer pain" (how much does this negatively affect the customer?), "Ease to solve," "Effect on other systems," and "Speed to solve." Originally the criteria "Ease to solve" was written as "Difficulty to solve," but that wording reversed the rating scale. With the current wording, on each criteria a high rating defines a condition that would encourage selecting the problem: high customer pain, very easy to solve, high effect on other systems, and quick solution.

"Customer pain" has been weighted with 5 points, showing that the team considers it by far the most important criteria. "Ease to solve" and

"Speed to solve" have both been weighted 2. "Effect on other systems" has been weighted 1.

The team has chosen to rate each problem either high, medium, or low, with ratings of 3, 2, and 1. For example, let's look at the problem "Customers wait for food." The customer pain is medium (2), because the restaurant ambiance is nice. This problem would not be easy to solve (low ease = 1), as it involves waiters and kitchen staff. The effect on other systems is medium (2), because with this problem waiters have to make several trips to the kitchen. The problem would not be quick to solve (low speed = 1), as the kitchen design is cramped and inflexible. (Notice that the team has assumed the solution will involve kitchen redesign. This may or may not be a good assumption.)

Each rating is multiplied by the weight for that criteria. For example, the rating of high (3) for "Customers wait for host" under "Customer pain" (weight of 5) gives a score of 15. The scores are added across the rows to obtain a total for each problem. "Customers wait for host" has the highest score at 28. Since the next highest score is 18, that problem is probably a clear choice.

Considerations

- This matrix can be used to compare opinions. However, when possible, it is better to use it to summarize data that has been collected about the various criteria.

- Subteams may be formed to collect data on the various criteria.

- When evaluating choices by option 1, some people prefer to think about just one choice, rating each criteria in turn all across the matrix, then doing the next choice, and so on. Others prefer to think about one criteria, working down the matrix for all choices, then going on to the next criteria. Take your pick.

- Prioritization matrices, described in *The Memory Jogger Plus+* (Brassard), are three methods similar to and more detailed than this one for choosing among options. (See "Recommended Reading.")

- *The Team Handbook* (Scholtes) includes a good discussion about evaluating solutions. (See "Recommended Reading.")

Deployment Flowchart

Description

A deployment flowchart shows not only what happens in a process but who (which people or groups) performs each step.

When to Use

- When several different individuals or groups are involved in a process at different stages
- When the team is trying to understand or communicate responsibilities
- To allocate and track responsibilities on a project

Procedure

1. Brainstorm the major steps of the process. Write each on a card or Post-It™ note and arrange in sequence. If a top-down or detailed flowchart has already been drawn, you have an excellent start.

2. On a flipchart page or newsprint, list all players (individuals or groups) involved in the process. List them across the top or down the left side, whichever is the narrower dimension of the paper. Draw lines between each extending the full dimension of the paper.

3. Starting at the beginning of the process, place the card or note with the first step of the process in the column (or row) of the player responsible for that step. Place the second step a little farther along, to indicate later time sequence, opposite that step's key player. Continue to place all steps opposite the person or group responsible. Place them as though along a timeline, with time moving away from the names. If two steps happen simultaneously or the sequence is unimportant, place the cards or notes at equal distances along the timeline.

4. Some process steps involve two players: "Joe telephones Sally." For these, make a second card to place opposite the second name. Write the action from the point of view of the second player: "Sally receives phone call."

5. Draw arrows between cards to show the flow of the process.

Example

Figure 4.29 shows the deployment flowchart of the Parisian Experience Restaurant's process for seating guests, drawn by the team trying to solve the problem of guests waiting to be seated. The key players are the maitre d', the diners, the busser, the waiter, and lounge staff. Notice that several steps involve two players and are written twice, from both points of view: "Direct diners to lounge" and "Go to lounge"; "Seat diners" and "Take seats"; "Choose food" and "Take order."

The crossed arrows occur where there is an option in the process. Diners might be seated or directed to the lounge. If they go to the lounge, there is a long sequence of events that is skipped if they are immediately seated.

The team can identify some opportunities for changes from this diagram. For example, the lounge and the waiter have little to do until the diners are seated. Perhaps the diners could be given their menus and have their orders taken while they are waiting for a table.

Considerations

- You may wish to indicate primary and secondary or multiple responsibility by placing a step under two names with different symbols or colors.

- Often it is easier first to construct a standard flowchart and then to convert it to a deployment chart—especially if this tool is new to the team.

Effective–Achievable Matrix

Description

The effective–achievable matrix prioritizes possible choices. This matrix ranks each choice based on how effective the choice would be and how achievable it is.

When to Use

- After choices for potential courses of action have been listed and evaluated. Those choices may be solutions to implement, problems to investigate, or goals to achieve.

- After using a problem or solution matrix.

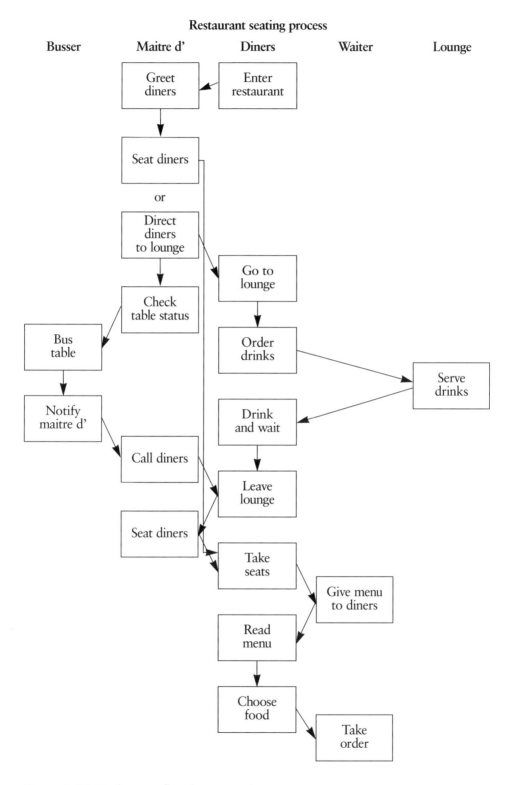

Figure 4.29. Deployment flowchart example.

Procedure

1. For each choice, ask the following two questions.

   First, how *effective* will this choice be? That is,

   - How well will this solution solve the problem? or
   - How well will solving this problem contribute to overall improvement? or
   - How well will achieving this goal support our overall mission?

   Second, how *achievable* is this choice? How easy will it be to accomplish? Consider what resources are required and the likelihood of success.

2. For each question, decide whether that choice rates "high" or "low." Finer distinctions than that are not necessary. Rate the choice in relation to the other choices, not on an absolute basis.

3. Write each choice in the box corresponding to its combination of effective and achievable ratings.

4. Choices should be chosen or prioritized in the following order:

   Highest—Box A
   2—Box B
   3—Box C
   Lowest—Box D

Example

Figure 4.30 shows an effective–achievable matrix used by a team to decide how to gather employee opinions. The team's six options were placed on the grid, based on group consensus of effectiveness and achievability.

Face-to-face interviews of a 10% random sample were judged to be low in achievability because they require a lot of time and people; but they were judged to be highly effective at gathering opinions. Low achievability and high effectiveness places that option in box B. Focus groups over lunch are highly achievable, inexpensive and quickly accomplished, but they were not considered to be very effective at getting a good sample of employee opinions. High achievability and low effectiveness places that option in box C. The other options were placed on the matrix similarly.

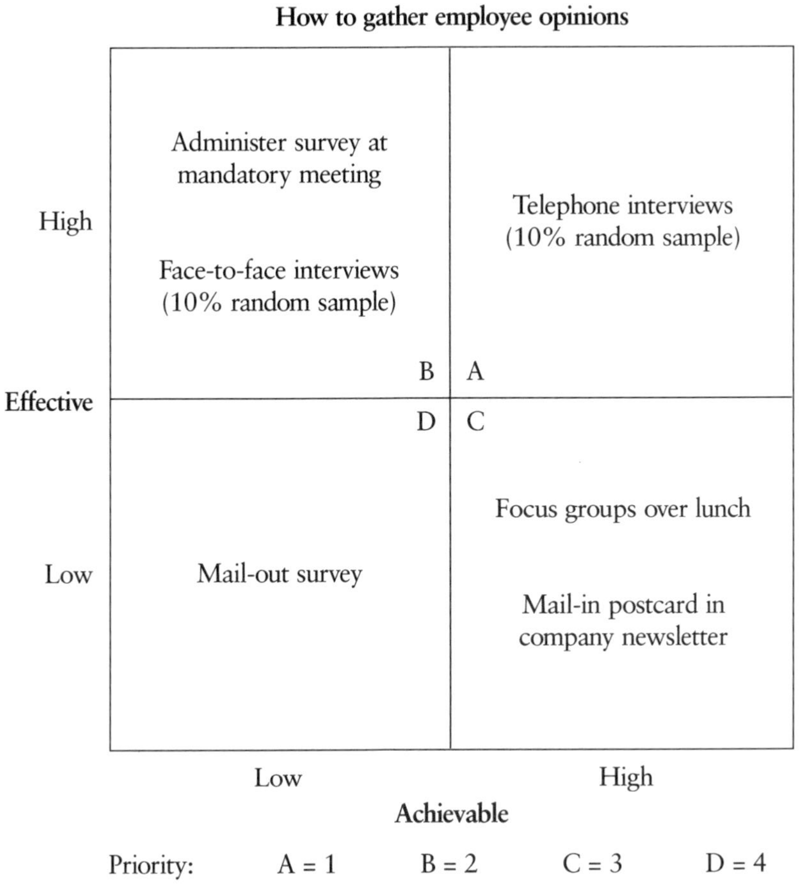

How to gather employee opinions

Administer survey at mandatory meeting Face-to-face interviews (10% random sample)	Telephone interviews (10% random sample)

High

Effective

Low

B │ A

D │ C

Focus groups over lunch

Mail-in postcard in company newsletter

Mail-out survey

Low   High

Achievable

Priority: A = 1   B = 2   C = 3   D = 4

Figure 4.30. Effective–achievable matrix example.

The group decided to start with telephone surveys, which was the only option both highly effective and highly achievable. If needed, group members would follow up with face-to-face interviews.

Considerations

- Ratings should be relative. Every choice is effective and achievable, or it would not be on your list. Compare choices to each other.
- Before using this tool, it can be useful to brainstorm evaluation criteria. What aspects of effectiveness need to be considered? Of achievability? You might use these aspects as headings for a decision matrix to evaluate each choice. Then use the effective–achievable matrix to summarize your understanding.

Fishbone Diagram

Cause-and Effect Diagram, Ishikawa Diagram

Description

The fishbone diagram relates causes and effects. It can be used to structure a brainstorming session. It immediately sorts ideas into useful categories.

When to Use

- When broad thinking about possible causes is desired
- When the team's thinking tends to fall into ruts

Procedure

1. Agree on a problem statement (effect).

2. Brainstorm the major categories of causes of the problem. If there is difficulty here, use generic headings: Method, Machines (equipment), People (manpower), Materials, Measurement, Environment.

3. Write the problem statement on a flipchart or board at the center right, draw a box around it, and draw a horizontal arrow running to it. Write the categories of causes as branches from the main arrow.

4. Brainstorm all the possible causes of the problem. Ask "Why does this happen?" As each idea is given, the facilitator writes it as a sub-cause branching from the appropriate main cause. Subcauses can be written in several places if there are multiple relationships.

5. Ask again, "Why does this happen?" about each subcause. Write sub-subcauses branching off the subcauses. Continue to ask "Why?" and generate deeper levels of causes. Layers of branches indicate causal relationships.

6. When the team runs out of ideas, focus attention to places on the fishbone where ideas are few.

Example

Figure 4.31 is the fishbone diagram drawn by the ZZ-400 team to try to understand the source of periodic iron contamination. The team used the six generic headings to prompt ideas. Several layers of branches show thorough thinking about the causes of the problem. For example, under the

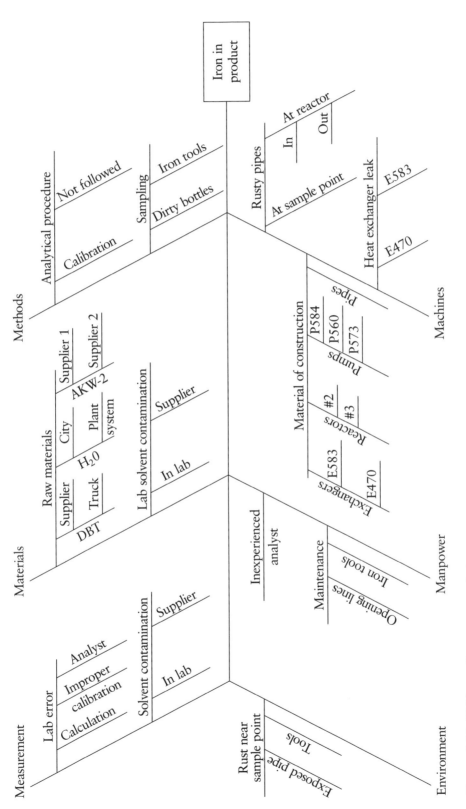

Figure 4.31. Fishbone diagram, example 1.

heading "Machines," the idea "materials of construction" shows four kinds of equipment and then several specific machine numbers.

Several ideas appear in two different places. "Calibration" shows up under "Methods," as a factor in the analytical procedure, and also under "Measurement," as a cause of lab error. "Solvent contamination" can be considered a "Materials" problem or a factor under "Measurement."

Another Example

The fishbone diagram in Figure 4.32 shows use of quality tools at home. It identifies reasons for being unable to load software on a personal computer (PC). In this example, the "Measurement" category doesn't provide any ideas, and "Environment" provides only one. If the problem occurs frequently, this list of causes from the fishbone could be made into a checklist for quickly pinpointing the source of the problem.

Variation 1: Cause Enumeration Diagram

1. Agree on the problem statement.

2. Brainstorm all possible causes, using any brainstorm technique. (See "Brainstorming" and "NGT" sections.) Record on Post-It™ notes or cards. Continue until the group has run out of ideas.

3. Using an affinity diagram, group the causes and determine headings.

4. Using the headings as main causes, arrange the ideas on a fishbone.

5. Use the fishbone to explore for additional ideas, especially where there are few ideas on the fishbone.

Variation 2: Process Fishbone
(Production Process Classification Diagram)

1. Identify the process to be studied and develop a flow diagram of the main steps. There should be fewer than 10. Draw them as a series of boxes running horizontally across a flipchart or board, with arrows connecting the boxes.

2. Brainstorm the main causes affecting the quality of each step. Draw fishbone arrows pointing to the appropriate step of the process. Also, consider the handoff from one step to another and the causes of quality problems that occur there.

3. Continue to brainstorm subcauses, as in the first procedure.

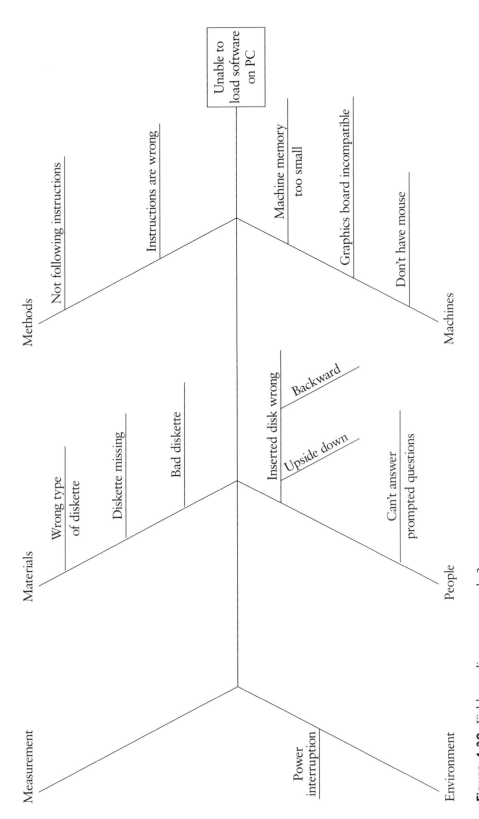

Figure 4.32. Fishbone diagram, example 2.

Variation 3: Time-Delay Fishbone

1. Begin a fishbone as in steps 1, 2, and 3 of the main procedure.

2. Hang the diagram in a well-travelled area with pens nearby. Allow people to add to the diagram over a certain time frame, say a week or two.

More people can participate this way. Even those who have not been trained in fishbones will catch on and join in.

Example

In the ZZ-400 unit, ideas were needed from everyone about the source of iron, but members of the four shifts were never all together. The team hung a flipchart page with the fishbone skeleton on the control room wall, and asked people to contribute ideas whenever they could. The result was a detailed fishbone that everyone had thought about for two weeks.

Variation 4: Desired-Result Fishbone

Instead of stating a problem, state a desired result. Then brainstorm ways to achieve the result. Or, state the desired result as a question, such as "How can we achieve our goal?"

Considerations

• The fishbone diagram broadens the team's thinking. We all tend to think in ruts at times. Determining major categories in advance, or using the generic ones, and then focusing on those categories where ideas are few will get a team out of its ruts.

• A traditional and widely used set of generic categories is the 5-Ms: machines, manpower, materials, methods, and measurement. Because they all begin with M, it is easy to remember them. However, many people consider the word *manpower* to be exclusionary. You may wish to use the 5-Ms to remember the categories, then substitute *people* for *manpower* on the diagram, as in Figure 4.32. Also, the word *equipment* is sometimes more meaningful to a group than *machines*.

• Think broadly about the problem. Consider the environment, policies, external factors. Consider all causes, not just those within your control. It can be useful to understand them all.

- The hardest part of facilitating a fishbone session is deciding where to write an idea. Let the group tell you where to write it. This gets members thinking about the relationships between the causes and the effect.

- Have someone outside the team review the diagram for fresh ideas.

- An affinity diagram can be used to determine the fishbone's categories.

Flowchart

Process Flow Diagram, Service Map

Description

A flowchart is a picture of the separate steps of a process in sequential order. It can show a sequence of actions, materials or services entering or leaving the process, decisions that must be made, and people who become involved. The process described can be anything: an administrative or service process, a manufacturing process, a plan for a quality improvement process.

When to Use

- When a team begins to study a process, as the first and most important step in understanding the process and finding improvements (sometimes called *as-is*)

- When designing an improved process (sometimes called *to-be*)

- When planning a project

- When better communication is needed between people involved with the same process

Procedure

Construction

This procedure is for a detailed flowchart, which is the most general kind. Other kinds of flowcharts are listed as separate tools because they can be used for different situations. See: "Arrow Diagram," "Deployment Flowchart," "Top-Down Flowchart," and "Work-Flow Diagram."

Materials needed: cards or Post-It™ notes, a large piece of flipchart paper or newsprint, marking pens.

1. Define the process to be diagrammed. Write it on a large card or Post-It™ note and place at the top of the work surface. Discuss and decide on the boundaries of your process: Where or when does the process start? Where or when does it end? Discuss and decide on the level of detail to be included in the diagram.

2. Brainstorm all the process steps that take place. Write each on a card. Sequence is not important at this point.

3. Arrange the steps in proper sequence.

4. Have you included steps that take place when something goes wrong or to correct problems? Have you included decisions that must be made and the alternate actions that depend on the decision? If not, add those.

5. List inputs and outputs of the process. Write each on a card and place at the appropriate point in the process flow.

6. When all steps are included and everyone agrees that the flow is correct, draw arrows to show the flow of the process.

7. Check with others involved in the process (workers, supervisors, suppliers, customers) to see if they agree that the process is as drawn.

Analysis

Some methods of analyzing flowcharts are

- Cost-of-quality analysis and critical-to-quality analysis
- Draw ideal flowchart and compare to actual
- Convert to deployment chart: Who does what when?
- Convert to work-flow diagram to identify physical inefficiencies
- Identify inputs and outputs; define suppliers, customers, and their requirements
- Identify time requirements and problems; label steps with time taken and/or required, holds or delays; find critical path; collect data if necessary
- Identify: large inventories, large lot sizes, long changeover times, long cycle time (*Note:* These production-derived terms apply to office work, too)

- Identify lack of consensus among those involved in the process over correct steps or sequence
- Identify common mistakes or problems at each step of process
- For big picture flowchart (often detected by little or no cost of quality): identify key steps (or problem steps, identified by the methods listed earlier) and flowchart these in more detail

Example

Figure 4.33 is a flowchart of the process for filling an order, from the time the order is received until the bill is mailed. An additional stopping point early in the process occurs if the potential customer's credit is not good. The flowchart also shows an output to and an input from the vendor in the middle of the process. The process is complicated enough that team members shuffled notes around several times and added forgotten steps, before they settled on the final flow.

Analysis reveals two delays ("Wait") and two recycle loops if product or raw materials aren't good. Cost-of-quality analysis also will reveal several inspection steps. (See the cost-of-quality analysis example and Figure 4.27.) Compare this flowchart with Figure 4.97, which is a work-flow diagram of the same process.

Considerations

- The following symbols are most commonly used in flowcharts:
    - ☐ Indicates one step in the process; the step is written inside the box. Usually, only one arrow goes out of the box.
    - ◇ Indicates a decision based on a question. The question is written in the diamond. More than one arrow goes out of the diamond, each one showing the direction the process takes for a given answer to the question. (Often the answers are Yes and No.)
    - → Shows the direction of moving from one step or decision to another.
- Don't worry too much about drawing the flowchart the right way. The right way is the way that helps those involved understand the process.
- Identify and involve in the flowcharting process all key people who are involved with the process. This includes those who do the work

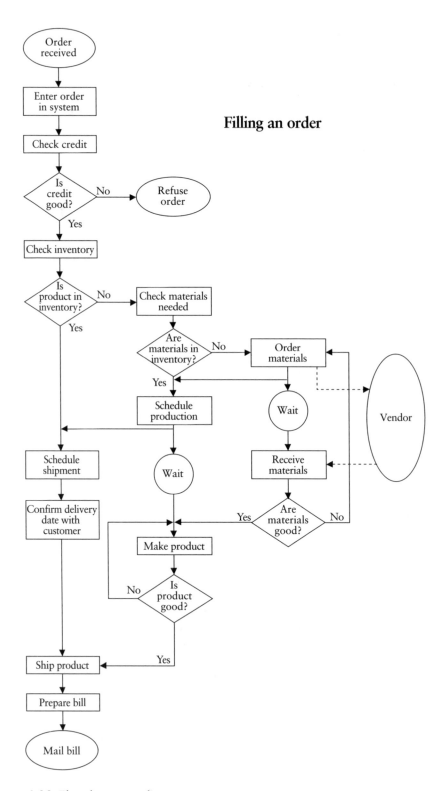

Figure 4.33. Flowchart example.

in the process: suppliers, customers, and supervisors. Involve them in the actual flowcharting sessions, by interviewing them before the sessions, and/or by showing them the developing flowchart between work sessions and obtaining their feedback.

- Do not assign a "technical expert" to draw the flowchart. People who actually perform the process should construct the flowchart.

- The facilitator's role is to be sure all members participate, to ask the right questions to uncover all aspects of the process, and to help team members capture all their ideas in the language of the flowchart.

- Keep all parts of the flowchart visible to everyone all the time. That is why flipchart or butcher paper should be used rather than transparencies or a board.

- Several sessions may be necessary. This allows members time to gather information or to reflect on the process. Even if the flowchart seems to be finished in one session, allow a review at a second session, to allow reflection time.

- Flowcharts are an excellent way to document the procedure for a process. They also are excellent for training.

- Here are good questions to ask as the flowchart is being developed.[13]

    —Where does the [service, material] come from?

    —How does the [service, material] get to the process?

    —Who makes the decision (if one is needed)?

    —What happens if the decision is yes?

    —What happens if the decision is no?

    —Is there anything else that must be done at this point?

    —Where does the [product, service] of this process go?

    —What tests or inspections are done on the product at each part of the process?

    —What tests or inspections are done on the process?

    —What happens if the test or inspection is failed?

    Note that these are "What, Where, How, Who?" questions. It is not helpful to ask "Why?" while flowcharting. Save that question for later.

Force Field Analysis

Description

Force field analysis is an analytical tool that clarifies opposing aspects of a desired change.

- Driving or positive forces that support an action or situation
- Restraining or negative forces that try to prevent it

When opposing forces are equal, no change can occur. When one set of forces becomes stronger than the other, change will occur. When all the forces have been considered, plans can be made that will encourage the desired change.

When to Use

- When the team is planning implementation of a solution
- When the team is identifying causes of a problem
- When the team is identifying problems in a process

Procedure

1. State a desired action or outcome.

2. Brainstorm all the positive, or driving, forces that cause that action to happen. Write them on the left side of a vertical line down the middle of a flipchart page, with arrows pointing right, toward the line.

3. Brainstorm all the negative, or restraining, forces that prevent that action from happening. Write them on the right side of the vertical line, with arrows pointing left, toward the line.

4. Discuss means to diminish or eliminate the restraining forces.

Example

Figure 4.34 is a force field analysis created by someone who wanted to lose weight. Let's call him Sam. Health threat, negative self-image, and clothes that don't fit were among the forces making him want to lose weight. Unsympathetic friends and family, genetic traits, and years of bad eating habits were among the forces preventing it.

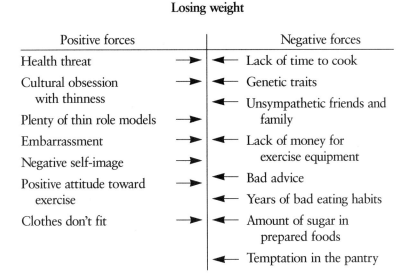

Figure 4.34. Force field analysis example.

For Sam, becoming more aware of health consequences, berating himself, or refusing to buy new clothes were not enough. Those were all ways to strengthen the driving forces. Instead, Sam explored ways to weaken or eliminate the restraining forces. For example, his friends and family could be coached on how to be supportive. Cooking lessons or cookbooks could show how to make healthy food attractive and interesting, to counteract years of bad eating habits. Unfortunately, some restraining forces, such as Sam's genetic traits, cannot be changed. But if enough restraining forces are weakened, Sam can lose weight.

Variation
When you are looking for causes of a problem, the action stated in step 1 will be the problem, which is undesirable. Then, in step 4, look for ways to diminish or eliminate the driving forces that support the problem.

Considerations
- Think of the driving forces as pushing the center line toward the right. Think of the restraining forces as pushing the center line toward the left. When the two sets of forces are equal, the current state will be maintained, with the line staying in the center. To accomplish a change, the center line must be moved by adjusting the forces.

- Strengthening the forces supporting a desired change often leads to a reaction that reinforces the opposing forces. It is more effective to develop ways to reduce or eliminate the opposing forces.

- It can be useful to assign relative strengths to each force, and then to focus attention on the strongest ones.

Graphs

Description

A graph is a visual display of numerical data to achieve deeper or quicker understanding of the meaning of the numbers.

When to Use

- When analyzing data
- When presenting data

Basic Procedure

1. Collect or assemble the data to be shown on your graph. Decide what you want to study or to show with the graph.

2. Decide what form the graph should take. See the variations section for different formats.

3. Determine the range (lowest number to highest number) you need to show on the graph for each set of data. Choose the scale for each set of data to be as large as or slightly larger than the range.

4. Draw the edge lines (called *scale lines*) and tick marks to show the numerical scale. Use no more tick marks than necessary, usually three to 10, depending on the range of the data. Write numbers (or labels, if appropriate) next to the tick marks.

5. Determine appropriate symbols for the data. Plot the data. If the data are in time sequence, connect points with lines.

6. If appropriate, draw reference lines for important values, such as the average, with which all the data must be compared. To note a significant number on the scale, such as the time a change was made, place a marker (an arrow and a note) along the scale line.

7. Complete the graph with title and date, a key for any symbols, and notes, if necessary.

8. Analyze the graph. What does it teach? What additional graphing, analysis, investigation, or data collection does it suggest?

Variations

There are many different kinds of graphs, some widely used and some very specialized. Several of the tools in this book are graphs designed for a particular use. See these tools for detail about when and how to use them:

- Box plot
- Control chart
- Histogram (also including stem-and-leaf display)
- Pareto chart
- Run chart
- Scatter diagram

Variations for Graphing Labeled Data

Sometimes you have a set of data where each number is accompanied by a description in words. For example, a list of problems, and with each problem the number of times it occurred. This is called *labeled data*. There are three common types of graphs to display this data: dot graph (which has several variations), bar graph, and pie graph.

Variation 1: Dot Chart

In the dot chart[14] (Figure 4.35), values are indicated by positions of dots opposite a scale, or sometimes also by the length of a line to the dot. This is an excellent way to display labeled data.

Procedure

Follow the basic procedure on page 144 except

4. At Step 4, write the labels along the left edge of the graph. Place tick marks and their numbers along the top and/or bottom edges.

5. Place a large dot for each data point opposite its label. Generally, it is most useful to the viewer to order the values from largest to smallest.

If there are many data points, use faint dotted lines between each data point and its label. If the numerical scale begins at 0, the length of the line as well as the position of the large dot will signal to the viewer the numerical value. If the numerical scale does not begin at 0, the length of the line is meaningless. To prevent the viewer from comparing meaningless lengths, continue the faint dotted line all the way across the graph to the right edge.

Example

In Figure 4.35, a dot chart shows the number of telephone calls processed each day for 10 different cities. Notice the faint dots helping the eye connect the city name (the label) with its dot. The faint dots continue across the entire graph, because the scale does not start at zero. If the dotted line stopped at the value dots, the eye would interpret the length of the dotted line to be proportional to the value. That is only correct when the numerical scale begins at zero.

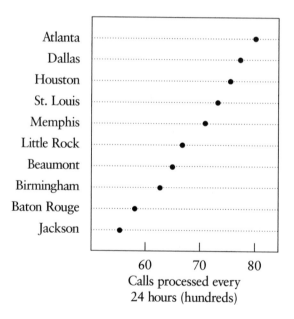

Figure 4.35. Dot chart example.

Variations: Two-Way Dot Chart; Grouped Dot Chart; Multi-Valued Dot Chart

These charts are different ways to show labeled data that can be sliced two ways: They are analyzed one way into a set of labels, and analyzed another way into a different set of labels. You want to show both groupings on one graph.

Variation 2: Two-Way Dot Chart

In the two-way dot chart,[15] each category from the second analysis is drawn as a separate dot chart, and the charts are placed side-by-side using one set of labels on the far left showing the first analysis. Each separate chart is titled at the top to show the labels of the second analysis.

Example

In Figure 4.36, a two-way dot chart analyzes average monthly automatic teller machine (ATM) volume for five different banks and for the four quarters of 1993. The first analysis is the five different banks; those labels are at the far left. The data for each time period is on a separate dot chart. This arrangement makes it easy to compare the five banks in each quarter.

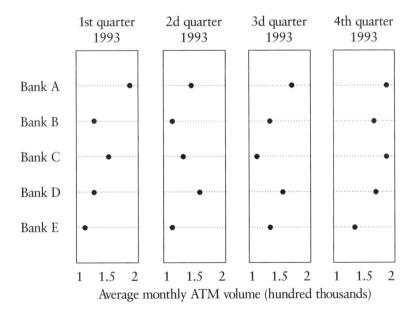

Figure 4.36. Two-way dot chart example.

Variation 3: Grouped Dot Chart

On the grouped dot chart,[16] the left edge of the graph shows labels for both ways of slicing the data. All the labels for the first analysis are grouped together for the first category of the second analysis. Then all the labels for the first analysis are grouped together for the second category of the second analysis, and so on.

Example

Figure 4.37 shows a grouped dot chart of the same ATM data. This time, all four quarters for Bank A are grouped together, then all four quarters for Bank B, and so on. This method of grouping allows easy quarter-to-quarter comparison for each bank. Notice that each bank's volume dropped in the second quarter—except Bank D. (Bank D installed some new ATM machines.)

The data could have been grouped the other way: All five banks for first quarter, then all five banks for second quarter, and so on. That grouping would have allowed easy bank-to-bank comparison for each quarter, but would have hidden the pattern we noticed between first and second quarters. So it is useful to try graphing your data several different ways to see what you can learn.

Variation 4: Multi-Valued Dot Chart

In the multi-valued dot chart,[17] all the values for the second analysis are placed on the same line opposite the label for the first analysis. Different symbols are keyed to the categories of the second analysis.

Example

In Figure 4.38, the first and second quarter ATM data is plotted for each bank. Bank D's second quarter increase shows up clearly, in contrast to the other banks' second quarter drops.

Variation 5: Bar Chart

In the bar chart, values are indicated by the length of a bar—a long, narrow rectangle. The histogram and Pareto chart are bar charts. Follow the basic procedure, except

4. Write labels either down the left side or across the bottom. Write the numerical scale on whichever edge does not have the labels. The

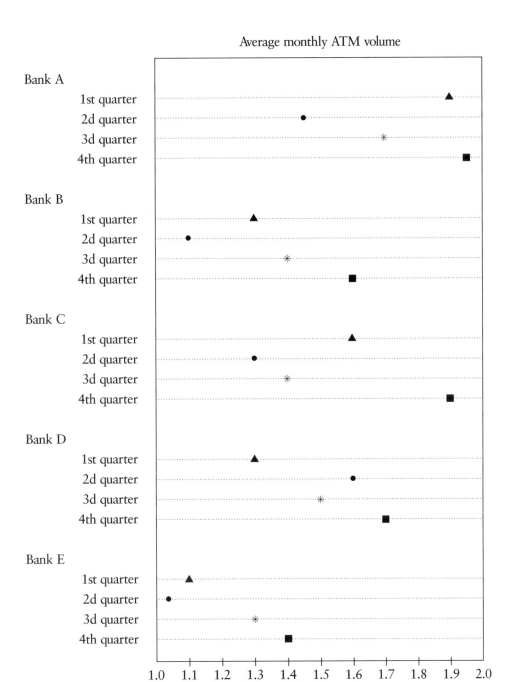

Figure 4.37. Grouped dot chart example.

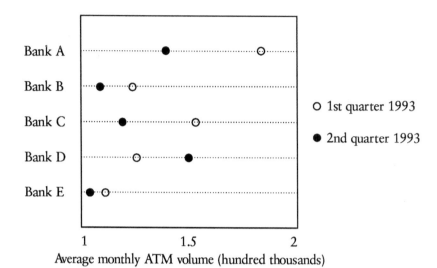

Figure 4.38. Multi-valued dot chart example.

numerical scale *must* start at 0, or the length of the line, the visual indicator of numerical value, will be meaningless.

5. Draw a bar for each value. Fill each bar with a light gray shading. Avoid cross-hatching, which is visually distracting. Even better, eliminate the edges of the bar and draw only the shading. Or, eliminate the bar and use a line to indicate length. This is preferable if a series of groupings of several bars must be compared. The bar creates redundant parallel lines which confuse the eye.[18]

Examples

There are many bar charts throughout this book. See the histograms in Figures 4.16, 4.45, and 4.47 through 4.54 and the Pareto charts in Figures 4.74 and 4.75.

Variation 6: Divided Bar Chart

This kind of chart is not recommended.[19] In the divided bar chart, one bar is divided into several sections along its length to show values of subgroups. The human eye and brain cannot compare lengths that are not aligned. In Figure 4.39, do time certificates increase, decrease, or stay the same from the first to second quarter of 1992?

Instead of a divided bar chart, use one of the variations of the dot chart, or a run chart with several lines if time is one of the groupings.

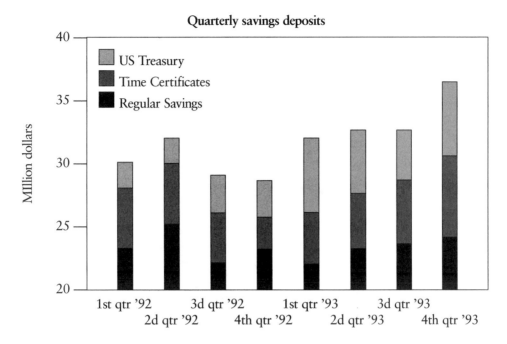

Figure 4.39. Divided bar chart example.

Variation 7: Pie Chart

This kind of chart is not recommended.[20] In the pie chart, a circle is divided into wedges to show relative proportions. The human eye and brain cannot compare angles very well. In Figure 4.40, which type of loan is a larger part of the loan portfolio: auto or conventional mortgage? Instead of the pie chart, use a dot graph or a bar chart, which do better jobs of comparing values.

The pie chart has one advantage: it emphasizes that the portions sum to 100%. If you need to use a pie chart for this reason, be sure to write the values or percentages on or beside each wedge.

Variations for Graphing Distributions

Sometimes you are measuring one variable and studying how it changes, over time or between groups. For example, your variable might be height, and you are measuring people who fall into the two groups of male and female, or 10 groups of ages. There are several graph variations that show the distribution of measurements of one variable.

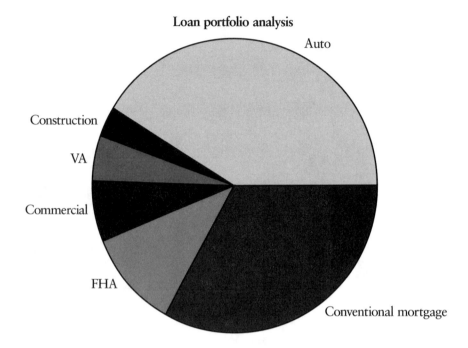

Figure 4.40. Pie chart example.

Variations 8 and 9: Histogram and Stem-and-Leaf Display

A histogram is a form of bar chart specially designed for showing distribution. The stem-and-leaf display is a variation on the histogram where the actual value is used as the symbol for the data point. See "Histogram" for more information on both these graphs and for examples.

Variation 10: Point Graph

A point graph is useful for showing distributions when there are few data points.[21] Each piece of information is graphed along a line with a small circle. This graph becomes ineffective when circles start overlapping so much that the viewer cannot tell how many circles lie together. A histogram should be used in that case.

Example

Figure 4.41 shows a point graph that compares two distributions: the time required to process invoices before making changes and the time required after the process has been reengineered. The improvement is clear.

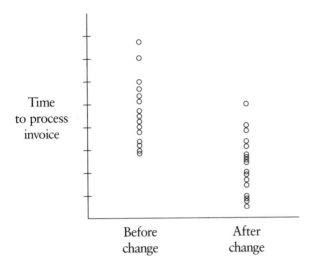

Figure 4.41. Point graph example.

Variation 11: Percentile Graph

The percentile graph plots each data value against its percentile.[22] A value's percentile is a statistical way of measuring the proportion of data that are less than or equal to that value. The range of percentiles will be 0 to 100. Follow the basic procedure, except

5. List all the values in the data set in sequence from smallest to largest. Give them sequence numbers from 1, the smallest, to the largest. If there are n values altogether, the percentile for each number is

$$\text{percentile} = \frac{\text{sequence number} - 0.5}{n} \times 100$$

Plot the value on one axis and the percentile on the other.

Example

To make the calculation clear, this example uses only seven numbers. The method is more valuable with a larger data set. The heights of seven children are (in inches)

62, 57, 55, 62, 56, 58, 60

Now these are listed in sequence from smallest to largest, with the sequence numbers and the percentile.

Sequence number	Value	Percentile
1	55	$0.5 \div 7 \times 100 =\ \ 7.1$
2	56	$1.5 \div 7 \times 100 = 21.4$
3	57	$2.5 \div 7 \times 100 = 35.7$
4	58	$3.5 \div 7 \times 100 = 50.0$
5	60	$4.5 \div 7 \times 100 = 64.2$
6	62	$5.5 \div 7 \times 100 = 78.6$
7	62	$6.5 \div 7 \times 100 = 92.9$

The resulting percentile graph is Figure 4.42. The points are closer together at the lower end, spacing apart at the top end. This shows that just a few children are much taller than the rest. Of course, with only seven points, you could easily figure that out by looking at the numbers. But with a large data set, the percentile graph is useful for showing where the data clump together.

Variation 12: Box Plot

The box plot is a graph that shows several important percentiles rather than all the data. It is especially useful for accurately comparing distributions. See "Box Plot" for the procedure and an example.

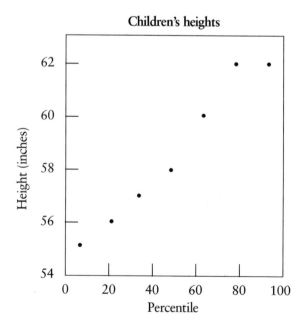

Figure 4.42. Percentile graph example.

Variations for Graphing Two Variables

Often two variables are plotted against each other to show their relationship. Two common examples include a measurement taken repeatedly over time and two variables that are suspected of having a cause–effect relationship. Tools used for plotting measurements over time include the control chart and the run chart. To look for a cause–effect relationship, use a scatter diagram. All three of these graphs are described separately in their own sections.

Considerations

These considerations have been summarized from Cleveland and Tufte (see "Recommended Reading").

- The two most important principles of good graphs are:

  —Make it easy for the viewer to quickly see the data.

  —Eliminate anything unnecessary.

- Unnecessary elements include grid lines, many tick marks, many numbers opposite tick marks, notes and labels inside the graph area, cross-hatching, bars instead of lines.

- Make every mark on the graph do enough work to earn the right to be there.

Symbols

- Make symbols dark and big—easy to see.

- If several symbols will fall on top of one another and be hard to distinguish, use symbols that look like Y, X or ✳. The number of lines radiating from the center of the symbol indicates how many data values fall on that spot. Or, you can use more sophisticated graphs, such as logarithmic scales or plot residuals, to eliminate overlap.

- If you must place labels next to data symbols, place them so that the eye can easily distinguish just the data. Place the labels outside a central area occupied by just the data symbols. If that is not possible, make the data symbols very prominent and the label lettering thin and unobtrusive.

Lines

- Connect points only when showing time sequence and when short-term variation is significant. Use straight lines to connect points.

Make sure the data points are big enough to show up, unless individual values are not important.

- Sometimes there are several data lines on the same graph, such as when two different measurements are being tracked over the same period of time. Be sure the viewer can tell the lines apart, especially where they cross. If this is a problem, place two separate graphs side-by-side. When you do this, there is always a tradeoff between the eye being able to distinguish the data sets and having to jump back and forth between two graphs to make comparisons.

- Sometimes two lines are graphed with the intent of comparing their values. If the slopes of the lines are changing, the eye will not be able to make accurate comparisons. Instead, plot the differences between the two data sets.

Scales and Scale Lines

- It is conventional to show time along the bottom edge of a graph, proceeding left to right. For cause-and-effect graphs, show cause along the bottom edge and effect along the left edge.

- Choose a scale that is only as large as or slightly larger than the range of data. Try not to have any areas of the graph that aren't working to show your data. The scale does not have to include zero. *Exception:* With a bar graph, the scale must include zero or the bar lengths are meaningless. Notice how in Figure 4.39, where the scale starts with 20, the bar lengths convey no real information.

- If two graphs will be compared, their scales must be the same. If this is impossible because of very different absolute values (say, one graph with data around 10 and another with data around 1000) then at least be sure that the lengths that represent one unit are the same.

- Use a scale break when a large region of the graph will have no data in it. Scale breaks must extend across the entire graph, as in Figure 4.43, not just across the scale line. Do not connect data symbols across a scale break. Do not use scale breaks with bar graphs.

- When using a bar graph or dot chart, think about whether larger or smaller will be considered good, and translate the data so that a larger number is good. For example, don't graph "% decrease in complaints" where a long bar means a larger decrease and therefore fewer complaints. Instead, graph the actual number of complaints, where a series of shortening bars shows complaints decreasing.

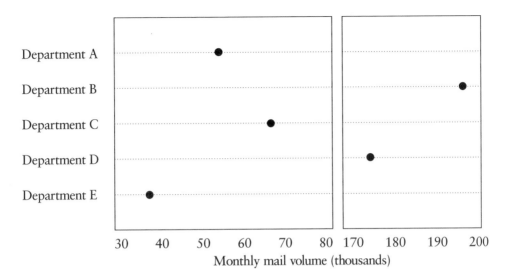

Figure 4.43. Scale break.

- Consider using two different scales on opposite sides of the graph when the data can be calculated in two different ways. For example, actual values on one scale and percent change on the other. Or percent purity and percent impurity. Or logarithmic values and original data values.

- Use a logarithmic scale when percent change or ratio comparisons are the point of the graph.

Reproduction

- Graphs copied on a machine often become harder to read, especially if they are reduced. A good test: Copy it at two-thirds reduction, then copy the copy at two-thirds reduction. If it survives that test, it will be readable under most conditions.

- Don't use color to differentiate symbols or lines if the graph is likely to be copied.

Histogram

Description

A histogram is a bar graph that shows the distribution of a set of data: how often the different values occur. In a histogram, individual data values cannot be seen. A variation, the stem-and-leaf display, preserves the individual values.

When to Use

- To analyze quickly whether a process can meet the customer's requirements
- To see whether a change has occurred from one time period to another
- To determine whether the output of a process is distributed approximately normally
- To communicate the distribution quickly and easily to others

Procedure

Construction

1. Collect at least 50 consecutive data points from a process. If you don't have that much data, use a point graph, described under the graph section.

2. Use the histogram worksheet (Figure 4.44) to set up the histogram. It will help you determine the number of bars, the range of numbers that go into each bar, and the labels for the bar edges. After calculating W in step 2, use your judgment to adjust it to a convenient number. For example, you might decide to round 0.9 to an even 1.0. The value for W must not have more decimal places than the numbers you will be graphing.

3. Draw X and Y axes on graph paper. Mark and label the Y axis for counting data values. Mark and label the X axis with the L values from the worksheet. The spaces between these numbers will be the bars of the histogram.

4. For each data point, mark off one count above the appropriate bar with an X or by shading that portion of the bar. For numbers that fall directly on the edge of a bar, mark the bar to the right.

Analysis

1. Before drawing any conclusions from your histogram, satisfy yourself that the process was stable during the time period being studied. If any unusual events affected the process during the time period of the

Process:_____

Data dates:_____

Calculated by:_____

Date:_____

Step 1. Number of bars

Find how many bars there should be for the amount of data you have. This is a ballpark estimate. At the end, you may have one more or less.

Number of data points	Number of bars *(B)*	
50	7	
	8	
	9	
100	10	$B =$ _____
	11	
150	12	
	13	
200	14	

Step 2. Width of bars

Total range of the data = R = largest value – smallest value

= _____ – _____ = _____

Width of each bar   = W = R ÷ B

= _____ ÷ _____ = _____

Adjust for convenience. W must not have more decimal places than the data.

W =   _____

Step 3. Find edges of the bars

Choose a convenient number, $L1$, to be the lower edge of the first bar. This number can be lower than any of the data values. The lower edge of the second bar will be W more than $L1$. Keep adding W to find the lower edge of each bar.

$L1$ $L2$ $L3$ $L4$ $L5$ $L6$ $L7$ $L8$ $L9$ $L10$ $L11$ $L12$ $L13$ $L14$

—   —   —   —   —   —   —   —   —   —   —   —   —   —

Figure 4.44. Histogram worksheet.

histogram, your analysis of the histogram shape probably will not be valid.

2. Analyze the meaning of your histogram's shape. See the considerations section for some typical shapes and their meanings.

Example

The Bulldogs bowling team wants to improve its standing in the league. Team members decided to study their scores for the past month. The 55 bowling scores are

103	107	111	115	115	118	119	121	122	124	124
125	126	127	127	129	134	135	137	138	139	141
142	144	145	146	147	148	148	149	150	151	152
153	153	154	155	155	155	156	157	159	160	161
163	163	165	165	167	170	172	176	177	183	198

Using the table on the histogram worksheet, they estimate B to be 7. The highest score was 198 and the lowest was 103, so the range of values is

$$R = \text{largest} - \text{smallest}$$
$$= 198 - 103$$
$$= 95$$

Then the width of each bar is

$$W = R \div B$$
$$= 95 \div 7$$
$$= 13.6$$

The bowling scores have no decimal places, so the bar width must have no decimal places either. They round 13.6 up to 14. Because 14 is an awkward number to work with, they decide to adjust W to 15.

Choosing 100 to be the lower edge of the first bar, the lower edges of the other bars are:

100 + 15 = 115

115 + 15 = 130, and so on

Figure 4.45 shows the histogram they drew. They seem to have a double-peaked, or bimodal, distribution: a group of players who score in the low 100s and another more talented group that scores in the mid-100s. To improve the team's standing, members can try to improve everyone's score,

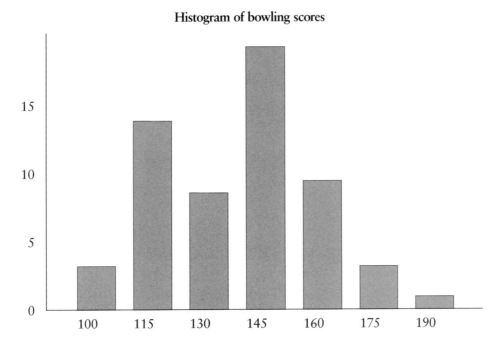

Figure 4.45. Histogram example.

which would shift the entire histogram to the right. Or they could focus their efforts on improving the poorer players, which would narrow the distribution, making the team as a whole more consistent.

Variation: Stem-and-Leaf Display

The stem-and-leaf display[23] uses the last significant digit of each value as the symbol marking that value on the graph. Thus, the stem-and-leaf display is a type of histogram that shows individual data values.

Procedure

1. Decide which digits in the data are changing. Out of this group, choose the two or three on the left that are most important. Of these digits, the one on the right will be the *leaf,* and the one or two on the left will be the *stem.*

2. Draw a vertical line on the page. To the left of the line, write the stems in order from smallest to largest in a column.

3. To the right of the line, write opposite each stem the leaf of each data value which has that stem. Do not use any digits to the right of the leaf.

4. Write a legend on the graph indicating how to read the numbers.

Example

Figure 4.46 shows the Bulldog's bowling scores in a stem-and-leaf display. The stems are the digits 10, 11, 12, and so forth. The leaves are the digits 3, 7, and so on. The first row,

$$10 \mid 37$$

indicates the scores 103 and 107. The display shows the same double-peaked distribution we saw with the histogram.

Considerations

- The following describe typical histogram shapes and what they mean.

  Normal: The most common pattern is the bell-shaped curve known as the *normal distribution* (Figure 4.47). In a normal distribution, points are as likely to occur on one side of the average as on the other.

  Skewed: The skewed distribution (Figure 4.48) is lopsided because a physical limit prevents outcomes on one side of the average. For example, a distribution of analyses of a very pure product might be skewed, because the product cannot be more than 100% pure.

Bowling scores

10	37
11	15589
12	124456779
13	45789
14	124567889
15	012334555679
16	0133557
17	0267
18	3
19	8

Leaf = 1
10 | 3 = 103

Figure 4.46. Stem-and-leaf display example.

Double-peaked or *Bimodal:* The bimodal distribution (Figure 4.49) looks like the back of a two-humped camel. The outcomes of two processes with normal distributions are combined in one set of data. For example, a distribution of production data from a two-shift operation might be bimodal, if each shift produces a different distribution of results. Stratification often reveals this problem.

Plateau: The plateau (Figure 4.50) might be called a *multimodal* distribution. Several processes with normal distributions are combined. Because there are many peaks close together, the top of the distribution resembles a plateau.

Comb: In a comb distribution (Figure 4.51), the bars are alternately tall and short. This distribution often results from a combination of rounded-off data and an incorrectly constructed histogram. For example, temperature data rounded off to the nearest 0.2 degree would show a comb shape if the bar width for the histogram were 0.1 degree.

Truncated or *Heart Cut:* The truncated distribution (Figure 4.52) looks like a normal distribution with the tails cut off. The supplier might be producing a normal distribution of material and then relying on inspection to separate what is within specification limits from

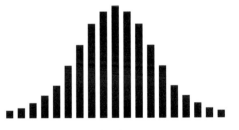

Figure 4.47. Normal distribution.

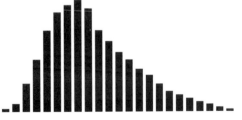

Figure 4.48. Skewed distribution.

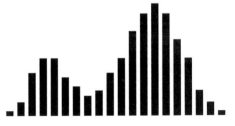

Figure 4.49. Bimodal (double-peaked) distribution.

Figure 4.50. Plateau distribution.

what is off-spec. The resulting shipments to the customer from inside the specifications are the heart cut.

Edge peak: The edge peak distribution (Figure 4.53) looks like the normal distribution except that it has a large peak at one tail. Usually this is caused by faulty construction of the histogram, with several bars of data lumped together into a bar labeled "greater than. . . ."

Dogfood: The dogfood distribution (Figure 4.54) is missing something—results near the average. If a customer receives this kind of distribution, someone else is receiving a heart cut. Even though what the customer receives is within specifications, the product falls into two clusters: one near the upper specification limit and one near the lower specification limit. This variation often causes problems in the customer's process.

- Take care before acting based on your histogram if the data is old. The process may have changed since your data were collected.

- If there are few data points, interpret the histogram cautiously. Any conclusions for a histogram with less than 50 observations should be seriously questioned.

Figure 4.51. Comb distribution.

Figure 4.52. Truncated or heart cut distribution.

Figure 4.53. Edge peak distribution.

Figure 4.54. Dogfood distribution.

- Any interpretation of a histogram shape is only a theory that must be verified with direct observation of the process.

- A histogram cannot be used to definitely conclude that a distribution is normal. There are other distributions that are similar in appearance. Statistical calculations such as the normal probability plot or Kolmogorov–Smirnov test must be used to prove a normal distribution. Of course, a histogram can show that a distribution definitely is not normal.

- If a process is stable, the histogram can predict future performance. If a process is not stable, the histogram merely summarizes past performance.

- See the section on graphs for more information.

Importance–Performance Analysis

Description

The importance–performance analysis analyzes the perceptions of customers about both the importance and the performance of products and services that a supplier provides. It helps organize discussions with customers about their needs and perceptions.

When to Use

- Early in a quality improvement process, to identify areas where improvement would have the greatest potential impact on customer satisfaction

- When you want to learn from the customer which elements of a particular service offer the best opportunities for improvement

- When management wants to set priorities for quality improvement efforts based on customer perceptions

Procedure

Data Collection

1. Identify your customers, products, and services. Useful tools for this include brainstorming, NGT, multivoting, the requirements matrix, and the requirements-and-measures tree.

2. Select key customers and ask them to rate on a scale of 1 to 5 the products and services provided. Ask them to rate both how important the product or service is to them (Importance) and how well you provide that product or service (Performance).

Importance

   5 = Critical

   4 = Important, but not critical

   3 = Of some value

   2 = Nice to have, but not necessary

   1 = Not needed

Performance

   5 = Greatly exceeds expectations

   4 = Exceeds expectations

   3 = Adequate products and services

   2 = Needs some improvement

   1 = Consistently lacking

3. Rate yourself. On the same 1 to 5 scale, rate how important your product or service is to the customer and rate your performance in providing the product or service.

4. Record the customer's ratings and your ratings on a table like Table 4.5.

Table 4.5. Importance–performance analysis rating table.

Service	Importance by supplier	Importance by customer	Performance by supplier	Performance by customer

Analysis

1. *Importance and performance: Customer's perception.* For each product or service, plot the customer's importance and performance perceptions on a matrix like Figure 4.55. Find the customer's importance rating on the left side and the customer's performance rating across the bottom. Then find the box where the importance row intersects with the performance column. (See the example.)

   • Box I is the most desirable. Products and services in that box are important to the customer and, according to the customer, are being done well.

   • Box II contains the most pressing needs for improvement. The customer believes that products and services important to the customer are not being done well.

   • Improvement of products and services in box III may be desirable, but the priority is lower than in box II.

   • Box IV may indicate areas where resources can be shifted to products and services that are more important to the customer.

2. *Importance: Customer compared to supplier.* Plot a point for each product or service on an importance matrix like Figure 4.56.

   • In boxes II and IV, the customer's view and your view do not match. These could be fruitful areas of discussion with the customer.

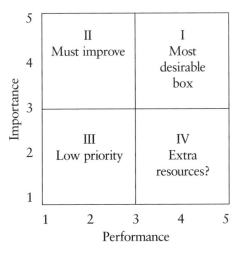

Figure 4.55. Customer's importance–performance comparison.

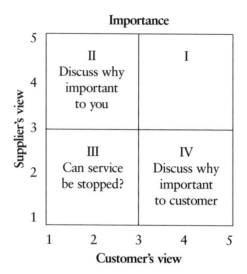

Figure 4.56. Supplier–customer comparison: Importance.

- In box III, both the customer and you rate importance 1 or 2. Talk with the customer about replacing the service with something of more value.

3. *Performance: Customer compared to supplier.* Plot a point for each product or service on a performance matrix like Figure 4.57.

- Again, areas of disagreement (boxes II and IV) are fruitful areas for discussion.

- If both you and your customer think performance is poor (box III), be sure to talk about why.

- If you both perceive a particular product or service to be a strength (box I), find out why. Maybe you will learn something that can be transferred to other services.

Example
The products and services that a restaurant provides to customers are listed in Table 4.6. An importance–performance questionnaire given to restaurant customers and to management and employees resulted in the ratings shown.

Customer Importance–Performance Comparison
For each service, a code placed on Figure 4.58 shows the customer's perception of importance and performance.

Performance

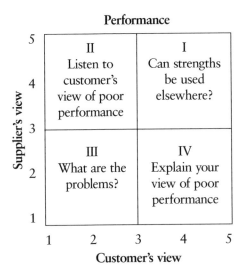

Figure 4.57. Supplier–customer comparison: Performance.

Table 4.6. Importance–performance analysis example: Rating table.

Service		Importance by restaurant	Importance by customer	Performance by restaurant	Performance by customer
Breakfast	(B)	4.1	4.2	4.9	3.9
Lunch	(L)	4.7	4.9	4.4	4.1
Dinner	(D)	4.9	4.9	4.6	4.4
Lounge/bar	(BAR)	2.2	3.2	3.1	4.8
Carry out	(C)	1.8	1.5	2.8	4.6
Private parties	(P)	3.9	4.7	4.1	2.5

- Breakfast (B) was rated 4.2 in importance and 3.9 in performance, so it goes in box I. Lunch, dinner, and bar all fall in box I, which is most desirable.

- Private parties was rated high (4.7) in importance but low (2.5) in performance. It falls in box II. The restaurant should take action to understand the gap and to improve performance.

- Carry-out (C) was rated low in importance (1.5) although it was high in performance (4.6), so it falls in box IV. The restaurant might want to divert resources from this area to improve private party service.

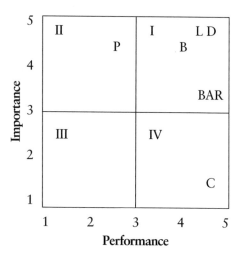

Figure 4.58. Importance–performance analysis example: Customer's comparison.

Importance: Customer–Supplier Comparison
The importance ratings of the customers and the restaurant are shown in
Figure 4.59.

- Both the customers and the restaurant consider carry out (C) relatively unimportant. The restaurant may want to revamp this service
  to be of greater value to the customers, or eliminate carry-out and
  assign those resources to more valued services.

Performance: Customer–Supplier Comparison
The performance ratings of the customers and the restaurant are shown in
Figure 4.60.

- Both the customers and the restaurant rate performance high for
  breakfast (B), lunch (L), and dinner (D). By discussing these services
  the restaurant may learn how to improve private parties (P), where the
  restaurant rates its performance much higher than the customers do.

- The customers' high evaluation of the bar is interesting. Maybe the
  bar employees are missing some well-deserved positive feedback.

- Overall, private parties (P) look like a great opportunity for improvement. Both customers and employees rate importance high, but the
  employees overrate their own performance, in the eyes of the
  customers.

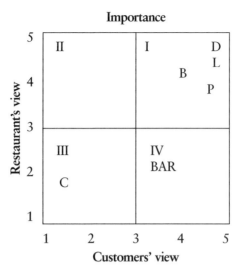

Figure 4.59. Importance–performance analysis example: Importance comparison.

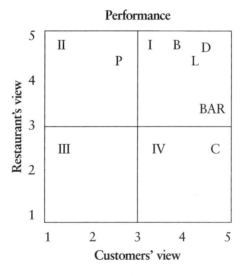

Figure 4.60. Importance–performance analysis example: Performance comparison.

Considerations

- The comparisons are made to learn from, rather than to argue with the customer. The customer's perception is always "right." Our job is to learn why the customer feels that way and then to apply that knowledge toward improvement.

- See "Surveys" for general information about planning, carrying out, and analyzing a customer survey.

Is–Is Not Matrix

Description

The is–is not matrix, created by Kepner-Tregoe, identifies where to start looking for causes. By isolating who, what, when, and where about an event, it narrows investigation to factors that have an impact, and eliminates factors that do not have an impact.[24]

When to Use

- When looking for causes of a problem or situation
- When attempting to isolate the factors that affect the situation from those factors that do not
- When looking for a pattern in the circumstances surrounding the situation

Procedure

1. Describe the event in general terms so that everyone clearly understands the problem.

2. Using the "Is" column of the matrix (Figure 4.61), describe what did or does occur.

    a. Determine *what* objects are affected and *what* exactly occurs. Be as specific as possible.

    b. Determine *where* the event occurs. This can be geographical (Houston), a physical location (the widget department or on machine 1), or on an object (at the bottom of the page or on the back of the widget). Or, it can be a combination (at the left side of each widget coming off line 2).

    c. Determine *when* the event occurs. When did it happen first? When since? What patterns of occurrence have you noticed? Date, time, day, and season can all be important to the solution. Also, when the event occurs in relation to other events (before, after, during) can be significant.

    d. Determine the *extent* of the problem. How many objects or occurrences had problems? How many problems? How serious are they?

    e. Determine *who* is involved in the event. To whom, by whom, near whom does it occur? However, this analysis should never be used to assign blame—only to determine cause.

	Is Describe what does occur	Is not Describe what does not occur, though it reasonably might	Distinctions What stands out as odd?
What objects are affected? What occurs?			
Where does the problem occur? • Geographical • Physical • On an object			
When does the problem occur? When first? When since? How long? What patterns? Before, during, after other events?			
Extent of problem How many problems? How many objects or situations have problems? How serious is the problem?			
Who is involved? (Do not use this question to blame.) To whom, by whom, near whom does this occur?			

© Copyright, Kepner-Tregoe, Inc. Reprinted with permission.

Figure 4.61. Is–is not matrix.

3. Use the "Is not" column of the matrix to isolate the circumstances that could occur but do not. Use what, where, when, extent, and who.

4. Study the "Is" and "Is not" columns to identify what is different or unusual about the situations where the problem is compared to where it is not. What stands out as being odd? What changes have occurred? Write your thoughts in the column headed "Distinctions."

5. Study the distinctions and look for links to the original problem.

Example

In the ZZ-400 manufacturing unit, a subteam was trying to understand the source of iron in its product. This problem, which occurred periodically, caused product purity to drop below specification. The team had learned from a stratified scatter diagram that the problem only occurred in reactors 2 and 3, not reactor 1. An is–is not diagram (Figure 4.62) brought together everything the team learned about the situation from a variety of other analysis tools, historical data, and its members' expert knowledge.

One of the mechanics noticed that the calendar tracking when the problem occurred looked just like the calendar for pump preventive maintenance (PM). So the team marked "Often during same week as pump PM" and "Mechanic doing pump PM" on the is–is not diagram. Team members started investigating what happened during pump PM, and what was different for reactor 1 pump PM. They discovered that the spare pumps were switched on whenever the main pump was being serviced. P-584C was used only for reactors 2 and 3; a different spare was used for reactor 1. Sure enough, the team could match incidents of high iron with times that P-584C was run.

P-584C turned out to be made of carbon steel instead of the stainless steel necessary for that fluid. Apparently, the pump had been obtained from stores inventory during an emergency many years ago and was never replaced. When it was removed and a stainless steel pump installed, the incidents of high iron disappeared.

Considerations

- The greater the level of detail in describing an occurrence and non-occurrence, the greater the likelihood of determining the cause.

- Examples of specific descriptions of what occurs: "The AIC report begins and stops in loop three." "A grinding sound came from the engine, it slowed to 20 mph and stopped after two miles."

	Is Describe what does occur	**Is not** Describe what does not occur, though it reasonably might	**Distinctions** What stands out as odd?
What objects are affected? What occurs?	Purity drops Iron increases	Other metal impurities Increase in moisture Change in color	Only iron increases
Where does the problem occur? • Geographical • Physical • On an object	Reactors 2 and 3	Reactor 1	Not reactor 1
When does the problem occur? When first? When since? How long? What patterns? Before, during, after other events?	Lasts about 1 shift Happens about once a month Often during same week as pump PM When pump P-584C runs	Continuous Any particular shift Any other pump than P-584C	Just P-584C
Extent of problem How many problems? How many objects or situations have problems? How serious is the problem?	Purity drops from 99% range to 98% range Puts us out of spec Iron up to 0.65 (3× normal)	Purity below 98.2% Pluggage problem Other specification problems	
Who is involved? (Do not use this question to blame.) To whom, by whom, near whom does this occur?	Mechanics doing pump PM		Mechanics usually around

© Copyright, Kepner-Tregoe, Inc. Reprinted with permission.

Figure 4.62. Is–is not matrix example.

- Examples of specific descriptions of circumstances that might occur but do not: "It does not occur at the Pittsburgh location." "It does not occur on weekends or at night." "The problem does not occur when printing the daily reports." "It is not continuous." "It does not occur with A Team."

Kolmogorov–Smirnov Test for Normality

Description

The Kolmogorov–Smirnov test checks whether a set of data forms a normal distribution.[25] Tests like this one are called *goodness-of-fit* tests.

When to Use

- Before setting up a chart of individuals to determine whether that chart is appropriate for the data

- When choosing subgroup size for an $\bar{X}$ and R chart, to determine whether that subgroup size is large enough that the subgroup averages form a normal distribution

Procedure

1. Make a histogram of the observations to be tested. These values can be individual measurements or subgroup averages. See the section on histograms for help in setting it up, especially determining the number and width of bars. Shortcut: Determine the range of values that will go into each bar of the histogram. Drawing the histogram is not absolutely necessary, although it helps you to understand the data.

2. On the Kolmogorov–Smirnov worksheet (Figure 4.63), list the data observations in order from smallest to largest. If one value occurs several times, list it several times. Use the worksheet for the remaining calculations in this procedure.

3. Using all the data points, calculate the average ($\bar{X}$) and the standard deviation ($\hat{\sigma}$).

$$\bar{X} = \frac{\Sigma X_i}{N} \qquad\qquad \hat{\sigma} = \sqrt{\frac{\Sigma (X_i - \bar{X})^2}{N - 1}}$$

X_i are the data values, and N is the total number of data points.

$\bar{X} = \quad \Sigma X_i \quad \div \quad N \quad = \underline{\hspace{1cm}} \div \underline{\hspace{1cm}} = \underline{\hspace{1cm}}$

$\hat{\sigma} = \sqrt{\Sigma\,(X_i - \bar{X})^2 \div (N - 1)} = \sqrt{\underline{\hspace{1cm}} \div \underline{\hspace{1cm}}} = \underline{\hspace{1cm}}$

Critical value $= 1.36 \div \sqrt{N} = \underline{\hspace{1cm}}$ for $N \geq 35$ or

$\qquad\qquad$ from table $= \underline{\hspace{1cm}}$ for $N < 35$

Rank	X_i	X_B	$S = \dfrac{\text{rank}}{N}$	$Z = \dfrac{X_B - \bar{X}}{\hat{\sigma}}$	F	$d = \lvert F - S \rvert$

Figure 4.63. Kolmogorov–Smirnov worksheet.

4. X_B are the values at the right edges of the bars of the histogram, as shown in Figure 4.64. Write each X_B value in the box next to the highest X_i in that bar. In many cases, X_i and X_B will be the same number. If there is not an X_i equal to the X_B value, write X_B beside the next highest data point and proceed with all calculations using X_B. (See the example.)

5. For each X_B, calculate S, the fraction of data values that are less than or equal to X_B.

$$S = \frac{\text{rank}}{N}$$

6. For each X_B, calculate Z.

$$Z = \frac{X_B - \overline{X}}{\hat{\sigma}}$$

7. For each Z, look up F on the table of area under the normal curve (Table A.1). F is the fraction of the normal curve that lies to the left of X_B.

Table 4.7. Critical values of D.

N	Critical value of D
11	.391
12	.375
13	.361
14	.349
15	.338
16	.328
17	.318
18	.309
19	.301
20	.294
25	.270
30	.240
35	.230
Over 35	$\dfrac{1.360}{\sqrt{N}}$

8. Compare S with F at each X_B. Find the largest difference D.

$$d = |F - S| \qquad D = \max(d)$$

9. Look up the critical value of D on Table 4.7 using N, the number of data points. If your largest D is greater than the critical value, then the distribution is not normal. If N is greater than 35, the critical value is $1.36/\sqrt{N}$.

Example

Suppose we have the following 24 measurements.

Day 1	Day 2	Day 3	Day 4
48	28	32	33
24	36	37	39
35	41	42	44
29	25	27	34
15	44	31	30
45	17	36	33

Figure 4.64 is a histogram of the measurements. (Remember that with fewer than 50 data points, a histogram may not give a reliable picture of the true distribution.) The X_B values are 15, 20, 25, 30, 35, 40, 45, 50.

Figure 4.65 is completed with the calculations for S, Z, F, and D. The largest value of d is 0.045. The critical value of D is 0.275. D is smaller than the critical value, so we have not proved that the distribution is non-normal. These are individual measurements, so a chart of individuals can be used to plot them.

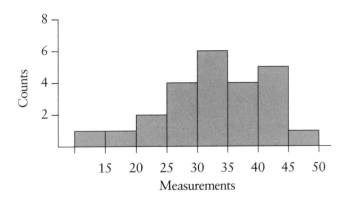

Figure 4.64. Kolmogorov–Smirnov example: Histogram.

$$\bar{X} = \quad \Sigma X_i \quad \div \quad N \quad = \quad \underline{805} \div \underline{24} = \underline{33.5}$$

$$\hat{\sigma} = \sqrt{\Sigma (X_i - \bar{X})^2 \div (N - 1)} = \sqrt{\underline{1640} \div \underline{23}} = \underline{8.444}$$

Critical value $= 1.36 \div \sqrt{N} = \underline{\qquad}$ for $N \geq 35$ or

from table $= \underline{.275}$ for $N < 35$

Rank	X_i	X_B	$S = \dfrac{\text{rank}}{N}$	$Z = \dfrac{X_B - \bar{X}}{\hat{\sigma}}$	F	$d = \lvert F - S \rvert$
1	15	15	.042	−2.191	.014	.028
2	17	20	.083	−1.599	.055	.028
3	24					
4	25	25	.167	−1.007	.157	.010
5	27					
6	28					
7	29					
8	30	30	.333	−.414	.340	.007
9	31					
10	32					
11	33					
12	33					
13	34					
14	35	35	.583	.178	.571	.012
15	36					
16	36					
17	37					
18	39	40	.750	.770	.779	.029
19	41					
20	42					
21	44					
22	44					
23	45	45	.958	1.362	.913	.045 ◄
24	48	50	1.000	1.954	.974	.026

Figure 4.65. Kolmogorov–Smirnov example: Calculations.

Considerations

- A histogram will not prove that a distribution is normal. Other distributions, such as the binomial, look like a normal distribution. A goodness-of-fit test like this one is necessary to have confidence that your distribution is normal.

- This goodness-of-fit test is recommended because it combines ease of use with power.

- Statisticians are never straightforward. They never say they have proved something to be true; they have only failed to prove that it is false. So, even this test does not *prove* a distribution to be normal. It can only prove that a distribution is not normal. If it fails to prove it nonnormal, it provides confidence that your distribution is close enough to normal that the formulas for your control chart will work.

- For the statisticians out there: The level of significance for $D = 0.05$.

- Figure 4.63 is a blank form for Kolmogorov-Smirnov calculations. Permission is granted to copy this form for individual use.

List Reduction

Description

List reduction is a set of techniques that are used to reduce a brainstormed list of choices (such as problems, solutions, measures) to a manageable number.[26]

When to Use

- After brainstorming or some other expansion tool has been used to generate a long list of choices

- When a list of choices has duplicate or irrelevant ideas

- When the group members together should think through the reasons for eliminating choices

Procedure

Wide Filter

1. Have the entire list of brainstormed ideas posted on flipchart pages so that everyone can see all items.

2. For each item individually, ask the question, "Should this item continue to be considered?" Get a vote of yeses and nos. A simple majority of yes responses keeps the item on the list. If an item does not get a majority of yes votes, mark it with brackets.

3. After all items have been evaluated by the wide filter, ask the team members, "Does anyone want to put any of the bracketed items back on the list?" Any items that are mentioned by even one team member are returned to the list.

Combining Ideas

4. Start with the first idea on the list. Label it number 1. Look at the second idea. Ask the team members, "Does anyone think this is a different idea from number 1?" If one person thinks the second idea is different, label the second idea number 2. If all agree that two items really are the same, eliminate one or develop new wording to combine the two ideas.

5. Similarly, compare item number 1 to all items on the list, one at a time. Then take item number 2 and compare it to each item below it on the list. Continue the procedure until all the ideas have been compared pairwise.

Criteria Filtering

6. Ask the team to suggest criteria for ranking the remaining ideas. Record the criteria on a flipchart.

7. Have the team rank order the criteria in terms of importance. The team should reach consensus on the rankings.

8. Evaluate each idea against the highest ranking criterion by asking for yes or no votes to the question, "Does this idea satisfy this criterion?" Then evaluate all ideas against the second criterion, and so on, until all the criteria have been addressed.

9. Tabulate the votes.

10. Discuss the results of this criteria ranking to help guide the team toward consensus. A numerical count of yes and no answers should not automatically generate the team's decision.

Example
The ZZ-400 manufacturing team used list reduction to reduce many possible performance measures to a set of just a few. Here is the list of

possible measures of maintenance effectiveness from the team's brain-storming and affinity diagram.

- Maintenance costs

- Number of emergency jobs

- Number of seal failures

- Hours downtime

- Percentage uptime

- Service factor

- Time between turnarounds

When the facilitator asked about each item, "Should this item continue to be considered?" the number of seal failures was eliminated.

Then items were compared to see if they were really different ideas. "Maintenance costs" was labeled 1 and compared one at a time to the rest of the items. They were all different. Then item 2, "number of emergency jobs," was compared to 3 "hours downtime," 4 "% uptime," 5 "service factor," and 6 "time between turnarounds." No duplicate ideas were found.

But when item 3, "hours downtime," was compared to item 4, "% uptime," everyone agreed that they really were the same idea. "Hours downtime" was preferred, because it is a more direct measurement, with no calculation involved. The facilitator crossed out item 4. Some people thought item 5, "service factor," was also the same idea, but several thought it was different, so it remained on the list. The last comparisons, 3 to 6 and 5 to 6, provided no combinations.

Then the group was ready for criteria filtering. It generated this list of criteria for selecting one measurement and decided their relative importance as shown, with 1 the most important.

4 already have data (or easy to get it)

3 meaningful to everyone on site

1 overall measure of maintenance performance

2 focus on this metric supports other aspects of performance

The team evaluated each idea against each criterion, asking "Does this idea satisfy the criterion—yes or no?" There were some interesting discussions during this evaluation. For example, some of the group members were surprised to hear that costs and service factor aren't very meaningful to many people on site. Time, such as hours of downtime and time between turnarounds, was thought to be more direct and meaningful.

	Criteria			
	1	2	3	4
1 Maintenance costs	N	N	N	Y
2 No. of emergency jobs	N	Y	Y	Y
[No. of seal failures]				
3 Hours downtime	Y	Y	Y	Y
4 % uptime				
5 Service factor	Y	Y	N	Y
6 Time between turnarounds	N	N	Y	N

Figure 4.66. List reduction example.

Also, the group agreed that focusing on costs can hurt other aspects of performance, as corners are cut or preventive maintenance skipped. At first some thought that focusing on hours downtime could cause people to run the equipment into the ground, but then the group realized that doing that would soon cause even more downtime. Hours downtime reflects maintenance's impact on operations performance.

The facilitator recorded the results in a matrix. When it was finished, the flipchart looked like Figure 4.66.

Team members discussed the results briefly to make sure they weren't missing any key ideas. "Hours downtime," with "Yes" evaluations all the way across, remained their preferred overall measure of maintenance performance.

Considerations

- Any of the three sections can be used separately. However, because combining ideas and criteria filtering are more complex, they are easiest to use after the list has already been reduced at least one time by a wide filter.

- During wide filter and combining ideas, the opinion of one person is enough to keep an item on the list. It is valuable to listen to that person's reasons for keeping the item alive.

- Rankings determined by criteria filtering should be used only to guide the team toward consensus. For example, just because idea 1 received 12 yes votes and idea 3 received only 10, the team is not committed to proceed with idea 1. Discussion of the voting and the reasons behind it should lead to team consensus on the best choice.

- Criteria filtering is very similar to the decision matrix.

- If several choices remain after all the reduction steps, you may want to follow with multivoting.

Matrix Diagram

Description

The matrix diagram graphically shows the relationship between two, three, or four groups of information. At the same time, it can tell something about that relationship, such as how strong it is or the roles various individuals play.

When to Use

- When trying to understand how one group of items relates to another group

- When communicating how one group of items relates to another group

Some common uses of matrices:

- When allocating responsibilities among a group of people

- When relating customer requirements to elements of a process

- When sorting out which problems are affecting which products or which pieces of equipment

- When looking for reinforcement or conflicts between two plans that will be executed together

Basic Procedure

1. Decide what groups of items must be compared.

2. Choose the appropriate format for the matrix. See the variations for different formats.

3. Draw the lines forming the grid of the matrix.

4. List the items in each group along the axes of the matrix.

5. Decide what information you want to show with the symbols on the matrix. See considerations for commonly used symbols.

6. Compare groups, item by item. Mark the appropriate symbol in the box at the intersection of the two items.

7. Complete the matrix with a legend describing the symbols.

8. Analyze the matrix for patterns. You may wish to repeat the procedure with a different format or a different set of symbols to learn more about the relationships.

Variation: L-Shaped Matrix
The L-shaped matrix compares two groups of items to each other. It is the most basic and most common format.

Example
Figure 4.67 is the L-shaped matrix used by the ZZ-400 manufacturing team to summarize customers' requirements. The team placed numbers in the boxes to show numerical specifications and used checkmarks to show choice of packaging. In this and following examples, the axes have been shaded to emphasize the letter that gives the matrix its name. The L-shaped matrix actually forms an upside-down L.

Variation: T-Shaped Matrix
The T-shaped matrix compares three groups of items: groups 1 and 2 are each compared to group 3. Groups 1 and 2 are not compared to each other.

Customer requirements

	Customer D	Customer M	Customer R	Customer T
Purity %	> 99.5	> 99.5	> 99.7	> 99.0
Trace metals (ppm)	< 5	—	< 10	< 25
Water (ppm)	< 10	< 5	< 10	—
Viscosity (cp)	20–35	20–30	10–50	15–35
Color	< 10	< 10	< 15	< 10
Drum		✓		
Truck	✓			✓
Railcar			✓	

Figure 4.67. L-shaped matrix example.

Example
Figure 4.68 is an example of a T-shaped matrix relating four product models to their manufacturing locations and to their customers.

The matrix can be examined in different ways to focus on different information. For example, concentrating on Model A, it is produced in large volume at the Texas plant and in small volume at the Arkansas plant. Time Inc. is the major customer for Model A, while Arlo Co. buys a small amount. If we choose to focus on the customer rows, we learn that only one customer, Arlo, buys all four models. Zig buys just one. Time makes large purchases of A and D, while Lyle is a relatively minor customer.

Variation: Y-Shaped Matrix
The Y-shaped matrix compares three groups of items.[27] Each group is compared to the other two.

Example
Figure 4.69 is a Y-shaped matrix showing the relationships between two customer requirements (on-time delivery and product availability), four internal process metrics, and five departments involved. Different symbols show the strength of the relationships: primary relationships, such as the manufacturing department's responsibility for production capacity; secondary relationships, such as the the link between product availability and

Products—customers—manufacturing locations

	Model A	Model B	Model C	Model D
Texas plant	●		○	○
Mississippi plant		●		○
Alabama plant	○			●
Arkansas plant		○	●	
● Large volume ○ Small volume	Model A	Model B	Model C	Model D
Customer #1: Zig Corp.		●		
Customer #2: Arlo Co.	○	○	○	●
Customer #3: Lyle Co.			○	○
Customer #4: Time Inc.	●			●

Figure 4.68. T-shaped matrix example.

Responsibilities for performance to customer requirements

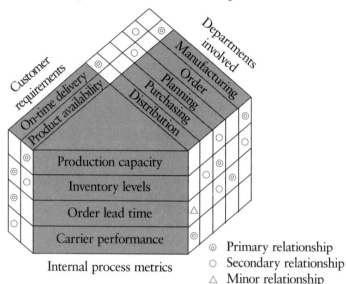

Figure 4.69. Y-shaped matrix example.

inventory levels; minor relationships, such as the distribution department's responsibility for order lead time; and no relationship, such as between the purchasing department and on-time delivery.

The matrix tells an interesting story about on-time delivery. The distribution department is assigned primary responsibility for that customer requirement. The two metrics most strongly related to on-time delivery are inventory levels and order lead time. Of the two, distribution has only a weak relationship with order lead time and none with inventory levels. The department has primary relationship with carrier performance, which is only moderately linked to on-time delivery. On the other hand, the planning department has primary responsibility for inventory levels and medium responsibility for order lead time. Yet no relationship is shown between planning and on-time delivery. Perhaps the responsibility for on-time delivery needs to be reconsidered.

Variation: X-Shaped Matrix

The X-shaped matrix relates four groups of items. Each group is related to two others. Group 2 is related to 1 and 3. Group 3 is related to 2 and 4. Group 4 is related to 3 and 1. Group 1 is related to 4 and 2.

Manufacturing sites—Products—Customers—Freight lines

						Model A	Model B	Model C	Model D
○		●	○	Texas plant		●		○	○
	○	●	●	Mississippi plant		○	●		○
		●	●	Alabama plant		○			●
○	○		○	Arkansas plant			○	●	
Red Lines	Zip Inc.	World-wide	Trans South			Model A	Model B	Model C	Model D
		●	○	Customer #1 Zig Corp.			●		
			●	Customer #2 Arlo Co.		○	○	○	●
○	○			Customer #3 Lyle Co.				○	○
	○	●		Customer #4 Time Inc.		●			●

● Large volume

○ Small volume

Figure 4.70. X-shaped matrix example.

Example

Figure 4.70 extends the T-shaped matrix example by including the relationships of freight lines with the manufacturing sites they serve and the customers who use them. Each axis of the matrix is related to the two adjacent ones, but not to the one across. Thus, the product models are related to the plant sites and to the customers, but not to the freight lines.

A lot of information can be contained in an X-shaped matrix. In this one, we can observe that Red Lines and Zip Inc., which seem to be minor carriers, are the only carriers that serve Lyle Co. Lyle doesn't buy much, but it and Arlo are the only customers for Model C. Each model has a plant site devoted primarily to that model, with another site that produces smaller amounts. The exception is Model D, which has two subsidiary sites. It also has two major customers, while the other models have just one. What other observations can you make?

Considerations

- Sometimes relationship is indicated with just an *X* or a blank, to indicate yes or no: involved or not, applicable or not, relationship exists or not. But the matrix is more useful with symbols that give more information about the relationship between the items. Two kinds of information are most common.

  —How strong the relationship is between the two items

  —If the items are a person and an activity, the role the person plays in that activity

- Here are some frequently used sets of symbols.

◎	Strong relationship	+	Positive relationship
○	Moderate relationship	0	Neutral relationship
△	Weak or potential relationship	–	Negative relationship
	No relationship		
S	Supplier	↑	Item on left influences item at top
C	Customer		
D	Doer	←	Item at top influences item on left
O	Owner		

  The arrows usually are placed next to another symbol indicating the strength of the relationship.[28] Feel free to create your own symbols or letters that are instantly recognizable to you or your audience.

- The L-shaped matrix is the most common, but it might not be the most useful for your application. Think about the groups of data you have and their possible relationships, review the other formats, then consider whether a different matrix might give more insight or show your point more clearly.

- Many tools in this book are matrices that are designed for a specific purpose. For example, the decision matrix is designed to relate potential choices to a list of criteria. For these specialized matrices, steps 1, 2, 3, and sometimes 5 of this matrix procedure are already done for you.

- *The Memory Jogger Plus+* (Brassard) has an excellent section on matrices. (See "Recommended Reading" at the end of this book.)

Mission Statement Checklist

Description

The mission statement checklist ensures that the entire team understands what it is supposed to accomplish and how.

When to Use

- During the first or second meeting of a new team
- When a team is given a new or modified mission

Procedure

Discuss the following questions.[29]

1. Is it clear what management expects of us?

2. Does our project cover only part of a larger process? Where do we fit in? Where does our part of the process start and end?

3. Are the boundaries of the project clear? What will be outside our jurisdiction?

4. Are the goals realistic?

5. Will this project work? Does the mission fit in with our knowledge about the process or system?

6. What resources, inside or outside the department, will we need?

7. Do we have the right people on this team to accomplish the mission?

8. What people not on the team will be crucial to our efforts?

9. Who will support our efforts? Who will be opposed? Who will be neutral? How can we reach all of these people?

10. How will opposition be expressed? How can we be sure that any opposition is brought out into the open?

11. Is it clear where this project fits into the organization's overall improvement plan?

12. How will we know that we have been successful? How will others decide whether we have been successful?

Considerations

- You may choose to divide into smaller groups, each assigned different questions to discuss, then reassemble to share results. The first three questions should be considered by everyone.

Mission Statement Wordsmithing

Description

Mission statement wordsmithing is a method for writing a statement that includes the ideas of everyone in the group. In a very short period of time, the critical concepts are surfaced and the impossible happens: composition by committee.

When to Use

- When writing a mission statement

- When writing any other brief statement, when it is important that the statement represent team consensus

Procedure

Materials needed: flipchart paper and marking pen for each person, masking tape.

1. Brainstorm thoughts and ideas around your team's issue. Capture the ideas on the flipchart.

2. *Optional:* For a mission or goal statement, discuss and decide where on the continuum of team goals the still-unknown statement should be.

3. Each member individually and silently drafts a statement. Give each person a flipchart page and marking pen to write his or her statement—in big letters—and then tape each page to the wall.

4. When all the statements are on the wall, everyone should walk around and examine all the statements. All team members underline words or phrases they believe should be in the final version of the statement. If someone has already underlined a phrase you like, underline it again. This is a voting process. Underline words on your own page, too.

5. Identify and discuss the most popular words and phrases. It also can be valuable to discuss minority opinions (single lines). Reach consensus on the key ideas that should be in the final version.

6. At this point, there are two options:

   • Sometimes it is obvious and easy to write the key words or phrases on a clean sheet of flipchart paper, add connecting words and phrases, and *eureka!* the statement is born.

   • If it doesn't seem obvious and easy, a few volunteers should wordsmith the popular phrases into a draft before the next meeting. The volunteers should take with them all the flipcharts from today's work and keep in mind the discussions from steps 1, 2, and 5.

7. The volunteers should communicate their draft to the entire team for feedback and/or confirmation. Does this statement capture the understanding of the team about its purpose? Check where the statement is on the continuum. Is it clear where it is? Is it in the right place?

8. Make the team's agreed modifications to the draft and finalize.

Example

A team from the Engineering Department was assigned to draft a mission statement for the entire department. The team brainstormed the following list of ideas.

• Design	• Easy to operate
• Build/construct	• Flexible
• Plan	• Safe
• Within budget	• Environmentally responsible
• Low cost	• Customers—plant operations
• Within schedule	• Easy to maintain
• Better than outsourcing	• Customers—maintenance
• Quickly—ASAP	• Community
• Best engineering know-how	• Manage contractors
• Current technology	• Maintain standards
• Business needs	

The group agreed that the final statement belonged at the far left of the continuum of goals, as the statement should encompass all services and activities of the department.

Next came the individual statements and the underlining. The following paragraphs show what was hanging on the walls after 12 minutes.

> The Engineering Department's mission is to <u>design and construct new manufacturing plants and plant expansions</u> at <u>best total cost and schedule.</u>

> The Engineering Department <u>serves</u> the <u>business units</u> and <u>manufacturing department</u> by <u>designing and building facilities</u> that <u>serve the needs</u> of those <u>customers.</u>

> To <u>ensure</u> that facilities exist to manufacture <u>products for our customers</u>, and that those facilities are built and operate as <u>efficiently</u> and <u>effectively</u> as possible.

> The role of the Engineering Department is to build <u>safe, environmentally responsible, easily maintained and operated facilities</u> according to the <u>best available practices.</u>

> To do the <u>best</u> possible job of building the <u>best</u> possible plants.

Several volunteers took all the flipcharts and over the next week developed the following statement, which was adopted by the team and the entire department.

> The Engineering Department serves the business units, manufacturing department, and our customers by being the best at designing and constructing safe, environmentally responsible, easily maintained and operated facilities—better, faster, and at lower total cost than anyone else.

Considerations

- This process usually takes 30 to 45 minutes up to step 6.
- The more discussion you have in steps 1 and 2, the less you will need in step 5. For most groups, it works best to discuss the ideas thoroughly before trying to generate words.
- If there has already been a lot of discussion about the topic, you can minimize or even skip steps 1 and 2. Get your initial ideas out on paper, then discuss more thoroughly in step 5.

Multivoting

Description

Multivoting narrows a large list of possibilities to a smaller list of the top priorities or to a final selection. Multivoting is preferred over straight voting because it allows an item that is favored by all, but not the top choice of any, to rise to the top.

When to Use

- After a brainstorming session
- To choose problems to tackle, causes to address, or solutions to implement

Procedure

1. Brainstorm a list of items. Combine duplicate items. Affinity diagrams can be useful to organize large numbers of ideas and eliminate duplication and overlap.

2. Number (or letter) all items.

3. Decide how many choices each team member will vote for. That number should be at least one-third the total number of items on the list.

4. Each member writes down the number (or letter) of his or her choices.

5. Tally votes. If secrecy is necessary, collect papers and tally. If not, use a show of hands as each item is called out.

6. Reduce the list by eliminating the items with the fewest votes. Sometimes there is an obvious difference between the popular few and the unpopular many. If not, here is a rule of thumb for determining which items to eliminate, based on the team's size:

   Five or fewer members: eliminate items with one or two votes

   Six to 15 members: eliminate items with three or fewer votes

   More than 15 members: eliminate items with four or fewer votes

7. Repeat steps 3 through 6 with the reduced list of items. Continue until a clear favorite emerges. If the list is reduced to only a few items with no clear favorite, stop the multivoting and have the team discuss the decision.

Example

The Technical Support Department survey team must develop a list of key customers to interview. First members brainstormed a list of possible names. Since they wanted representation of customers in manufacturing, marketing, and R&D, they divided the list into three groups. Within each group, they used multivoting to identify four first-choice interviewees.

The team numbered the 15 names on the manufacturing list. Each team member got $\frac{1}{3} \times 15 = 5$ votes in the first round of voting. Here are each member's votes and the tallied list of manufacturing names. (Names are fictitious, and any resemblance to real individuals is strictly coincidental.)

Rhonda's votes:	2, 4, 8, 9, 12
Terry's votes:	6, 9, 10, 12, 15
Pete's votes:	2, 4, 6, 9, 14
Martha's votes:	8, 10, 11, 12, 15
Al's votes:	4, 6, 8, 10, 11

1. Buddy Ellis
2. Susan Legrand ✓✓
3. Barry Williams
4. Lisa Galmon ✓✓✓
5. Steve Garland
6. Albert Stevens ✓✓✓
7. Greg Burgess
8. Joan McPherson ✓✓✓
9. Donald Jordan ✓✓✓
10. Sam Hayes ✓✓✓
11. Mike Frost ✓✓
12. Luke Dominguez ✓✓✓
13. Joe Modjeski
14. Paul Moneaux ✓
15. Chad Rusch ✓✓

The group narrowed the list to the six names that received three votes: Lisa, Albert, Joan, Donald, Sam, and Luke. Because they needed four final choices, they decided to discuss the six choices rather than voting again.

They quickly reached consensus that Lisa, Albert, and Sam would provide broad representation of opinions. There was quite a divergence of opinion on the other three choices, with only Al holding a strong opinion. He was insistent that Joan should be included because of her particular involvement in projects in Al's area. Because no one else had such a strong opinion, the group agreed to make Joan the fourth choice.

Variation 1: NGT Multivoting or 3–2–1 Voting

1. Follow steps 1 and 2 from page 195.

2. Decide how many choices each member will vote for. Use the following as a guideline.

For this many items	Vote for this many choices
up to 10	2
10–15	3
15–25	4
20–35	6
more than 35	8

3. Members rank their choices in order of priority and assign points according to how many votes are allowed. For example, if each member has three votes, a top priority would receive three points, a second choice would receive two points, and a third choice would receive one point.

4. Tally votes. If secrecy is required, collect the papers. If not, go around the room and have members state how many points they have given to each choice. It is easiest for the scribe to record votes with tally marks next to each choice.

5. Identify the item(s) with the most votes. The team may want to do another round of multivoting on a reduced list of items.

   Alternatively, include in the tally the number of people voting for each item and each person's first choice. After tallying, identify

   • The highest total points

   • The highest number of votes

   • Top priorities for any participant

Use this information for further discussion, investigation, data collection, or further multivoting.

Example

Suppose the survey team had used this method of multivoting, still allow-
ing each person five choices. (As they will select four names, it is appropriate to allow more choices than the guideline.) Each member would give five
points to the top choice, four to the second choice, and so on down to one
point to the fifth choice. Then the votes and tally would look like this:

Rhonda's votes: 4, 9, 12, 2, 8

Terry's votes: 6, 10, 12, 9, 15

Pete's votes: 2, 9, 14, 4, 6

Martha's votes: 10, 8, 15, 12, 11

Al's votes: 8, 6, 11, 10, 4

  1. Buddy Ellis

  2. Susan Legrand   ‖‖‖ ‖

  3. Barry Williams

  4. Lisa Galmon   ‖‖‖ ‖‖

  5. Steve Garland

  6. Albert Stevens   ‖‖‖ ‖‖‖

  7. Greg Burgess

  8. Joan McPherson   ‖‖‖ ‖‖‖

  9. Donald Jordan   ‖‖‖ ‖‖‖

10. Sam Hayes   ‖‖‖ ‖‖‖ ‖

11. Mike Frost   ‖‖‖‖

12. Luke Dominguez   ‖‖‖ ‖‖

13. Joe Modjeski

14. Paul Moneaux   ‖‖‖

15. Chad Rusch   ‖‖‖‖

There is a separation of the top seven choices: 2, 4, 6, 8, 9, 10, and
12. Note that this is the same set as before plus choice 2. Number 2 is the
lowest ranked of the seven, but with seven votes it clearly belongs in the
group of the top choices. The next lowest choice has only four votes. The
group can proceed to discuss these choices and then come to consensus or
vote again.

Variation 2: Weighted Voting

This variation normally results in fewer ties and allows the members to express the relative strength of their preferences better than 3–2–1 voting.

1. Follow steps 1, 2, and 3 of the basic procedure.

2. Each member has a number of points equal to either the number of items or 1½ times the number of items. The members distribute those points over their choices. For example, one may wish to assign all points to one choice about which the member cares fervently, or another may equally distribute points among three top choices.

3. Continue with steps 4 and 5 as in variation 1.

Example

This time the survey team gives each member 15 points (same as the number of names) to distribute. The results are

Rhonda's votes:	6 to #4, 5 to #9, 4 to #12
Terry's votes:	3 to #6, 3 to #10, 3 to #12, 3 to #9, 3 to #15
Pete's votes:	5 to #2, 5 to #9, 5 to #14
Martha's votes:	4 to #10, 4 to #8, 4 to #15, 3 to #12
Al's votes:	7 to #8, 3 to #6, 3 to #11, 2 to #10

Notice that Al's strong opinion about Joan is expressed by giving her almost half his votes. Terry is at the other extreme: he has given three points to each of five choices to show low preference. Pete's opinion is equally divided among three medium-strong choices, while Rhonda has preferences among her three choices. Martha has four almost-equal choices; number 12 ranks slightly lower than the other three.

The tallies are

1. Buddy Ellis
2. Susan Legrand   ﬀﬀ
3. Barry Williams
4. Lisa Galmon   ﬀﬀ ﬀﬀ
5. Steve Garland
6. Albert Stevens   ﬀﬀ |
7. Greg Burgess

8. Joan McPherson   ‖‖‖ ‖‖‖ |

9. Donald Jordan   ‖‖‖ ‖‖‖ |||

10. Sam Hayes   ‖‖‖ ||||

11. Mike Frost |||

12. Luke Dominguez   ‖‖‖ |

13. Joe Modjeski

14. Paul Moneaux   ‖‖‖

15. Chad Rusch   ‖‖‖ ||

This voting method separated the choices more than the other methods did. Number 9 is the top choice, 8 the second choice (due to Al's strong opinion and Martha's support), 4 the third choice, and 10 the fourth choice. There is a gap between the fourth choice with nine votes and the fifth choice with seven votes, but the group should still discuss whether these results reflect group opinion and are acceptable.

Notice that the top choices are in a different order than with the NGT multivoting. Then, 10 was top; this time, 10 is fourth. This time, 4 ranks third; then it tied for fifth. This is why it is always a good idea to discuss the top group of choices to ensure consensus.

Considerations

- Multivoting does not necessarily guarantee consensus. Consensus is a decision that all individuals can support—and can "live with." Discussion after multivoting will indicate whether the team has reached consensus.

- Discussion after each round of multivoting can be very useful in arriving at the best choice and in reaching consensus. Are the results surprising? Are there objections? Does the group want to discuss pros and cons of the top choices and vote again?

- It can be valuable to begin a multivoting session by brainstorming and discussing a list of criteria that are important for the current decision.

- To determine the most critical problem or the most significant root cause, multivoting should not be used in place of good data collection and analysis.

Nominal Group Technique (NGT)

Description

Nominal Group Technique (NGT) is a structured method for group brainstorming that encourages contributions from everyone.

When to Use

- When some group members are much more vocal than others
- When some group members think better in silence
- When there is concern about some members not participating
- When the group does not easily generate quantities of ideas
- When all or some group members are new to the team
- When the issue is controversial or there is conflict

Procedure

1. State the problem to be solved or the decision to be reached. Clarify the statement as needed.

2. Each team member silently thinks of and writes down as many ideas as possible, for a set period of time (5–10 minutes).

3. Record ideas. Each member in turn states aloud one idea. Facilitator writes it on a flipchart, overhead transparency, or board.

   - No discussion is allowed, not even questions for clarification.
   - Ideas given do not need to be from the team member's written list; indeed, as time goes on, many ideas will not be.
   - A member may "pass" his or her turn, and may then add an idea on a subsequent turn.

   Continue around the group until all members pass or for an agreed-upon length of time.

4. Discuss the ideas to clarify intent or to combine duplicates. Wording may be changed only when the idea's originator agrees. Ideas may be stricken from the list only by unanimous agreement. Discussion should be restricted to clarifying meaning. Relative merits of ideas are not discussed.

Considerations

- Often it is useful to follow an NGT exercise with an affinity diagram to organize the ideas.

- NGT often concludes with a prioritization process. However, using the brainstorming process alone is valuable, so this book separates the two processes. See "Multivoting" (page 195) and "List Reduction" (page 181) for methods to prioritize and/or narrow the list generated by brainstorming.

Normal Probability Plot

Quantile–Quantile or Q–Q Plot

Description

This is a method for checking whether a set of data takes the form of a normal distribution. Modified, it can be used to determine whether the data form any known distribution, such as binomial or Poisson.

When to Use

- Before setting up a chart of individuals to determine whether that chart is appropriate for the data

- When choosing subgroup size for an $\bar{X}$ and R chart, to determine whether that subgroup size is large enough that the subgroup averages form a normal distribution

- For best results, when you have 50 or more data points

Procedure

1. Sequence the data from the lowest to the highest value. Number them from 1 to n. Call the lowest value $x_{(1)}$, the second lowest $x_{(2)}$, and so on up to the highest value $x_{(n)}$.

2. Calculate the quantile number for each value.

$$\text{Quantile number} = \frac{i - 0.5}{n}$$

3. Find the value of the normal distribution that matches each quantile number. On the table of area under the normal curve (Table A.1), locate the F that equals the quantile number. Then find Z opposite that F. This is called the *normal quantile*; we'll call it Z_i.

   Note of caution: In this step, you use the table backward. Look up the quantile number in the body of data in the center and find the Z value on the edge.

4. Plot each value against the matching Z_i. Put the data value on the Y axis and the normal distribution's Z on the X axis. You will plot n pairs of numbers.

5. Draw a line that fits most of the data. If your data were a perfect normal distribution, the dots would form a straight line. Examine the shape of the dots compared to the line you have drawn to judge how well your data compare to the normal distribution. See the considerations for typical shapes.

Example

This example uses only 20 values to make the calculations easier to follow. Table 4.8 has the 20 values in numerical order, in the column labeled "Process data." They have been numbered from 1 to 20.

The next step is calculating the quantile numbers. For the first value, 9, the calculation is

$$\text{Quantile number} = \frac{i - 0.5}{n} = \frac{1 - 0.5}{20} = \frac{0.5}{20} = 0.025$$

Similarly, for the second value, the calculation is

$$\text{Quantile number} = \frac{1.5}{20} = 0.075$$

And you can see the pattern now: the third quantile number is $2.5 \div 20$, the fourth is $3.5 \div 20$, and so on to the last one, $19.5 \div 20$.

Now look up the Z_i values on the normal curve table. In this table, the first two digits for Z are at the left end of the row, and the last digit is at the top of the column. The first quantile number, 0.025, is in the row starting with –1.9, in the column headed by 0.06. So Z = –1.96. Each quantile number is looked up in the same way.

Table 4.8. Normal probability plot example calculations.

	Process data	Quantile number	Z
1	9	.025	–1.960
2	11	.075	–1.440
3	11	.125	–1.150
4	13	.175	–0.935
5	14	.225	–0.755
6	15	.275	–0.595
7	16	.325	–0.455
8	17	.275	–0.320
9	19	.425	–0.190
10	21	.475	–0.065
11	23	.525	0.065
12	25	.575	0.190
13	26	.625	0.320
14	26	.675	0.455
15	28	.725	0.595
16	32	.775	0.755
17	36	.825	0.935
18	37	.875	1.150
19	43	.925	1.440
20	62	.975	1.960

Some of the quantile numbers are between two values on the table, so they need to be interpolated. For example, the fourth quantile number, 0.175, is about halfway between 0.1736 and 0.1762. The Z for 0.1736 is –0.194, and the Z for 0.1762 is –0.193. Halfway between those numbers is $Z = -0.935$.

Now plot the process data against the Zs. Figure 4.71 shows the result, with the best straight line drawn through the points. Notice that the points are above the line at either end. That is typical of right-skewed data. Compare with the histogram of the data, Figure 4.72.

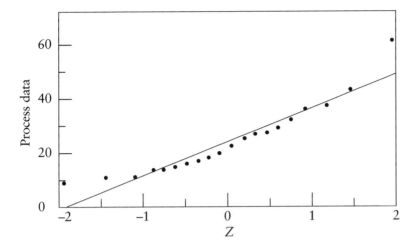

Figure 4.71. Normal probability plot example.

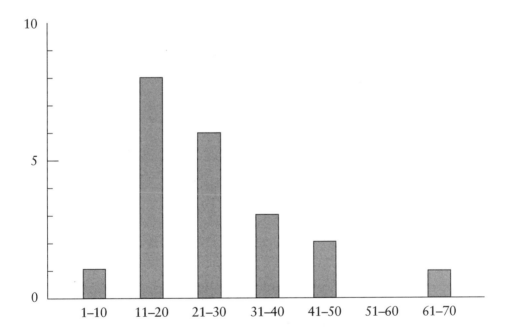

Figure 4.72. Histogram of normal probability plot data.

Variation

This method can be used to check data against any known distribution. Instead of looking up the quantile numbers on the table of the normal distribution, look them up on a table for the distribution in which you are interested.

Considerations

- Figure 4.73 shows how some common distortions of the normal distribution look on a normal probability plot.

  Short tails: If tails are shorter than normal, the shape of the points will curve above the line at the left and below the line at the right—an *S* (for *short*) if you tip your head to the right.

  Long tails: If tails are longer than normal, the shape of the points will curve below the line at the left and above the line on the right—a backward *S*.

  Right-skewed: A right-skewed distribution has a short tail on the left and a long tail on the right. Therefore, the shape of the points forms an upward curve, or *U*, compared to the line.

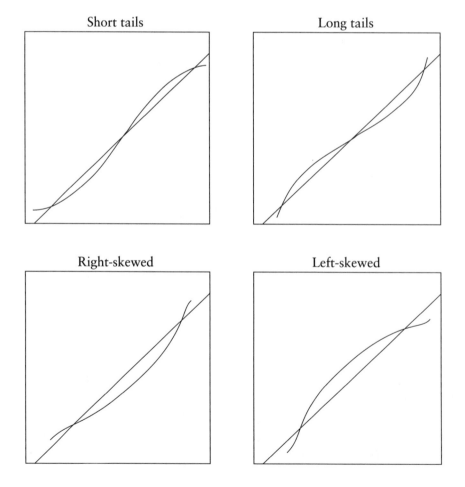

Figure 4.73. Shapes of normal probability plots.

Left-skewed: A left-skewed distribution has a long tail on the left and a short tail on the right. Therefore, the shape of the points forms a downward curve compared to the line.

- Remember that your process should be in control to make valid judgments about its shape.

- Most statistical software will do this calculation and plotting for you, which is especially useful for large sets of data.

- In usual statistical terminology, $x_{(i)}$ is the $(i - 0.5)/n$ quantile of the data, and Z is the $(i - 0.5)/n$ normal quantile.

Operational Definitions

Description

Operational definitions are usable definitions of important terms and procedures in measurement or data collection. They remove ambiguity from words or operations that can be interpreted in different ways. The purpose of operational definitions is obtaining results that are consistent and meaningful.

When to Use

- When developing and using any form of data collection
- When establishing metrics to monitor performance
- When establishing customer requirements
- When establishing any agreement or contract

Procedure

1. Ask

   - What characteristic will we measure?
   - How will we measure this characteristic?

2. Mentally or actually run through the data collection procedure. Note opportunities for differences in

   - Equipment
   - Procedures

- Criteria

- Data collectors themselves

Identify all potential variation and decide how each will be handled. Define an operational definition for each.

3. Consider three elements for each operational definition.

   a. How will data be sampled?

   b. What procedure or test will be followed?

   c. What are the criteria to be satisfied?

4. Discuss the definitions until consensus is reached.

5. If possible, conduct a trial run, with all data collectors observing the same data. Compare the data collected and resolve any differences. Repeat the trial run until variation is minimized.

Example

An organization had a goal of increasing customer satisfaction by 25%. It needed operational definitions for measuring this goal. Discussion led to these definitions:

> We will survey a random sample of 10% of our population each quarter, using questionnaire B. The customer satisfaction rating will consist of the overall average of all sampled customers' scores and the standard deviation of the responses (formulas attached). Our goal will be to increase the average by 25% while maintaining or reducing the standard deviation.

A team member pointed out that this definition covered the test of step 3b with the survey and the criteria of step 3c by stating the method of calculation, but the method of sampling still was not defined. The team added the following operational definition for *random sample of 10%*:

> Say we have *n* customers. We will run our computer's random-number-generating routine to generate a set of random numbers between 1 and *n*. We will generate *n*/10 random numbers. Using the numbered customer database, we will choose the customers whose numbers correspond to those random numbers.

Considerations

- Operational definitions are easily overlooked because we all make assumptions without realizing it.

- Think about an operational definition in the following way.

  Operational: Do we all agree what to do?

  Definition: Do we all agree what every word means?

- Two good sources of more information on operational definitions are W. Edwards Deming's *Out of the Crisis* (chapter 9) and *The Team Handbook* by Scholtes (pp. 2-28–2-29). (See "Recommended Reading" at the back of this book.)

Pareto Chart

Description

A Pareto chart is a bar graph. The length of the bars represent frequency of occurrence or cost (money, time). Therefore, the chart visually shows which situations are more significant.

When to Use

- When analyzing data by groups, to reveal unnoticed patterns

- When trying to focus on the most significant problem or cause

- When communicating with others about your data

- When relating cause and effect, by comparing a Pareto chart classified by causes with one classified by effects

- When evaluating improvement, by comparing before and after data

Procedure

1. Decide what categories you will use to group items.

2. Decide what period of time the chart will include.

3. Decide what measurement to use—frequency, percent, cost, time, quantity.

4. Collect the data.

5. Determine the appropriate number scale for your chart. Mark the scale on your chart.

6. Construct and label bars for each category. Place the tallest at the top or far left, then the next tallest, and so on. If there are many categories with small measurements, they can be grouped as "other."

Steps 7 and 8 are optional, but are very useful for analysis and communication.

7. Calculate the percentage for each category: the total for that category divided by the total for all categories. Label each bar with its percentage, or draw a right vertical axis and label it with percentages.

8. For this step, draw a right vertical scale labeled with percentages. Calculate and draw cumulative values:

   • Add the measurements for the first and second categories, and place a dot above the second bar indicating that value.

   • Place a dot above the third bar indicating the sum of the first, second, and third categories.

   • Continue the process for all the bars.

   Connect the dots, starting at the top of the first bar. The last dot should reach 100% on the right vertical scale.

Example

Figures 4.74 and 4.75 are nested Pareto charts. Figure 4.74 shows how many customer complaints were received in each of five categories. Figure 4.75 takes the largest category from Figure 4.74, "Documents," breaks it down into six categories of document-related complaints, and shows cumulative values.

If all complaints cause equal distress to the customer, working on eliminating document-related complaints would have the most impact, and of those, working on certificates of analysis (C of A) should be most fruitful.

Considerations

• This chart is based on the Pareto principle: 80% of the trouble comes from 20% of the causes. While the percentages may not be always exactly 80/20, there usually are "the vital few and the trivial many."

Figure 4.74. Pareto chart, example 1.

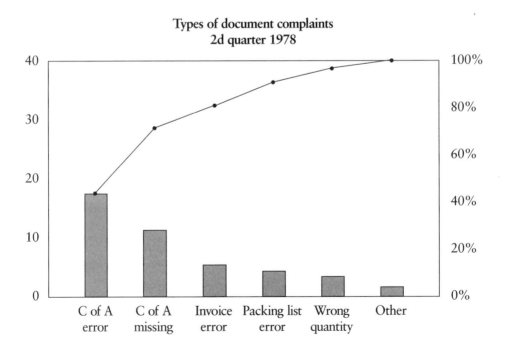

Figure 4.75. Pareto chart, example 2.

- The best Pareto chart uses a measurement that reflects cost to the organization.[30] If the number of items is proportional to the cost or pain to the organization, then it is a good measurement. However, it may be more useful to measure dollars, time, or some other indicator of cost to the organization.

- If you use two measurement scales, one for raw measurements and the other for percentages, be careful to make the two scales match. For example, the left measurement that corresponds to one-half should be exactly opposite 50% on the right scale.

- Figure 4.76 is a blank worksheet that can be used to collect data or to draw a Pareto chart. Permission is granted to copy it for individual use.

Performance Index

Objectives Matrix

Description

The performance index provides a way of monitoring performance when several characteristics contribute to overall quality. A family of several measurements are rolled into one overall number.

When to Use

- When there are several customer requirements to consider as you measure overall performance

- When monitoring step-by-step improvement toward a goal

- When monitoring large amounts of information for problems and trends

Procedure

Setting Up the Chart

1. Define the mission or objectives of the organization, system, or job to be measured.

2. Select key performance indicators based on the mission or objectives. Three to seven is a typical number of indicators. Write the performance indicators in the boxes across the top of the chart.

Process or variable		Time beginning ———	Ending ———		

Variable or factor	Occurrences	Count	%
Total			

Figure 4.76. Pareto chart worksheet.

3. Establish current performance levels for each indicator. As a rule of thumb, about three months' performance should be reviewed to determine current performance. Enter current performance levels in the boxes on the chart (Figure 4.77) opposite the number 3.

4. Establish goals. Choose a specific time period (say, a year) and determine realistic goals for that period. Enter these goals in the boxes opposite the number 10.

5. Establish minigoals to correspond to the boxes between 3 and 10. Consider whether different resources and effort will be required to accomplish each minigoal. If so, you may want to make the numerical distance between minigoals smaller when more resources or effort are required. If there are no such considerations, you can set the mini-goals so the distance from each one to the next is equal. Write the minigoals in the boxes opposite the scores of 4 to 9.

6. Establish minimum performance levels. These will be the lowest performance levels you can imagine occurring. Enter these levels in the boxes opposite the 0.

7. Determine performance levels for scores of 1 and 2, taking into consideration slow periods and slumps. Write these in the appropriate boxes.

8. Assign weights to each indicator to show relative importance. The sum of the weights must equal 100. Enter weights in the boxes opposite "Weight" at the bottom of the chart.

9. Make copies of this chart to use each time you calculate the index.

10. Monitor performance for several cycles of your process(es). If needed, adjust the current performance levels, the weights, the number of indicators, and so on.

Using the Chart

11. On a regular predetermined frequency (weekly, monthly, quarterly) collect data and record results on the chart. Enter the actual measure for each indicator opposite "Performance."

12. Circle the actual performance for each indicator. If a minigoal is not obtained, circle the next worse performance level.

13. For each indicator, determine the performance score (0–10) opposite the circled performance number. Write that number opposite "Score" at the bottom of the chart.

Date: _____

								Criteria
								Performance
								10
								9
								8
								7
								6
								5
								4
								3
								2
								1
								0
								Score
								Weight
								Value
								Index =

Jan	Feb	Mar	Apr	May	Jun	Jul	Aug	Sep	Oct	Nov	Dec

(James Riggs and Glenn Felix, *Productivity by Objectives,* ©1983, pp. 225, 233. Adapted by permission of Prentice Hall, Englewood Cliffs, N.J.)

Figure 4.77. Performance index.

14. Multiply each score by its weight factor to generate the weighted value. Write this number opposite "Value."

15. Add all the "Values." The sum is the performance index.

16. You may wish to plot performance indexes on a graph, with time on the X axis and the index on the Y axis. When you begin, the index should be 300, because that is the score for current performance. The goal is 1000.

Example

Figure 4.78 is the performance index form for June for a manufacturing group. The italicized numbers were written on the photocopied form this month. Note that pounds made has deteriorated since the chart was established, although the other measures have remained steady or improved.

Considerations

- Do not change the numbers used to calculate the chart within a monitoring period, or comparisons will be meaningless.

- You may wish to revise the chart annually or on some other long time frame. When you do, ask whether important current indicators are missing, whether some are no longer needed, whether priorities have changed. Also ask whether customers are still satisfied with the goals and whether you have become capable of better performance than the goal indicates.

- Involve your customers when you determine indicators and set goals, minimums, and weights.

- Don't let an overall good score mask difficulties on a single indicator.

- This approach was developed by James L. Riggs and Glen H. Felix and originally called an objectives matrix. This procedure is based on a booklet from Dow Chemical U.S.A., Louisiana Division, titled *Performance Indexing: A Tool for Continual Improvement*, that was adapted from a booklet by Northern Telecom entitled *Managing by Productivity Indexing*.[31]

Date: _June, 1992_

% rework	Hrs downtime	Pounds made	Safety & envir flags	$ / pound			Criteria
26	28	42	9	278			Performance
0	0	70+	0	–143			10
2	5	69	1	164			9
6	10	67	2	185			8
11	15	65	4	206			7
16	20	60	6	227			6
21	25	55	8	248			5
24	(30)	50	(10)	269			4
(28)	40	45	12	(290)			3
31	50	(40)	13	311			2
34	60	35	14	332			1
36+	70+	–30	15+	353+			0
3	4	2	4	3			Score
25	15	15	20	20			Weight
75	60	30	100	60			Value
						Index	= 325

Jan	Feb	Mar	Apr	May	Jun	Jul	Aug	Sep	Oct	Nov	Dec
			300	315	325						

(James Riggs and Glenn Felix, *Productivity by Objectives*, ©1983, pp. 225, 233. Adapted by permission of Prentice Hall, Englewood Cliffs, N.J.)

Figure 4.78. Performance index example.

Plan–Do–Check–Act Cycle

Deming Cycle, Shewhart Cycle

Description

The plan–do–check–act (PDCA) cycle (Figure 4.79) consists of four steps to follow for improvement or for making changes. Just as a circle has no end, the PDCA cycle should be repeated again and again for continuous improvement.

When to Use

- When starting a new improvement project
- When stuck moving from one phase to another of a project
- To plan data collection and analysis in order to verify and prioritize problems or root causes
- When implementing a solution
- When reviewing your improvement process for what you learned

Procedure

1. *Plan:* Recognize an opportunity and plan the change.
2. *Do:* Test the change. Carry out a small-scale study.

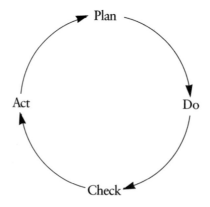

Figure 4.79. Plan–do–check–act cycle.

3. *Check:* Review the test, analyze the results, and identify learnings.

4. *Act:* Take action based on what you learned in the check step. If you were successful, incorporate the learnings from the test into wider changes. If the change did not work, go through the cycle again with a different plan.

Example

The safety subteam of the ZZ-400 manufacturing unit was brought an idea about a novel approach to improving safety behavior. The subteam went through a thorough *plan* step: exploring and evaluating the idea, analyzing causes of safety incidents and attitudes, identifying barriers to implementation, developing a rollout plan, and preparing the rest of the unit for this new approach. The *do* step began when the subteam rolled out the new approach.

In a few weeks, the subteam will begin to *check,* surveying the team to learn how the approach is being received and whether it is working. If there are any problems, the subteam will modify the approach in the *act* step. If the approach works well, the *act* step will be used to firmly establish the new approach in the unit's routine, putting it on the calendar, establishing rotating coordination responsibilities, and so forth.

The subteam has ideas that the same approach might work with environmental issues, so it will start a new cycle of PDCA, *plan*ning how to modify the approach to help environmental performance.

Considerations

- The quality improvement process is an expansion of PDCA. Steps 1 to 6 are *plan,* 7 is *do,* 8 is *check,* and 9 and 10 are *act.*

- *Check* is sometimes called *review, study,* or *learn.*

- *The Team Handbook* (Scholtes) and *Kaizen* (Imai) have good discussions of the PDCA cycle. (See "Recommended Reading" at the back of this book.)

Plan–Results Matrix

Description

Typically, we look at results on a one-dimensional scale—were we success-ful or weren't we? It is more useful to look at two dimensions.

- Did we accomplish the plan we developed?

- Did we achieve our desired results?

The plan–results matrix looks at both dimensions. It is an analytical tool to guide the team's thinking about the outcome of a project and to determine the next steps.

When to Use

- When a project has been completed, whether an entire mission or one implementation stage

- When a project is floundering, about to be or already labeled dead

Procedure

1. Think about the plan, solution, or strategy that your team put in place and carried out. Was it successfully accomplished? Were you able to do what you had planned to do? Choose "Not accom-plished" or "Accomplished" on the "Plan" edge of the matrix, Figure 4.80.

2. Think about the results that your plan was intended to accomplish. Were they successfully accomplished? Choose "Not accomplished" or "Accomplished" on the "Results" edge of the matrix.

3. The two points you have chosen on the two edges lead into one of the four boxes of the matrix. The words in the box provide guidance about how to think about your results and your next actions.

   - *Results accomplished, plan accomplished.* This is the ideal situa-tion. Everything seems to have worked well. Move on to the next step in your improvement process.

   - *Results not accomplished, plan accomplished.* Something was wrong with the plan. It may not have been effective or appro-priate. Or it may not be addressing the true root cause of the problem. Some more analysis will tell you which is the case, and whether you need to recycle to solutions or causes.

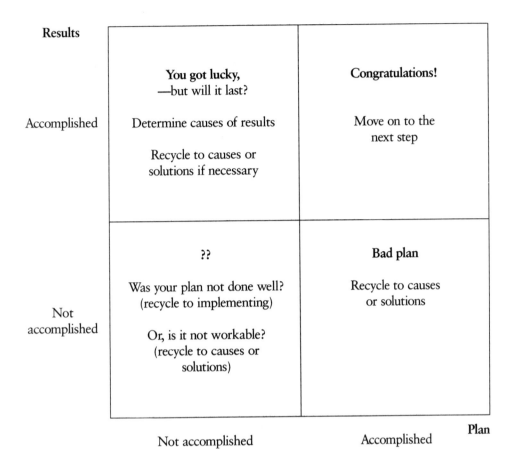

Figure 4.80. Plan–results matrix.

- *Results not accomplished, plan not accomplished.* In this situation, you cannot know if the problem lies with the execution of the plan or the plan itself. Usually, you should first go back and carry out the plan correctly. If you recognize that the plan is no good, you should find a better plan or reanalyze the root cause.

- *Results accomplished, plan not accomplished.* Somehow you got lucky. Determine the causes of the results. Analyzing process measures, not just results measures, can help indicate what is going on. If your analysis shows that the results are temporary, you may need to recycle. Return to implementing a better plan, choosing a better solution, or finding the true root cause.

Example

There was a continuing problem with mail being delivered late or not at all. The Pony Express team developed a new system for mail collection, sorting, and delivery. Team members developed and taught a training class for all mailroom employees to introduce the new system.

Case A: The training classes and rollout of the new system went without a hitch. A month later, data show that mail is still late and lost.

Analysis: Results not accomplished, plan accomplished. (See Figure 4.81.) Something was wrong with the plan. Maybe the training was ineffective, or maybe the new system doesn't address the real problems.

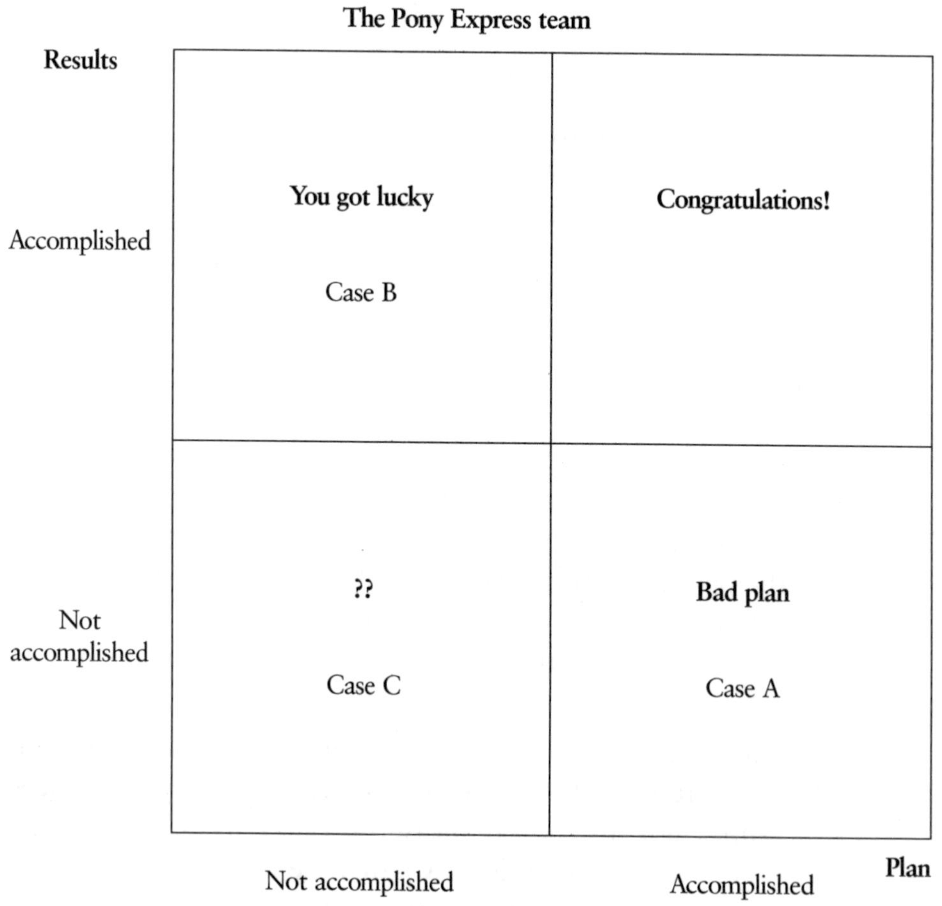

The Pony Express team

Results		
Accomplished	**You got lucky** Case B	**Congratulations!**
Not accomplished	**??** Case C	**Bad plan** Case A
	Not accomplished	Accomplished **Plan**

Figure 4.81. Plan–results matrix example.

Case B: Results on a quiz administered after training averaged 58% correct, and spot checks show that the new system is not being followed. Yet, to everyone's surprise, results after a month show far fewer lost and late pieces of mail.

Analysis: Results accomplished, plan not accomplished. Maybe the Hawthorne effect is at work here: there was a lot of attention focused on correct mail delivery. But will those results slide after the attention goes away? The team may need to repeat the training or revise the system so it is more user-friendly.

Case C: There was much complaining during training about the new system being confusing and harder to use than the old one. And mail is still late and lost.

Analysis: Results not accomplished, plan not accomplished. The problem could be execution: a poor rollout of the new system. Maybe better training is needed. Or it may be that the new system really isn't better than the old one, and the Pony Express team needs to go back to the drawing board.

Considerations

- Many groups never review projects or steps of a project. Regular reviews will improve your rate of success. This is the essential *check* step of the PDCA cycle.

- When results are not accomplished, do not get discouraged. Above all, do not quit. Use analytical tools to understand the cause of your difficulty. Cause analysis tools may be especially useful.

- Initial failures can yield valuable lessons that will make your second attempt successful.

- When results are accomplished, but plan was not: Too often we are tempted to collect our winnings and move on. Before you give in to that temptation, think about what caused the good results. Were they caused by a special cause, a temporary environmental factor, or a Hawthorne effect? Will they last?

- The Hawthorne effect is named after a famous study of the relationship between lighting conditions and productivity. Researchers found that just focusing attention can create positive results. Raising the lighting improved productivity—and so did lowering it! The problem with the Hawthorne effect is that the positive results are temporary. The Hawthorne effect often is alive and well in quality improvement efforts as unusual attention is focused on specific areas.

- Many groups are quick to claim success and move to the next challenge. Understanding what caused your results is important for the success of the rest of this project and future ones.

PMI

Description

PMI stands for *plus, minus, interesting.*[32] This process structures a discussion to identify the pluses, minuses, and interesting points about an idea.

When to Use

- When evaluating an idea, such as a proposed solution
- When the group is being one-sided in its thinking, aware only of advantages or only of disadvantages
- When members of the group are polarized and arguing

Procedure

1. Review the topic or problem to be discussed. Often it is best phrased as a why, how, or what question. Make sure the entire team understands the subject of the PMI.
2. Brainstorm pluses—positive aspects of the idea.
3. Brainstorm minuses—negative aspects of the idea.
4. Brainstorm interesting points about the idea. These might be neutral aspects, points to explore, or unusual features.

Example

A subteam of the ZZ-400 manufacturing unit was looking for ideas to improve safety performance. One day Chris told the subteam about the safety approach her neighbor's company used, which involved shift safety circles where individuals could confront co-workers' unsafe behavior. The immediate reaction of the team members was skeptical and uninterested, but George suggested that they evaluate the idea before discarding it. They used PMI to explore various aspects of the concept.

Addressing pluses first, they generated the following list.

More attention to safety

Focus on behavior

Raise awareness of unsafe acts

Up close and personal

Support for confronting unsafe behavior

Creates more teamwork

Learn to be honest with each other

Positive effect in other areas of our lives

Keep each other alert

Then they focused on minuses.

Too personal!

What would we talk about

People wouldn't say what they really think

Too busy to take the time

No one to lead group

Could cause hard feelings

Usual people would dominate

Already have safety training and meetings

Finally, they listed interesting points.

Peer pressure doesn't just affect kids

Ownership for safety belongs where?

We want to be best

Learn how it worked at XYZ Company

Different from safety approach we've had

Each person's behavior affects everyone else's safety

At the end of the exercise, the group decided the approach had real possibility and wanted to pursue it further.

Considerations

- It is important to do one step at a time, in the sequence listed. For example, do not go back and forth between pluses and minuses. By directing attention to one side of an issue at a time, a better view of the entire issue is developed.

- The entire group should look at each side of the issue together. Do not modify the procedure to assign pluses to one subgroup, minuses to another, and interesting points to a third. Thinking together, individuals can drop assumptions and positions to arrive jointly at a better evaluation of the idea.

- Interesting points can lead to modifications and adaptations of an idea that in its present form is not practical.

- This tool can be used by individuals as well as by groups.

Process Capability

Process Spread, Capability Index, Cp_k, Cp, Performance Index, Pp_k, Pp

Description

Process capability refers to the capability of a process to make products that meet specifications. Many ways have been devised to measure and numerically report process capability.

When to Use

- When a numerical measurement of process performance is needed
- When the process is monitored by a control chart

Variation: Process Limits and Process Spread

1. If you are using an $\overline{X}$ and R chart, calculate process limits.

$$\hat{\sigma}_X = \frac{\overline{R}}{d_2}$$

upper limit $= \overline{\overline{X}} + 3\hat{\sigma}_X$ \qquad lower limit $= \overline{\overline{X}} - 3\hat{\sigma}_X$

Read d_2 from Table 4.9. The subgroup size is n.

Table 4.9. d_2 for capability calculations.

n	d_2
2	1.128
3	1.693
4	2.059
5	2.326
6	2.534
7	2.704

2. If you are using a chart of individuals or attribute chart, the process limits are the upper and lower control limits from the chart. The value for $3\hat{\sigma}_X$, which will be needed in step 4, can be taken directly from your control chart calculation worksheet.

3. Compare the process limits to the specifications or tolerances for the product. If the process limits are within the specifications, the process is in an ideal state. Stop here. If either of the process limits falls outside its specification, continue to step 4.

4. Calculate the process spread.

$$\text{process spread} = 6\hat{\sigma}_X$$

5. Calculate the spread between specification limits.

$$\text{specification spread} = \frac{\text{USL} - \text{LSL}}{\hat{\sigma}_X}$$

USL = upper specification limit

LSL = lower specification limit

6. Compare the process spread to the specification spread. If process spread is greater, work to reduce the variation in the process. If the process spread is smaller, work to center the process within the specifications.

Variation: Capability Indexes Cp_k and Cp

When to Use

- Only when the process is in statistical control
- Only when the process forms a normal distribution

Procedure

1. Establish that the process forms a normal distribution, using the normal probability plot or Kolmogorov–Smirnov test.

2. Establish that the process is in statistical control, using a control chart.

3. Use the capability index worksheet (Figure 4.82) to calculate Cp_U and Cp_L. The smaller of the two numbers is Cp_k.

   Note: If there is only one specification, calculate Cp_U or Cp_L for just that side; that is also the Cp_k.

4. Larger Cp_k values are better. If Cp_k is less than 1.0 (or the value designated by your customer), work to reduce variation or to center the process within specifications.

5. Calculate Cp.

$$Cp = \frac{USL - LSL}{6\hat{\sigma}_X}$$

   If Cp is greater than or equal to 1.0, the process would be capable of meeting specifications if it were centered.

Example

Figure 4.83 shows a normal process distribution. To make the calculations and relationships easier to see, it is drawn so that $\sigma = 1$. The process is in control, so Cp_k and Cp can be calculated.

process limits = 3 and 9

specification limits = 0 and 8

The upper process limit falls beyond the upper specification limit, so out-of-spec product is being made in the range from 8 to 9, as shown by the shaded area.

$$\text{process spread} = (9 - 3) \div 1 = 6$$
$$\text{specification spread} = (8 - 0) \div 1 = 8$$

Process: _____

Data dates: _____

Calculated by: _____

Date: _____

Note: Before calculating a capability index for a process, control charts *must* be used to establish that the process is in statistical control.

Step 1. Record specifications.

Upper specification = USL = _____   Lower specification = LSL = _____

Step 2. Record from control charts.

Process average = $\bar{\bar{X}}$ = _____

Average range   = $\bar{R}$ = _____ $\Big\}$ only if $\bar{X}$-R chart used

Subgroup size   = n = _____

Step 3. Standard deviation.

3a. If using $\bar{X}$-R charts: Look up d_2.

n	d_2	n	d_2
2	1.128	5	2.326
3	1.693	6	2.534
4	2.059	7	2.704

d_2 = _____

3b. If using chart of individuals:

Record $3\hat{\sigma}_x$ from control chart calculation.

$3\hat{\sigma}_x$ = _____

Estimate $\hat{\sigma}_x$ = $\bar{R}$ ÷ d_2

= _____ ÷ _____ = _____

Calculate $3\hat{\sigma}_x$ =   3 × $\hat{\sigma}_x$

=   3 × _____ = _____

Step 4. Calculate upper capability and lower capability.

C_{pU} = $(USL - \bar{\bar{X}})$ ÷ $3\hat{\sigma}_x$

= (_____ − _____) ÷ _____

= _____ ÷ _____

= _____

C_{pL} = $(\bar{\bar{X}} - LSL)$ ÷ $3\hat{\sigma}_x$

= (_____ − _____) ÷ _____

= _____ ÷ _____

= _____

Step 5. Select C_{pk} = the smaller of C_{pU} and C_{pL} = _____

Figure 4.82. Capability index worksheet.

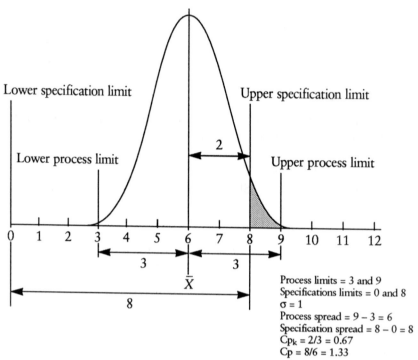

Figure 4.83. Incapable process.

$$Cp_U = (8 - 6) \div 3 = 0.67$$
$$Cp_L = (6 - 0) \div 3 = 2.7$$
$$Cp_k = Cp_U = 0.67$$
$$Cp = (8 - 0) \div 6 = 1.33$$

The Cp of 1.33 reflects how the process would be capable of performing if it were centered between the specification limits. Figure 4.84 shows the centered process.

Variation: Performance Indexes Pp_k and Pp
When to Use

- When the process is not in statistical control
- Only when the process forms a normal distribution

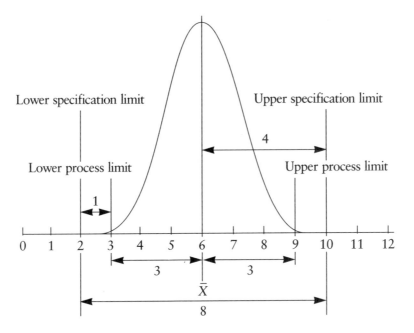

Figure 4.84. Capable process.

Procedure

1. Establish that the process forms a normal distribution, using the normal probability plot or Kolmogorov–Smirnov test.

2. Determine the upper specification limit (USL), and the lower specification limit (LSL). Determine the average of the process values $\bar{X}$.

3. Calculate the root mean square deviation s, using all the data from the time period being considered.

$$s = \sqrt{\sum \frac{(X_i - \bar{X})^2}{n - 1}}$$

Many electronic calculators use this formula to calculate σ.

4. Calculate Pp_U and Pp_L.

$$Pp_U = \frac{USL - \bar{X}}{3s} \qquad Pp_L = \frac{\bar{X} - LSL}{3s}$$

The smaller of the two numbers is Pp_k.

Note: If there is only one specification, calculate the Pp_U or Pp_L for just that side; that is also the Pp_k.

5. Larger Pp_k values are better. If Pp_k is less than 1.0 (or the value designated by your customer), work to reduce variation or to center the process within specifications. Also, work to bring the process into control.

6. Calculate Pp.

$$Pp \ = \ \frac{USL - LSL}{6s}$$

If Pp is greater than or equal to 1.0, the process would be capable of meeting specifications if it were centered.

Considerations

- The purpose of measuring and reporting process capability is to be able to predict how well the process will perform in the future. This is only possible if the process is in control. If the process is out of control, all you can measure and report with any certainty is past performance of the process.

- To understand the capability of your process, you must consider both the width of the process and whether it is centered. The process in Figure 4.83 is narrow enough to fit the specifications, but because it is off-center, it is producing out-of-specification product, represented by the shaded area.

- Cp_k and Pp_k take into account both the width of the process and whether it is centered. The process in Figure 4.83 has a Cp_k of .67, because the process is not centered between the specifications. The process in Figure 4.84 is the same width and has the same specifications, but because the process is centered, $Cp_k = 1.33$.

- Cp and Pp do not take into account whether the process is centered. They indicate whether the process would be capable *if* it were centered. Only when the process is centered will $Cp_k = Cp$ or $Pp_k = Pp$.

- When calculating capability for data being plotted on an $\bar{X}$ and R chart, do not use the process limits and the 3σ value calculated on the control chart worksheet (Figure 4.14). Those worksheet calculations are using the *subgroup averages*. For capability, you must use the original data. The calculations given in this section use the original data.

- Do not drop data from the calculation just because you have identified the cause of an outlier. Include all bad points unless you have truly eliminated forever and always the cause of the outlier.

- If you calculate Pp_k, be sure to not to mislabel it as Cp_k. The designation Pp_k clearly indicates that the process is not in control.

- Because a normal distribution has tails on either side, even a perfectly centered distribution with a Cp_k of 1.0 will have a small amount of product outside the specifications—0.26%, to be exact. (In the normal distribution, 99.74% of the distribution lies within 3σ of the average.) In addition, processes usually drift slightly. Therefore, many customers require their suppliers to demonstrate that their processes have higher Cp_k. With a Cp_k of 1.33, the specification lies 1σ beyond the process limit, which provides a comfortable cushion.

- The requirement for *six sigma* capability has been made famous by Motorola. Six sigma means that the distance from either specification limit to the target (the midpoint between the two limits) should be at least 6σ. So the total specification spread should be 12σ. The process average should be no more than 1.5σ from the target. You might want to test your understanding of capability by calculating the corresponding Cp and Cp_k. (Answer: Cp = 2.0 and Cp_k = 1.5.)

- If the process is not normal, you cannot calculate a capability index or performance index. There are three other options.[33]

  1. Transform the data. For example, a skewed distribution can be transformed into a normal distribution using natural logarithms.

  2. If you know the process' distribution (binomial, Poisson, and so on), directly calculate from that distribution the values that correspond to a given Cp_k and compare to your data.

  3. Do not calculate a capability index. Instead, calculate directly the percentage of the process that is outside specifications.

  Consult one of the books listed in "Recommended Reading" or obtain expert help.

- Use of a capability index is controversial. All too often the number is improperly calculated and is misleading.[34] Be sure to follow the rules about statistical control and normal distribution. Using process limits and process spread avoids some of these problems.[35]

Relations Diagram

Interrelationship Digraph

Description

The relations diagram shows cause-and-effect relationships. Just as important, the process of creating a relations diagram helps a group analyze the natural links between different aspects of a complex problem.

When to Use

- A complex issue is being analyzed for causes

- A complex issue is being implemented

- After generating an affinity diagram, cause-and-effect diagram, or tree diagram, to more completely explore the relations of ideas

Basic Procedure

Materials needed: Cards or Post-It™ notes, large paper surface (newsprint or two flipchart pages taped together), marking pens, tape.

1. Write a statement defining the issue that the relations diagram will explore. Write it on a card or Post-It™ note and place it at the top of the work surface.

2. Brainstorm ideas around the issue and write them on cards or notes. If another tool has preceded this one, take the ideas from the affinity diagram, the most detailed row of the tree diagram, or the final branches on the fishbone diagram. You may want to use these ideas as starting points and brainstorm additional ideas.

3. Place one idea at a time on the work surface and ask, "Is this idea related to any others?" Place ideas that are related near the first. Leave space between cards to allow for drawing arrows later. Repeat until all cards are on the work surface.

4. For each idea, ask "Does this idea cause or influence any other idea?" Draw arrows from each idea to the ones it causes or influences. Repeat the question for every idea.

5. Analyze the diagram.

   - Count how many arrows in and out each idea has. The ones with the most arrows are the key ideas.

- Note which ideas have primarily outgoing (from) arrows. These are the basic causes.

- Note which ideas have primarily incoming (to) arrows. These are final effects that also may be critical to address.

Be sure to check whether ideas with fewer arrows are also key ideas. The number of arrows is only an indicator, not an absolute rule. Draw bold lines around the key ideas.

Example

A computer support group is planning a major project: replacing the mainframe computer. The group drew a relations diagram (Figure 4.85) to sort out a confusing set of elements involved in this project. "Computer replacement project" is the card identifying the issue. The ideas that were brainstormed were a mixture of action steps, problems, desired results, and less-desirable effects to be handled. All these ideas went onto the diagram together. As the questions were asked about relationships and causes, the mixture of ideas began to sort themselves out.

After all the arrows were drawn, key issues became clear. They are outlined with bold lines. "New software" has one arrow in and six arrows out. "Install new mainframe" has one arrow in and four out. Both ideas are basic causes. Also, "Service interruptions" has three arrows in, and the group identified it as another key issue. "Increased processing cost" also has three arrows, but the group decided it was not a key issue.

Variation: Matrix Relations Diagram

Use a matrix to compare ideas to each other one at a time. This variation can be more methodical and neater.[36] It might not visually emphasize relationships as well.

1. Write a statement defining the issue that the relations diagram will explore.

2. Brainstorm ideas around the issue on a flipchart. If another tool has preceded this one, take the ideas from the affinity diagram, the most detailed row of the tree diagram, or the final branches on the fishbone diagram. You may want to use these ideas as starting points and brainstorm additional ideas.

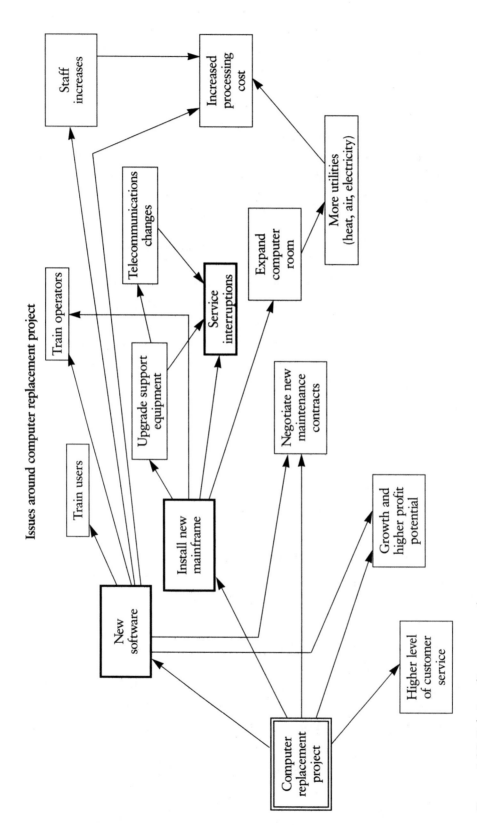

Figure 4.85. Relations diagram example.

3. Draw a matrix with as many rows and columns as there are ideas. Write the ideas down the left side of a matrix. Number each one. Write the numbers across the top of the matrix.

4. Go through the matrix methodically, comparing each idea on the left to each idea across the top, and asking, "Does the first idea cause or influence the second?" In the grid box, draw an arrow pointing up to indicate the idea in the row causing or influencing the idea in the column.

5. Reflect the matrix. Every place there is an arrow pointing up, draw an arrow pointing left in the other box where those two ideas intersect. For example, if row 2, column 3 has an upward arrow, then row 3, column 2 must have a left-pointing arrow.

6. To analyze the matrix, count the "to" arrows (pointing left) and the "from" arrows (pointing up) on each row. Add for the total number of arrows to and from that idea. Continue to analyze for key ideas as in step 5 of the basic procedure.

Example

The same project, replacement of the mainframe computer, and the same issues are shown in the matrix relations diagram of Figure 4.86. There's an upward arrow in row 1, column 2. Idea 1 influences or causes idea 2. Similarly, the arrow pointing left in row 3, column 2 means idea 2 influences or causes idea 3.

Every upward-pointing arrow is matched with a left-pointing one. For example, row 4 (train operators) has a left-pointing arrow at column 6. Row 6 has an upward-pointing arrow at column 4.

The last three columns sum the arrows pointing left (to), the ones pointing up (from), and the total. These are the same sums the team counted in the previous example to determine key issues.

Considerations

- Fifteen to 50 ideas is the best range of numbers for a relations diagram. Fewer than 15 and you do not need it; more than 50 and the diagram is too complex to handle.[37]
- Do not ask, "Is this idea caused or influenced by any others?" Look for ideas that cause others, and do that for every idea. Then the "caused by" question is unnecessary.[38]

	1	2	3	4	5	6	7	8	9	10	11	12	13	14	15	To	From	Total
1 Computer replacement		←				←				←			←		←	0	5	5
2 New software	↓		←	←	←					←		←	←			1	6	7
3 Train users		↓														1	0	1
4 Train operators		↓				↓										2	0	2
5 Staff increases		↓										←				1	1	2
6 Install new mainframe	↓			←			←		←		←					1	4	5
7 Upgrade support equipment						↓		←	←							1	2	3
8 Telecommunications changes							↓		←							1	1	2
9 Service interruptions						↓	↓	↓								3	0	3
10 Negotiate new maintenance contracts	↓	↓														2	0	2
11 Expand computer room						↓								←		1	1	2
12 Increased processing cost		↓			↓									↓		3	0	3
13 Growth and higher profit potentials	↓	↓														2	0	2
14 More utilities											↓	←				1	1	2
15 Higher level of customer service	↓															1	0	1

Figure 4.86. Matrix relations diagram example.

- Do not draw double-headed arrows. Force yourself to decide which cause or influence is strongest.[39]

- It can be useful to share the diagram with others and request their ideas and comments. Do this after step 4 (before the analysis) and when the analysis is completed.

- This tool also has been called the *interrelationship digraph*.[40] The name *relations diagram* is less intimidating and more easily remembered.

Requirements Matrix

Description

The requirements matrix is a format for recording customers and their requirements. It separates customers into four different categories and requirements into two categories. Thinking about the categories leads to a more complete list of customers and requirements.

When to Use

- When developing a list of customers
- When developing a list of customers' requirements

Procedure

1. Define the product or service. Write it at the top of the form.

2. Brainstorm a list of customers. Ask, "Who cares about the quality of what we do or how we do it?" Use these four categories to help develop a complete list.

   External: The purchaser or user of the product or service, or a representative. *External* means external to the process producing the product or service; this customer may be internal to your company.

   Internal: Those who run and manage the process that produces the product or service. This may be the person who operates the process or a supervisor.

   Society: Society has an interest in how we run our processes and in certain aspects of our products or services. Society's interests usually are represented by agencies such as the EPA, OSHA, certification boards, and so forth.

Supplier: Sometimes a supplier has an interest in how its materials are used or presented. There also may be requirements about when the supplier receives information or how the information is communicated.

3. For each customer, brainstorm requirements and write them in the appropriate columns. Consider the following two types of requirements:

Product: Requirements or needs about the product or service itself.

Process: Requirements or needs about how the product or service is prepared or made.

Example

Figure 4.87 shows the beginning of a requirements matrix for an engineering department. The product is a set of designs for a new manufacturing plant: equipment specifications, piping diagrams, electrical diagrams, site layout, and so on. This matrix analyzes the customers of that design and their requirements.

It is important to remember that the *product* is the set of designs for the new plant, not what it will produce. The *process* is how the design is done, the entire flow of activities for designing the plant, beginning with the assignment to the design engineers and ending with completion and final approval of all the pieces of the design.

Company ABC will be the customer for the product the new plant will produce. One of the purchasing agent's product requirements for the plant design is that it be capable of producing specification product, in this case 99% purity. There are probably many other product specification and packaging requirements that will be requirements for the design. Company ABC's process requirements for the design have to do with timing; the unit must be producing product by September. The external customers usually have few process requirements; they do not care how something is done as long as it *is* done.

The plant operations department has many product requirements for the new plant design. It must be safe and easy to operate, quick to start up, and so forth. The department has a process requirement also: As the engineers work on the design, operations personnel want to be able to review the designs so they can provide input.

Note that the manager, an internal customer, has the same requirements as the customers who will use the product. Typically, management wants the customers to get whatever they want. In addition, management usually

Product or service: Design for new manufacturing plant		
Customer	**Product requirements**	**Process requirements**
External Purchasing agent, Company ABC	Produces product of 99% purity	Unit producing product by September
Internal Plant operations Manager	Safe to operate Quick start-up Easy to operate Produces product of 99% purity Safe to operate Quick start-up Easy to operate	Allowed to review designs early Producing product by September Within budget Designed without overtime
Society OSHA EPA	Complies with all regulations Complies with all regulations	
Supplier Equipment vendor		8-week lead time for equipment specifications

Figure 4.87. Requirements matrix example.

has process requirements concerning time and cost. In this case, the design must be done within budget and without overtime.

Two regulatory agencies, OSHA and the EPA, represent society with regulations about safe design and equipment to prevent environmental accidents. Those regulations set requirements for the design itself. The agencies have no requirements for how the design is done.

Finally, a supplier has a process requirement. The equipment vendor needs to receive equipment specifications eight weeks before the equipment delivery date. This requirement sets a deadline for completing equipment specifications and anything else that must be finished before the equipment specifications.

Considerations

- The reason for categorizing requirements as process or product is to make sure that you think about both types.

- When you are listing requirements for a report or form, include not only what information must be there, but also requirements like arrangement for easy reading or use, format as a graph or table, number of copies, legibility, and so on.

- Table 4.10 shows the kinds of requirements that concern each type of customer.

Requirements-and-Measures Tree

Description

The requirements-and-measures tree organizes customers, their requirements, and related measurements for a product or service. The relationships between all the customers, requirements, and measures become visible.

When to Use

- When developing requirements or measures

- To organize a complex set of requirements and/or measures

- To visually describe a set of requirements and measures and their relationships

Table 4.10. Categories of customers and their requirements.

Those who care about quality	What is produced (product requirements)	How it is produced (process requirements)
External	Specifications Consistency	Price Time from request to delivery
Internal	Internal specifications	Production safety Cost, including labor
Society	Product liability Product safety	Employee and community health and safety
Suppliers		Safe use of supplies When and how information is received

Procedure

1. Identify one process output. Write it on a Post-It™ note and place at the top of a flipchart page.

2. Identify all customers of that output. Write each one on a Post-It™ note and place on the page under the output.

3. For each customer, identify all requirements. Be as specific as possible, using operational definitions. For example, don't say "Timely." Instead say, "Received by Friday noon." Write each requirement on a note and place under the customer's name.

4. At this point, some requirements may be duplicated, or natural groupings may be obvious. Reorganize the requirements if desired. Draw lines to show connections between customers and requirements.

5. For each requirement, brainstorm potential measurements. Follow good brainstorming techniques and try uncritically to generate as many as possible. Then discuss and evaluate the measures. Reduce the list to a manageable number.

6. For each measurement, identify how it will be tracked: what tool, where data are obtained, what frequency, who is responsible.

Example

Figure 4.88 shows the beginning of a requirements-and-measures tree for an engineering department. The product is a set of designs for a new manufacturing plant. This is the same situation that was described in the requirements matrix example. Refer to that example for a discussion of the requirements.

This requirements-and-measures tree shows the branches for plant operations and for the design engineers' manager. There would be branches for any other internal or external customers. One of the manager's requirements is shown, "Within budget," and dotted lines indicate that the manager shares plant operations' requirements.

"Within budget" would be measured by variance from the budget, which can be monitored by a control chart. "Safe to operate" can be measured by completion of any changes required by a safety review; this would

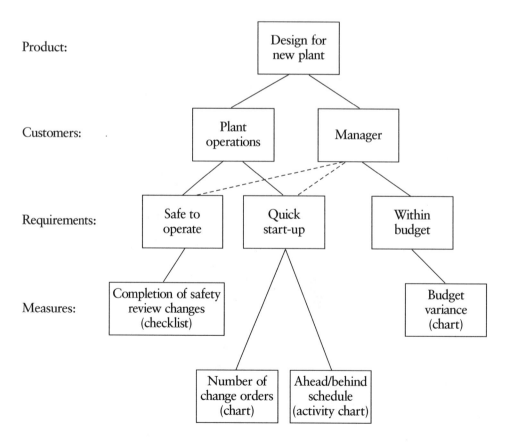

Figure 4.88. Requirements-and-measures tree example.

be monitored with a checklist. "Quick start-up" could be measured by the number of change orders, monitored on an attribute control chart, and by the amount the project is ahead or behind schedule, as shown by an activity chart.

This chart is not complete. Every requirement for every customer should be identified.

Considerations

- Do not neglect process requirements—*how* this output is produced. Be sure to include them.

- An affinity diagram can be useful when organizing the requirements that have been brainstormed.

- When developing measures, it helps to switch the time frame of your thinking. Think about how to collect measurements of many occurrences over time rather than a single occurrence of the output. For example, if the product is a check request, a requirement might be "contains authorized signature." For one request, that is a yes–no measurement. On a weekly basis, one could record on an attribute control chart the percentage of requests lacking an authorized signature.

- When evaluating and deciding on measures, you can use other tools such as the decision matrix, multivoting, and list reduction.

- At step 2 of the quality improvement process, you may wish to generate only the top branches of the tree, down through requirements. Later in your quality improvement process, when you are ready to measure, you can return to the tree and complete the measurements section.

Run Chart

Description
A run chart is a graph that shows a measurement (on the vertical axis) against time (on the horizontal axis), with a reference line to show the average of the data (Figure 4.89). It is similar to a control chart but does not show control limits.

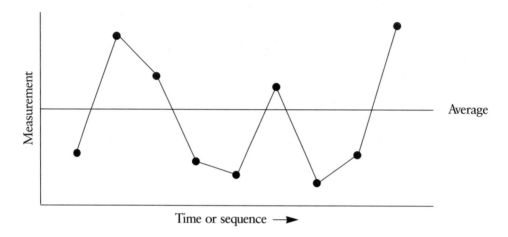

Figure 4.89. Run chart.

When to Use

- During data collection, before enough points have been collected to draw a control chart

- To look for trends or changes in the average

- To look for cycles, autocorrelation, or other patterns

Procedure

1. Decide on the vertical scale, based on the range of measurements you expect to see. Decide on the horizontal time scale, based on the frequency of measurements. Mark and label the scales.

2. If you already have a set of historical data, calculate the average:

$$\text{average} = \frac{\text{sum of the values}}{\text{number of values}}$$

Draw across the chart a reference line showing the average.

3. Plot each measurement in the time order it occurs. Connect points with straight lines.

4. Look for patterns in the data, using tests for out-of-control situations.

Considerations

- Run charts are not as powerful as control charts for analyzing process data and identifying problems.

- Common out-of-control tests are

  Run: Too many consecutive points on one side of the average. A run can be seven points in a row, 10 points on one side out of 11 in a row, 12 points on one side out of 14 in a row.

  Trend: A series of points heading up or down. Use the method described in the scatter diagram section (page 248) to divide the chart into four quadrants and count points in opposite quadrants. Use the trend test table (Table 4.11) in that section to decide if the number of points indicates a trend.

  Number of runs: The average line is crossed too few or too many times. Use the number of runs table (Table 4.2) for this test. Count the total number of points, skipping any points lying directly on the average line. Determine the number of runs by counting the number of times the line between data points crosses the average line. If the data line touches the average line and then returns to the same side, do not count it as crossing.

- These tests for patterns are based on statistics. They test whether the data are truly statistically random. If not, an underlying pattern needs to be identified.

- The tests do not judge whether patterns are desirable or undesirable. For example, a trend may be toward better performance or toward worse performance. It is just as important to do something to understand and keep good performance as it is to eliminate bad performance.

Scatter Diagram

Description

The scatter diagram helps identify relationships between two variables.

When to Use

- When trying to identify potential root causes of problems

- After brainstorming causes and effects using a fishbone diagram, to determine objectively whether a particular cause and effect are related

- When determining whether two effects that appear to be related both occur with the same cause

Procedure

1. Collect paired data for variables where a relationship is suspected.

2. Plot all the variable pairs on a graph, with one variable on the horizontal axis and the other variable on the vertical axis.

3. Look at the pattern of points to see if a relationship is obvious. If the data clearly form a line, you may stop now. Otherwise, complete steps 4 through 7.[41]

4. Divide points on the graph into four quadrants. If there are X points on the graph,

    Count $X/2$ points from top to bottom and draw a line.

    Count $X/2$ points from left to right and draw a line.

    Label the four quadrants as shown in Figure 4.90.

   Note: If you have an odd number of points, the line will pass through a point.

5. Count how many points are in each quadrant. Do *not* count points on a line.

6. Calculate

    A = the number of points in Quadrant I + Quadrant III

    B = the number of points in Quadrant II + Quadrant IV

    Q = the smaller of A and B

    $N = A + B$

7. Look up the limit for N on the trend test table (Table 4.11).

   - If Q is less than the limit, the two variables are related.

   - If Q is greater than the limit, the pattern could have occurred from random chance.

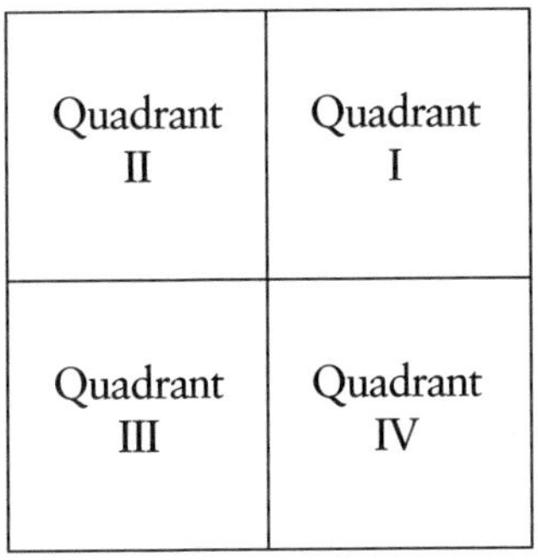

Figure 4.90. Scatter diagram quadrants.

Table 4.11. Trend test table.

N	Limit	N	Limit
1–8	0	51–53	18
9–11	1	54–55	19
12–14	2	56–57	20
15–16	3	58–60	21
17–19	4	61–62	22
20–22	5	63–64	23
23–24	6	65–66	24
25–27	7	67–69	25
28–29	8	70–71	26
30–32	9	72–73	27
33–34	10	74–76	28
35–36	11	77–78	29
37–39	12	79–80	30
40–41	13	81–82	31
42–43	14	83–85	32
44–46	15	86–87	33
47–48	16	88–89	34
49–50	17	90	35

Example

The ZZ-400 manufacturing team suspects a relationship between product purity (% purity) and the amount of iron (measured in parts per million or ppm). Purity and iron are plotted against each other as a scatter diagram in Figure 4.91.

There are 24 data points. Median lines are drawn so that 12 points fall on each side for both % purity and ppm iron.

To test for a relationship, calculate

A = the number of points in Quadrant I + Quadrant III

= 4 + 3 = 7

B = the number of points in Quadrant II + Quadrant IV

= 8 + 9 = 17

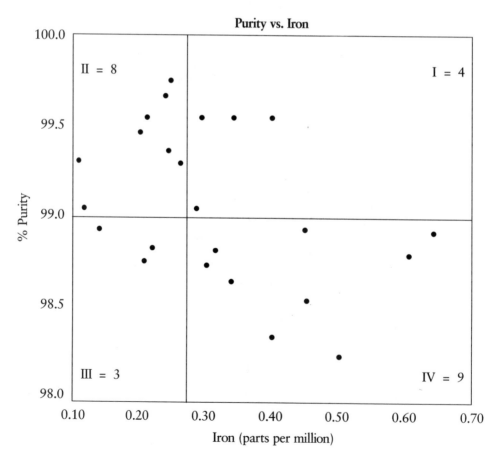

Figure 4.91. Scatter diagram example.

$$Q = \text{the smaller of } A \text{ and } B$$

$$= \text{the smaller of 7 and } 17 = 7$$

$$N = A + B$$

$$= 7 + 17 = 24$$

Look up the limit for N on the trend test table (Table 4.11). For $N = 24$, the limit is 6.

If Q is less than the limit, the two variables are related. If Q is greater than the limit, the pattern could have occurred from random chance. In this example,

$$Q = 7 \text{ which is greater than 6}$$

Therefore, the pattern could have occurred from random chance, and no relationship is demonstrated.

Considerations

- In what kind of situations might you use a scatter diagram? Here are some examples. Variable A is the temperature of a reaction after 15 minutes. Variable B measures the color of the product. You suspect higher temperature makes the product darker. Plot temperature and color on a scatter diagram. Or, variable A is the number of people trained on new software, and variable B is the number of calls to the computer helpline. You suspect that more training reduces the number of calls. Plot number of people trained versus number of calls.

- Even if the scatter diagram shows a relationship, do not assume that one variable caused the other. Both may be influenced by a third variable.

- When the data are plotted, the more the diagram resembles a straight line, the stronger the relationship.

- If a line is not clear, statistics (N and Q) determine whether there is reasonable certainty that a relationship exists. If the statistics say that no relationship exists, the pattern of the diagram could have occurred by random chance.

- If the scatter diagram shows no relationship between the variables, consider whether the data might be stratified. See "Stratification" on page 255 for more details.

- Think creatively about how to use scatter diagrams to discover a root cause.

Storyboard

Description

A storyboard is a visual display of thoughts.[42] It makes all facets of a process, organization, plan, or concept visible at once to anyone. It taps both the creative right brain and the analytical left brain to yield breakthrough thinking.

When to Use

- When developing new ideas
- When planning a project
- When developing a process flow diagram
- When planning a presentation
- When using an exhibit to communicate ideas, project activities, or organizational relationships and responsibilities[43]

Procedure

Materials needed: cards or Post-It™ notes in three different sizes, large piece of newsprint or pinboard, marking pen for each participant.

1. Define the topic of the storyboard. Write it on a large card and place it at the top of the work surface (paper or pinboard).

2. Brainstorm important subjects to be considered. Write these on large header cards. The first one should be "Purpose" or "Why work on this topic." Continue to brainstorm headers until the flow of ideas stops.

3. Critically discuss each heading. Identify duplicates and subjects that are less important and should be dropped. Some headings will be a subcategory under another heading and should be set aside. Team members can object to anything on the work surface. The team tries to remove the objection by *plussing* (improving) the idea. Change the card if it is *plussed;* remove it if the objection cannot be resolved. Continue the discussion until the group has determined the important headers.

4. Choose one header and brainstorm ideas. Write them on small cards and place under the heading. These are called *subbers.* Brainstorm until the group has exhausted all ideas.

5. Critically discuss the subbers, as in step 3. Where choices need to be made, the team may use other tools (such as decision matrix, list reduction, or multivoting) to narrow the list.

6. Continue to generate subbers for each of the headings in turn. Always do a complete brainstorm first and follow with a discussion session.

7. Arrows or string may be used to connect ideas and to show relationships.

8. Small cards with notes, called *siders*, can be placed next to any card to make comments or amplify ideas.

Example

The ZZ-400 safety subteam used the storyboard of Figure 4.92 on the control room bulletin board to introduce a new approach to safety to the rest of the unit. The topic card reads "SAFE–ZZ." The header cards are "Purpose," "Focus," "What," "How," and "Who Else?" Under each header, subbers describe the approach.

String between cards shows relationships. For example, the idea "Discuss incidents" is linked to two "Focus" subbers: "Honesty" and "Directness." "Learn to speak up" is linked to "Building trust."

The sider "Chris' neighbor" next to "Ozzi Inc." adds a side comment that will be interesting to the group.

Considerations

- Storyboarding requires a small group. Between four and 10 participants is the ideal size.

- Storyboarding alternates between creative brainstorming and critical review. It is essential to keep the two modes separate. Mixing the two is deadly: a group cannot be creative when some members are being critical. It is the facilitator's role to keep the team in the right mode. One helpful technique is to pin a card on the board with "creative" on one side and "critical" on the other, signaling to the team which type of thinking is in play.[44]

- The decision to switch from creative to critical mode or vice versa can be made by the facilitator or suggested by a team member.

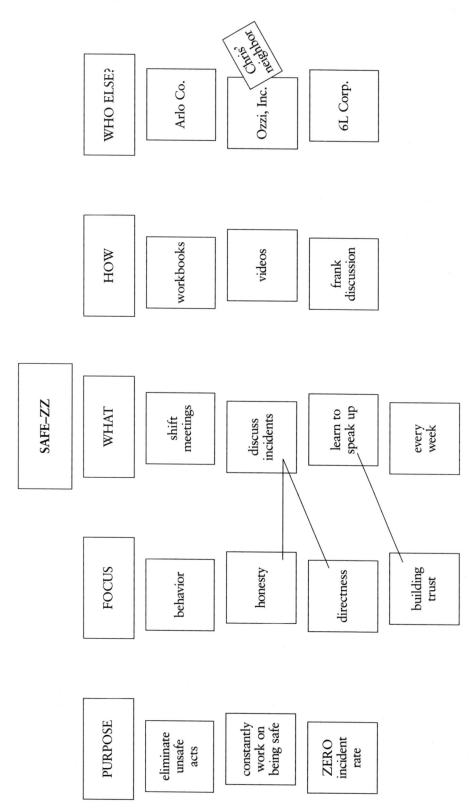

Figure 4.92. Storyboard example.

- Common subject headers include purpose, future state, who, what, when, how, cost, and miscellaneous.[45] The headers you use will depend on your topic.

- To speed the creative process, have participants themselves write their own ideas on the cards.

- The better defined the topic statement is, the better the final result will be and the easier it will be to get there.

- Use marking pens. With regular pens, it is hard to read ideas from any distance.

- Using cards of different colors for the different header subjects helps the eye and brain sort the different ideas.

- See "Brainstorming" on page 71 for more ideas about that part of the process.

- See "Flowchart" on page 137 for a storyboarding method for developing a flowchart.

- See "Requirements-and-Measures Tree" on page 242 for a storyboarding method for developing requirements and measures.

Stratification

Description

Stratification is a technique used in combination with other data analysis tools. When data from a variety of sources or categories has been lumped together, the meaning of the data can be impossible to see. This technique separates the data so that patterns can be seen.

When to Use

- When using a checksheet, scatter diagram, control chart, histogram, or similar data collection or analysis tool

- When data come from several sources, such as several shifts, days of the week, lots, suppliers, pieces of equipment, and so on

Procedure

1. Before collecting data, consider what information about the sources of the data might have an effect on the results. Set up the data

collection so that you collect that information also. The following list gives examples of typical information that requires data to be stratified.

Machines	Materials	Day of the week
Equipment	Shifts	Products
Workers	Time of day	Suppliers

2. When plotting or graphing the collected data on a scatter diagram, control chart, histogram, or other analysis tool, use different marks or colors to distinguish data from various sources. Data that are distinguished in this way are said to be *stratified.*

3. Analyze the subsets of stratified data separately. For example, on a scatter diagram where data are stratified into data from source 1 and data from source 2, draw quadrants, count points, and determine the critical value for just the data from source 1, then for just the data from source 2.

Example

The ZZ-400 manufacturing team drew a scatter diagram (Figure 4.91) to test whether product purity and iron contamination were related. The diagram did not demonstrate a relationship. Then a team member realized that the data came from three different reactors. The team member redrew the diagram, using a different symbol for each reactor's data (Figure 4.93).

Now patterns can be seen. The data from reactor 2 and reactor 3 are circled. Even without doing any calculations, it is clear that for those two reactors, purity decreases as iron increases. However, the data from reactor 1, the solid dots that are not circled, do not show that relationship. Something is different about reactor 1.

Considerations

- If you might photocopy your graph, use different marks rather than different colors to stratify the data.

- On your graph or chart, include a legend that identifies the marks or colors used. In Figure 4.93, the legend tells which symbol refers to which reactor.

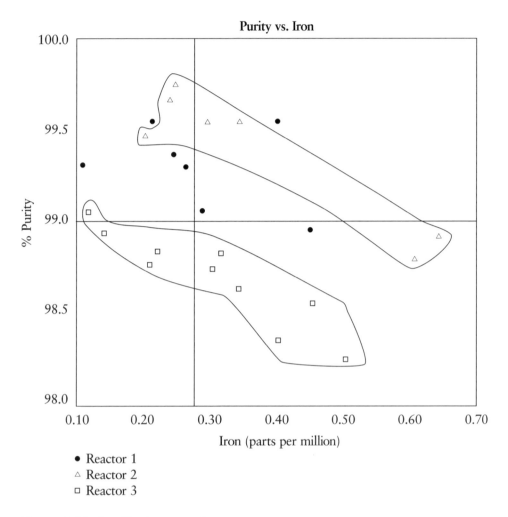

Figure 4.93. Stratification example.

Survey

Questionnaire, Interview, Focus Group

Description

Surveys are used to collect data about the knowledge and opinions of a targeted group of people. Common types of surveys are written questionnaires, face-to-face or telephone interviews, and focus groups. Surveys are commonly used in quality improvement to discover customers' views of their supplier's performance. They also can be used to determine internal views.

When to Use

- When identifying customer requirements
- When assessing performance against requirements
- When identifying or prioritizing problems to address
- When assessing whether an implemented solution was successful
- Periodically, to confirm that improved performance is being maintained

Basic Procedure

1. Decide what you want to learn from the survey and how you will use the results. Also decide the group you need to survey.

2. Decide the most appropriate type of survey. See the variations for when to use each type.

3. Decide whether the survey's answers will be numerical rating, numerical ranking, yes–no, multiple choice, or open-ended—or a mixture.

4. Brainstorm questions and the answer choices. Keep in mind what you want to learn and how you will use the results. Narrow down the list of questions to the absolute minimum that you must have to learn what you need to learn.

5. Decide who should be surveyed. Identify groups, and if they are too large to survey everyone, decide how to narrow the list to ensure a representative sample. Decide what demographic information is needed to analyze and understand the results.

6. Print the questionnaire or interviewers' question list.

7. Test the survey on a small sample group. Collect feedback.

   - Which questions were confusing?
   - Were any questions redundant?
   - Were the answer choices clear? Were they interpreted as you intended?
   - Was there anything they wanted to give feedback about that was not requested?
   - How long did it take?
   - For a questionnaire, were there any typos or other printing errors?

Also test tabulating and analyzing the results. Is it easy? Do you have all the data you need? Revise accordingly.

8. Administer the survey. See the variations for details.

9. Tabulate and analyze the data. Decide how you will follow through. Report results and plans to everyone involved.

Variation: Written Questionnaire

Note: Many of the tips for the survey variations and considerations come from the excellent booklet *Surveys from Start to Finish*, by Lori Long.[46]

When to Use

- When collecting data from a large group
- When possible responses to the questions are known and need only be quantified
- For example, after an initial set of interviews or focus groups has identified key issues
- When data are not needed immediately
- When a low response rate can be tolerated
- When resources (money, people) for collecting data are limited

Procedure

Follow the basic procedure. Add the following details at steps 6 and 8.

6. Print the survey in a format that is easy to read and easy to fill out. Leave generous space for answers to open-ended questions. Design the form so that tabulating and analyzing data will be easy. At the top, print instructions for completing and returning it.

8. There are three options for administering the questionnaire.

- Send out the questionnaire with a cover letter. A cover letter should include the reason for the survey, how recipients were chosen, a deadline and instructions for returning questionnaires, and thanks. Include a stamped and addressed envelope.
- Hand deliver the survey. Ask the recipient for an appointment for 10 minutes. At the appointment explain the purpose of the survey and ask for the recipient's help. This method usually gets a better response rate.

- Hold a meeting, if all respondents are at the same location. Send a memo explaining the purpose of the survey and the time required. At the meeting, repeat the purpose before handing out the survey.

For mailed or hand-delivered questionnaires, follow up with non-respondents to increase the response rate. Send another copy of the survey with a new cover letter.

Variation: Face-to-Face Interviews

When to Use

- When possible answers to the questions are not known, such as when you first begin studying an issue
- When the questions to be asked are sensitive
- When the people to be surveyed are high-ranking, important, or otherwise deserving of special attention
- When the group to be surveyed is small
- When close to 100% response rate is needed
- When ample resources (time, people, and possibly travel expenses) are available for the survey

Procedure

Follow the basic procedure. Add the following details at steps 3, 6, and 8.

3. Almost all the questions should be open-ended. You might start with a few simple yes–no questions.

6. Print the interviewers' question list with lots of space to write notes directly under the question.

8. There are four contacts with each interviewee.

- Send a letter to each interviewee explaining the survey's purpose and stating who will call to make interview arrangements.

- The interviewer should call the interviewee to request an interview. Introduce yourself, describe the survey again briefly, and state how much time is needed. Set an appointment.

- The interview itself: At the beginning of the interview, restate the purpose of the survey and the time needed. See the considerations for interviewing tips.

- Send a follow-up thank-you letter to the interviewee.

Variation: Telephone Interview

When to Use

- When most possible answers to the questions are known
- When data are needed quickly
- When a high response rate is needed
- When people's time is available for making calls

Procedure

Follow the basic procedure. Add the following details at steps 6 and 8.

6. Print the interviewers' question list with lots of space to write notes directly under the question. Make one copy for each interview to be conducted. Also prepare a checksheet with columns for name, phone number, busy signals, message left, and interview completed. (See "Checksheet" on page 74 for more information.)

8. Fill out the checksheet as calls are made. At the beginning of the phone interview, introduce yourself and explain the survey and its purpose. State how much time will be needed and ask if this is a convenient time. If not, make an appointment to call back. See the considerations for interviewing tips.

Variation: Focus Group

When to Use

- When the subject of the survey is so unfocused that questionnaire or interview questions cannot be written
- As a first step, before surveying with a questionnaire or interviews
- When resources are ample

Procedure

A focus group brings together up to a dozen people to discuss their attitudes and concerns about a subject. Leading, documenting, and analyzing a focus group requires an experienced facilitator. Ask for help from your human resources or training departments or from a consultant.

Considerations

Writing Questions

- When surveying customers about your performance, ask also about the importance of each item. See "Importance–Performance Analysis" on page 165 for a way to ask and analyze those kinds of questions.

- Write and rewrite your questions to be short and clear. Try to imagine how the respondent will perceive the question.

- Group the questions by topic and start with easy ones. Put the hardest ones in the middle.

- Avoid jargon, duplicate questions, leading questions, questions phrased in the negative, sensitive or emotional questions, questions that ask two things at once.

- Demographic information that often is important includes age, years of experience, location, type or level of job, size of company or group, which company or group. Often what you ask is a compromise between maintaining the respondents' confidentiality and ensuring necessary analysis later. Carefully think through what demographics you will need to analyze the data. When you are analyzing results, it will be too late to ask for the information.

Responses

- Questions with forced-choice answers—numerical ratings, rankings, yes–no, or multiple choice—are simple to answer and score, can be analyzed statistically, and can be repeated on periodic surveys to observe trends. Open-ended questions can reveal insights and nuances and tell you things you would never think to ask. A good compromise on a questionnaire or telephone interview is mostly forced-choice questions with a few open-ended ones at the end.

- Use only five numbers in the numerical scale unless you describe each number with words that clearly differentiate the responses. It is hard to make value decisions when asked to rate something on a scale of 1 to 10. What's the difference between a 7 and an 8?

- Write specific descriptions of each rating. For example, instead of "from poor (1) to excellent (5):"

  1 = Often encounter problems

  2 = Sometimes encounter problems

  3 = Meets expectations

4 = Sometimes goes beyond expectations

5 = Often goes beyond expectations

- Always set up your numerical scale so that a high number means a good response. People expect that, so with a scale running the opposite direction some respondents will answer incorrectly. Your data will be unreliable.

- Check that the choices in a multiple choice answer are mutually exclusive. If not, allow people to select as many as apply.

Choosing Respondents

- Remember that an average response rate for a blind, random questionnaire is about 35%. Be sure enough questionnaires are sent out that a 35% response rate will give you enough data.

- It can be useful to survey not only current customers but also potential and past customers.

- Be sure a random sample is truly random. For example, for a 20% sample, take every fifth name from an alphabetical list. If subgroups must be equally represented, sample randomly within each subgroup.

Interviewing

- If there are several interviewers, they should agree on procedures for recording, summarizing, and analyzing responses. See "Operational Definitions" on page 207.

- When reading questions, speak distinctly.

- Strive for a tone of voice that does not suggest a particular response. Do not react to answers. You should talk as little as possible.

- On open-ended questions, ask follow-up questions to explore the interviewee's thinking. Ask for clarification if you do not fully understand an answer.

- Take complete notes on each question. You will not remember later. It is all right to ask the interviewee to wait a few moments while you write.

- Always ask for permission if you want to tape record the interview. It is illegal to tape a telephone conversation without permission. Take notes to supplement the interview. What if the interviewee's voice cannot be heard on the tape?

- If the interview is not done within the time estimated, ask for permission to continue.

- Always thank the interviewee for his or her time.

- Transcribe your notes as soon as possible after the interview.

Analysis and Reporting

- For numerical responses, study the range of responses as well as the average. Responses that vary from 1 to 5 mean something very different from responses that are all 3s and 4s, although both may average 3.4. Standard deviation of the responses is a useful number to calculate, report, and study.

- Use graphical techniques for better analysis and communication of the results. See the sections on graphs, histograms, importance–performance analysis, matrix diagram, performance indexing, and stratification.

- Whenever you sample from a group, there will be variation in the results. The data you get may not exactly represent the data of the entire group. The larger your sample, the smaller the variation. You can calculate what the variation is; consult your local statistics expert.

- Results can be biased for many reasons: respondents chosen nonrandomly, poor wording of a question, a questionnaire's format. If the survey is critical, get help from an expert in marketing, sociology, or psychology to design and administer it.

- Analyze open-ended questions by reading and summarizing the responses, question by question. Establish a uniform procedure and format if several people are analyzing responses.

- If confidentiality was promised to respondents, maintain confidentiality at all costs.

- A complete report of the results and analysis should have an appendix with all the raw data, including responses to open-ended questions. Mask any responses that reveal the respondent's identity or refer to individuals.

- Send everyone who received a survey a summary of the results and what you plan to do. This is not only a courtesy, but can improve the response rate the next time you conduct a survey.

Top-Down Flowchart

Description

A top-down flowchart shows the most important steps of a process or project and the first layer of substeps. This kind of flowchart emphasizes the big picture.

When to Use

- When you are beginning to study a complex process and need to start with the big picture
- When beginning to plan a project
- Whenever you need to get an overview of a process or project
- When you want to focus on the ideal process
- When you can't see the forest for the trees

Procedure

1. Define the process to be diagrammed. Write it on a large card or Post-It™ note and place at the top of the work surface. Discuss and decide on the boundaries of your process: Where or when does the process start? Where or when does it end?

2. Brainstorm the main steps in the process. There should be about six or eight. Write each on a card or note and place them in a line across the top of your paper.

3. Brainstorm the major substeps of the first main step. Again, there should be no more than six or eight. Write each on a card and place them in order vertically below the first main step.

4. Repeat for each main step.

5. When the group agrees that you have all the steps and substeps and that the sequence is correct, draw horizontal arrows leading from one main step to the next. Draw arrows pointing down from each main step to the first substep. You can draw arrows pointing down between substeps, but they are not necessary. Do not draw an arrow below the last substep of each vertical column.

6. Check with others involved in the process (workers, supervisors, suppliers, customers) to see if they agree that the process is as drawn.

Example

A group beginning a quality improvement project drew a top-down flow-chart (Figure 4.94) to guide the first phase of the effort. The major steps are

1. Determine customer needs.

2. Determine current state.

3. Identify focus area(s).

Under each major step are three to six substeps that detail what must be done to accomplish each step.

Considerations

- This is a fast method for flowcharting a process.

- This flowchart focuses on the essential components of a process or project. By comparing it to the way things are really done, the sources of waste and complexity can quickly become obvious.[47]

- Use the top-down flowchart to get an overview of the entire process or project, then construct detailed flowcharts of particular steps as needed.[48]

- See "Flowchart" on page 137 for information about analyzing a flowchart and for additional considerations.

Tree Diagram

How–How Diagram

Description

The tree diagram identifies actions to solve a problem or implement a solution. Developing the tree diagram moves one's thinking logically from broad goals to specifics.

When to Use

- When developing logical steps to achieve an objective

- When developing actions to carry out a solution

- When the objective is broad and vague

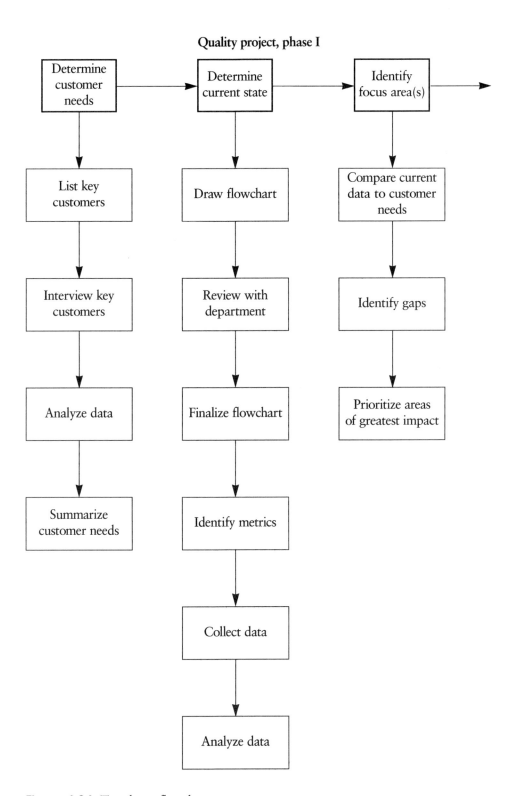

Figure 4.94. Top-down flowchart.

- When the task or objective is complex

- When the action plan must be complete and thorough

- During evaluation of a list of potential solutions, to understand implementation issues for each solution

- After an affinity diagram or relations diagram has uncovered key issues

- As a communication tool, when the many potential actions need to be explained to others

Procedure

Materials needed: cards or Post-It™ notes, large writing surface (newsprint or flipchart paper), marking pens, tape.

1. Develop a statement of what needs to be achieved: the cause to be remedied or objective to be accomplished. Write it on a card and place at the far left of the horizontal work surface.

2. Ask "How can this be accomplished?" Brainstorm all possible means. The answers may be a subgroup of issues that need to be addressed to accomplish the goal. If an affinity diagram or relationship diagram has been done previously, ideas may be taken from there. Write each idea on a card and place the cards in a vertical tier to the right of the objective.

3. Each of the new idea statements now is a problem statement. Again ask "How can this be accomplished?" for each one. Create another tier of statements and show the relationships to the first tier of ideas with arrows.

4. Continue to turn each new idea into a problem and ask "How can this be accomplished?" Do not stop until you reach specific actions that can be carried out.[49]

5. With each new idea, check its relevance by asking, "Will doing this help to accomplish the original objective?" If not, the idea does not belong on the diagram.

6. If this diagram is intended to develop all action steps for a project or program, do a "necessary and sufficient" check of the entire diagram. Are all the specific actions necessary to accomplish the objective? If all the specific actions are done, are they sufficient to accomplish the objective?

Example

Figure 4.95 is a tree diagram used to answer the question, "How can we achieve extraordinary safety performance?" This is a diagram intended to help understand implementation issues for several possible approaches.

The second level answers the question with broad concepts: develop a new approach, modify behavior, or focus attention on safety. The third level expands the concepts with programs that might be pursued, such as publicity to focus attention or benchmarking top performers to develop a new approach. The fourth level shows specific actions for implementing the programs. If the program were benchmarking, a specific action would be assigning a benchmarking team. If the program were publicity, a specific action might be a safety newsletter.

Notice that items can be related to two of the previous levels. "Regular safety meetings" is a specific action that could be used for publicity or training. "Safety council" can be used for employee involvement and senior management attention.

Obviously, not all of these ideas would be used. The purpose of this diagram is to clarify what action steps would be needed for each approach. A team could then evaluate and prioritize these options. In other situations, a tree diagram can be used to lay out all facets of a program or project. In that case, every item on the diagram would have to be completed.

Variation: Why–Why Diagram

The tree diagram can be used to uncover multiple causes of a problem, until the root cause is revealed. See "Why–Why Diagram" on page 271 for a separate description of this use.

Variation: Requirements-and Measures Tree

The tree diagram format can be used to work through the customers, requirements, and measures of a product or service. See "Requirements-and-Measures Tree" on page 242 for a separate description of this use.

Considerations

- The team may prefer to follow one branch to its end before addressing other branches.
- Ideas in a later tier may be related to several earlier ideas.

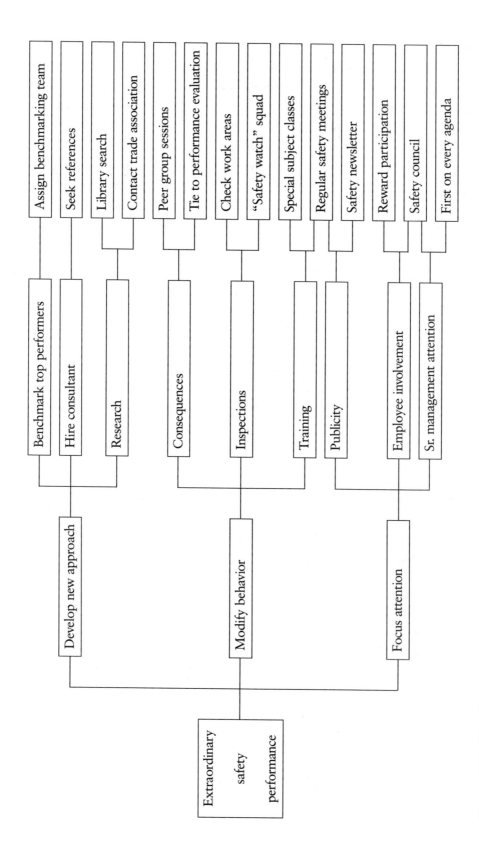

Figure 4.95. Tree diagram example.

- It is a good idea to review the completed diagram with those who will be involved in the actions. Ask for their comments and be willing to make changes based on their suggestions.

- When the tree diagram is used to solve a problem, it is sometimes called a how–how diagram.

- A good description of the tree diagram can be found in *The Memory Jogger Plus+* (Brassard). (See "Recommended Reading" at the back of this book.)

Why–Why Diagram

Description
The why–why diagram helps to identify the root causes of a problem. In addition, the diagram helps the team to recognize the broad network of problem causes and the relationship among these causes. It can indicate the best areas to address for short- and long-term solutions.

When to Use
- When the team needs to probe for the root cause of a problem
- When the team's analysis of a problem is too superficial
- When the many contributing causes to a problem are confusing
- As a graphic communication tool, to explain the many causes of a problem to others

Procedure
Materials needed: cards or Post-It™ notes, newsprint or flipchart paper, marking pens, tape.

1. Develop a statement of the specific problem to be solved. Write it on a note and place it at the far left of the work paper.

2. Ask "Why?" this problem does or could occur. List all these causes on notes and place them in a column immediately to the right of the problem.

3. Each of the cause statements now becomes a new problem state-ment. Again ask "Why?" Sometimes the question needs to be

phrased, "Why does this situation cause the problem?" Create another column of cause statements. Show the relationships to the first column of causes with arrows.

4. Continue to turn each cause into a problem and ask "Why?" Do not stop until you reach an answer that is fundamental (company policy or procedure, systems, training needs, and so forth).

Example

Figure 4.96 is a why–why diagram that tries to uncover the reasons that "making travel arrangements is a time-consuming hassle." At the second level, there are two answers to the question "Why?" The secretary interrupts with questions about the travel arrangements, or the tickets arrive with wrong arrangements and must be sent back.

When the question is asked, "Why does the secretary interrupt?" there are six different answers for various types of information the secretary needs. When "Why?" is asked again for each of those, the answers come back to three possibilities: the secretary doesn't know the traveler's requirements, doesn't know company policies, or doesn't know if the trip is firm. Notice that the end of one chain of causes involving the secretary is a very broad systemic problem: no training program exists.

Look at the cause, "Traveler's requirements not known by secretary." One cause of that is "Temporary secretary." It is not useful to ask "Why is there a temporary secretary?" That question diverts us from our original problem. The appropriate question is "Why does having a temporary secretary cause this problem?" Then the answer is, "Poor communication of requirements to secretary."

Considerations

- You can construct the diagram directly on flipchart paper or a board, but using Post-It™ notes makes construction of the diagram easier.

- The team may prefer to follow one cause statement to its end before thinking about other causes.

- Causes in a column on the right may be related to more than one earlier cause.

- If you prefer, place your problem statement at the top of a vertical board or flipchart and list causes in rows under it.

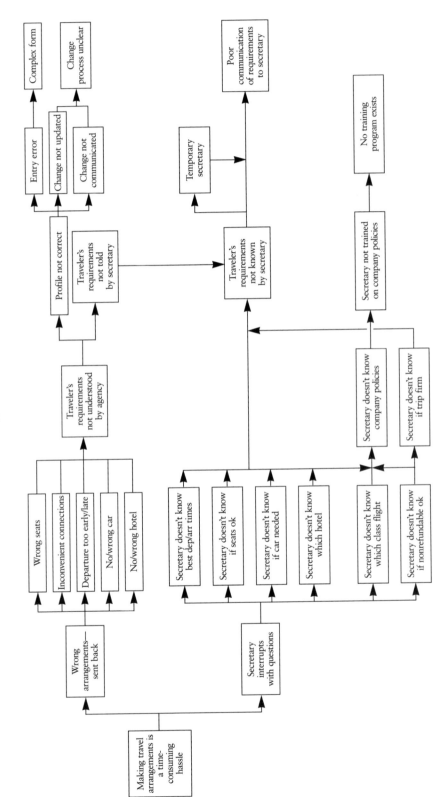

Figure 4.96. Why–why diagram example.

- Don't stop when you reach a "who." Keep asking why. "Whos" are convenient ways to point fingers, but they are not root causes.

- The longer the chain of causes to the end point, the more likely it is that the end point deals with system issues such as management policies.[50] These deeper causes usually lead to a more complete, fundamental solution to a problem. Addressing causes that arise early in the chain often amounts to applying a Band-aid™; addressing deeper causes provides long-term solutions to the problem.

- Tackling deeper causes also can solve other, related problems. When you respond to the surface causes of problems, each solution applies to only one problem. When you focus on one problem and dig deeper, you hit bedrock. The deeper cause usually involves fundamental, underlying systems. In digging that deep, you reach a cause whose solution will influence many other problems. For example, establishing a training program for secretaries on company policies would probably solve other problems in addition to travel arrangement hassles.

- The why–why diagram is a variation of the tree diagram.

Work-Flow Diagram

Description

A work-flow diagram is a picture that shows movement through a process. That movement might be of people, materials, paper, or information. The diagram consists of a map (such as a floor plan) of the area where the process takes place and lines showing all movements. The diagram graphically shows inefficiency—unnecessary movement.

When to Use

- When the process being studied involves movement of people, materials, paper, or information

- When trying to eliminate inefficiency

Procedure

1. Decide what it is that moves. This may be paper, a file, a person, a piece of information, or materials.

2. Determine the relevant area of movement. This may be an office, a form to be filled out, or five offices located around the world. Develop or obtain a representation of that area: a floor plan, a copy of the form, a map, and so forth.

3. Develop a list of the process steps, in sequence. The best way to do this is to develop or obtain a flowchart of the process.

4. Draw lines on the layout showing every movement of the item as the process proceeds from step to step. If the movement in a step follows the same path as the movement in a previous step, draw another line.

Example

The paper flow of the process for filling an order is tracked on the work-flow diagram of Figure 4.97. This is the same process flowcharted in

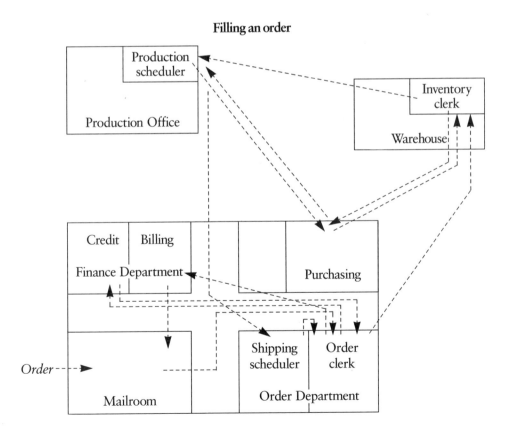

Figure 4.97. Work-flow diagram example.

Figure 4.33. The work-flow diagram follows the path of the pieces of paper that are needed to complete the process.

The map of the production office, warehouse, and main offices (located in three separate buildings) was drawn first. Then the team drawing the diagram mentally walked through the process, starting with the first step on the flowchart, "Order received." Each paper movement was drawn with an arrow. If a movement followed the same path as a previous movement, another arrow was drawn.

The paper does a lot of traveling. Notice that credit and billing are located together in the finance department, but they do not interact in this process. Perhaps physical arrangement according to paper flow would be more efficient than the present arrangement by departments.

Considerations

- Look for excessive, repetitive, or unnecessary movement.[51]

- Try to rearrange the layout or the process to reduce or eliminate movement.

- If information is passed electronically rather than on paper, the physical layout becomes irrelevant.

Appendix

Table A.1. Area under the normal curve.

z	0.00	0.01	0.02	0.03	0.04	0.05	0.06	0.07	0.08	0.09
−3.5	.00023	.00022	.00022	.00021	.00020	.00019	.00019	.00018	.00017	.00017
−3.4	.00034	.00033	.00031	.00030	.00029	.00028	.00027	.00026	.00025	.00024
−3.3	.00048	.00047	.00045	.00043	.00042	.00040	.00039	.00038	.00036	.00035
−3.2	.00069	.00066	.00064	.00062	.00060	.00058	.00056	.00054	.00052	.00050
−3.1	.00097	.00094	.00090	.00087	.00085	.00082	.00079	.00076	.00074	.00071
−3.0	.00135	.00131	.00126	.00122	.00118	.00114	.00111	.00107	.00104	.00010
−2.9	.0019	.0018	.0017	.0017	.0016	.0016	.0015	.0015	.0014	.0014
−2.8	.0026	.0025	.0024	.0023	.0023	.0022	.0021	.0021	.0020	.0019
−2.7	.0035	.0034	.0033	.0032	.0031	.0030	.0029	.0028	.0027	.0026
−2.6	.0047	.0045	.0044	.0043	.0041	.0040	.0039	.0038	.0037	.0036
−2.5	.0062	.0060	.0059	.0057	.0055	.0054	.0052	.0051	.0049	.0048
−2.4	.0082	.0080	.0078	.0075	.0073	.0071	.0069	.0068	.0066	.0064
−2.3	.0107	.0104	.0102	.0099	.0096	.0094	.0091	.0089	.0087	.0084
−2.2	.0139	.0136	.0132	.0129	.0125	.0122	.0119	.0116	.0113	.0110
−2.1	.0179	.0174	.0170	.0166	.0162	.0158	.0154	.0150	.0146	.0143
−2.0	.0228	.0222	.0217	.0212	.0207	.0202	.0197	.0192	.0188	.0183
−1.9	.0287	.0281	.0274	.0268	.0262	.0256	.0250	.0244	.0239	.0233
−1.8	.0359	.0351	.0344	.0336	.0329	.0322	.0314	.0307	.0301	.0294
−1.7	.0446	.0436	.0427	.0418	.0409	.0401	.0392	.0384	.0375	.0367
−1.6	.0548	.0537	.0526	.0516	.0505	.0495	.0485	.0475	.0465	.0455
−1.5	.0668	.0655	.0643	.0630	.0618	.0606	.0594	.0582	.0571	.0559
−1.4	.0808	.0793	.0778	.0764	.0749	.0735	.0721	.0708	.0694	.0681
−1.3	.0968	.0951	.0934	.0918	.0901	.0885	.0869	.0853	.0838	.0823
−1.2	.1151	.1131	.1112	.1093	.1075	.1057	.1038	.1020	.1003	.0985
−1.1	.1357	.1335	.1314	.1292	.1271	.1251	.1230	.1210	.1190	.1170
−1.0	.1587	.1562	.1539	.1515	.1492	.1469	.1446	.1423	.1401	.1379
−0.9	.1841	.1814	.1788	.1762	.1736	.1711	.1685	.1660	.1635	.1611
−0.8	.2119	.2090	.2061	.2033	.2005	.1977	.1949	.1922	.1894	.1867
−0.7	.2420	.2389	.2358	.2327	.2297	.2266	.2236	.2207	.2177	.2148
−0.6	.2743	.2709	.2676	.2643	.2611	.2578	.2546	.2514	.2483	.2451
−0.5	.3085	.3050	.3015	.2981	.2946	.2912	.2877	.2843	.2810	.2776
−0.4	.3446	.3409	.3372	.3336	.3300	.3264	.3228	.3192	.3156	.3121
−0.3	.3821	.3783	.3745	.3707	.3669	.3632	.3594	.3557	.3520	.3483
−0.2	.4207	.4168	.4129	.4090	.4052	.4013	.3974	.3936	.3897	.3859
−0.1	.4602	.4562	.4522	.4483	.4443	.4404	.4364	.4325	.4286	.4247
−0	.5000	.4960	.4920	.4880	.4840	.4801	.4761	.4721	.4681	.4641

Continued

Table A.1. *Continued.*

Z	0.00	0.01	0.02	0.03	0.04	0.05	0.06	0.07	0.08	0.09
0	.5000	.5040	.5080	.5120	.5160	.5199	.5239	.5279	.5319	.5359
0.1	.5398	.5438	.5437	.5517	.5557	.5596	.5636	.5675	.5714	.5753
0.2	.5793	.5832	.5871	.5910	.5948	.5987	.6026	.6064	.6103	.6141
0.3	.6179	.6217	.6255	.6293	.6331	.6368	.6406	.6443	.6480	.6517
0.4	.6554	.6591	.6628	.6664	.6700	.6736	.6772	.6808	.6844	.6879
0.5	.6915	.6950	.6985	.7019	.7054	.7088	.7123	.7157	.7190	.7224
0.6	.7257	.7291	.7324	.7357	.7389	.7422	.7454	.7486	.7517	.7549
0.7	.7580	.7611	.7642	.7673	.7704	.7734	.7764	.7794	.7823	.7852
0.8	.7881	.7910	.7939	.7967	.7995	.8023	.8051	.8079	.8106	.8133
0.9	.8159	.8186	.8212	.8238	.8264	.8289	.8315	.8340	.8365	.8389
1.0	.8413	.8438	.8461	.8485	.8508	.8531	.8554	.8577	.8599	.8621
1.1	.8643	.8665	.8686	.8708	.8729	.8749	.8770	.8790	.8810	.8830
1.2	.8849	.8869	.8888	.8907	.8925	.8944	.8962	.8980	.8997	.9015
1.3	.9032	.9049	.9066	.9082	.9099	.9115	.9131	.9147	.9162	.9177
1.4	.9192	.9207	.9222	.9236	.9251	.9265	.9279	.9292	.9306	.9319
1.5	.9332	.9345	.9357	.9370	.9382	.9394	.9406	.9418	.9429	.9441
1.6	.9452	.9463	.9474	.9484	.9495	.9505	.9515	.9525	.9535	.9545
1.7	.9554	.9564	.9573	.9582	.9591	.9599	.9608	.9616	.9625	.9633
1.8	.9641	.9649	.9658	.9664	.9671	.9678	.9686	.9693	.9699	.9706
1.9	.9713	.9719	.9726	.9732	.9738	.9744	.9750	.9756	.9761	.9767
2.0	.9773	.9778	.9783	.9788	.9793	.9798	.9803	.9808	.9812	.9817
2.1	.9821	.9826	.9830	.9834	.9838	.9842	.9846	.9850	.9854	.9857
2.2	.9861	.9864	.9868	.9871	.9875	.9878	.9881	.9884	.9887	.9890
2.3	.9893	.9896	.9898	.9901	.9904	.9906	.9909	.9911	.9913	.9916
2.4	.9918	.9920	.9922	.9925	.9927	.9929	.9931	.9932	.9934	.9936
2.5	.9938	.9940	.9941	.9943	.9945	.9946	.9948	.9949	.9951	.9952
2.6	.9953	.9955	.9956	.9957	.9959	.9960	.9961	.9962	.9963	.9964
2.7	.9965	.9966	.9967	.9968	.9969	.9970	.0971	.9972	.9973	.9974
2.8	.9974	.9975	.9976	.9977	.9977	.9978	.9979	.9979	.9980	.9981
2.9	.9981	.9982	.9983	.9983	.9983	.9984	.9985	.9985	.9986	.9986
3.0	.99865	.99869	.99874	.99878	.99882	.99886	.99889	.99893	.99896	.99900
3.1	.99903	.99906	.99910	.99913	.99915	.99918	.99921	.99924	.99926	.99929
3.2	.99931	.99934	.99936	.99938	.99940	.99942	.99944	.99946	.99948	.99950
3.3	.99952	.99953	.99955	.99957	.99958	.99960	.99961	.99962	.99964	.99965
3.4	.99966	.99967	.99969	.99970	.99971	.99972	.99973	.99974	.99975	.99976
3.5	.99977	.99978	.99978	.99979	.99980	.99981	.99981	.99982	.99983	.99983

Notes

1. Thomas Gilbert, *Human Competence* (New York: McGraw-Hill, 1978), 150–56.

2. Jeff D. Dewar, "If You Don't Know Where You're Going, How Will You Know When You Get There?" *Chemtech* (April 1989): 214–17.

3. Michael Brassard, *The Memory Jogger Plus+* (Methuen, Mass.: GOAL/QPC, 1989).

4. Ferdinand K. Levy, Gerald L. Thompson, and Jerome D. Wiest, "The ABCs of the Critical Path Method," in *Managing Projects and Programs* (Boston, Mass.: Harvard Business School Press, 1989).

5. Robert W. Miller, "How to Plan and Control with PERT," in *Managing Projects and Programs* (Boston, Mass.: Harvard Business School Press, 1989).

6. Levy, Thompson, and Wiest, "ABCs of the Critical Path Method."

7. This method was developed within Celanese Chemical Company and has been taught by Blanchard Pritchard, former Director of Quality Management for Celanese.

8. Blanchard Pritchard, personal communication, March 1986.

9. Pritchard, personal communication.

10. John W. Tukey, *Exploratory Data Analysis* (Reading, Mass.: Addison-Wesley Publishing Company, 1977).

11. Simple, modified, and modified-width box plot, and parentheses variations from Gerald B. Heyes, "The Box Plot," *Quality Progress* 18, no. 12 (December 1985): 12–17; ghost box plot variation from Gerald B. Heyes, "The GHOST Box Plot," *Statistics Division Newsletter,* ASQC (summer 1988); and box plot control chart from Boris Iglewicz and David C. Hoaglin, "Use of Boxplots for Process Evaluation," *Journal of Quality Technology* 19, no. 4 (October 1987): 180–90.

12. This tool was adapted from materials first published by Xerox and used by the U.S. Air Force Reserve in its quality management training.

13. John T. Burr, "The Tools of Quality; Part I: Going with the Flow(chart)," *Quality Progress* 23, no. 6 (June 1990): 64–67. Reprinted with permission.

14. William S. Cleveland, *The Elements of Graphing Data* (Monterey, Calif.: Wadsworth Advanced Books and Software, 1985).

15. Ibid.

16. Ibid.

17. Ibid.

18. Edward R. Tufte, *The Visual Display of Quantitative Information* (Cheshire, Conn.: Graphics Press, 1983).

19. Cleveland, *The Elements of Graphing Data.*

20. Ibid.

21. Ibid.

22. Ibid.

23. Tukey, *Exploratory Data Analysis;* and Berton H. Gunter, "Subversive Data Analysis, Part I: The Stem and Leaf Display," *Quality Progress* 21, no. 9 (September 1988): 88–89.

24. Kepner-Tregoe, *Analytic Trouble Shooting* (Princeton, N.J.: Kepner-Tregoe, 1966).

25. Charles W. Holland and Robert G. McMillan, *Advanced Statistical Quality Improvement Techniques* (Knoxville, Tenn.: Qual-Pro, 1988).

26. This tool was adapted from materials first published by Xerox and used by the U.S. Air Force Reserve in its quality management training.

27. Brassard, *The Memory Jogger Plus+*.

28. Ibid.

29. Questions 1 through 9 and 11: Peter Scholtes, *The Team Handbook* (Madison, Wis.: Joiner Associates, 1988): 7–32. All rights reserved. Reprinted by the author with permission.

30. Kaoru Ishikawa, *Guide to Quality Control* (Tokyo: Asian Productivity Organization, 1982).

31. James Riggs and Glenn Felix, *Productivity by Objectives* (Englewood Cliffs, N.J.: Prentice Hall, 1983); and Dow Chemical U.S.A., *Performance Indexing: A Tool for Continual Improvement* (Plaquemine, La.: Dow Chemical U.S.A., Louisiana Division, 1987).

32. Edward De Bono, *Serious Creativity* (New York: HarperCollins, 1992).

33. William H. McNees and Robert A. Klein, *Statistical Methods for the Process Industries* (Milwaukee, Wis.: ASQC Quality Press, 1991).

34. Kenneth E. Case and James S. Bigelow, *The Proper Use of Process Capability Indices in SPC,* paper presented at Institute of Industrial Engineers Integrated Systems Conference, Nashville, Tenn., 1987; Gunter, "The Use and Abuse of Cp_k," *Quality Progress* 22, no. 1 (January 1989): 72–73; ———, "The Use and Abuse of Cp_k," *Quality Progress* 22, no. 3 (March 1989): 108–9; ———, "The Use and Abuse of Cp_k," *Quality Progress* 22, no. 5 (May 1989): 70–71; and ———, "The Use and Abuse of Cp_k," *Quality Progress* 22, no. 7 (July 1989): 86–87.

35. Donald Wheeler and David Chambers, *Understanding Statistical Process Control* (Knoxville, Tenn.: Keith Press, 1986).

36. Brassard, *The Memory Jogger Plus+*.

37. Ibid.

38. Ibid.

39. Ibid.

40. Ibid.

41. Ishikawa, *Guide to Quality Control.*

42. Storyboards and storyboarding were created by Walt Disney Studios for developing cartoons.

43. Dick Shepard, "Storyboard: A Creative, Team-Based Approach to Planning and Problem-Solving," *Continuous Journey* 1, no. 2 (December 1992/January 1993): 24–32.

44. Ibid.

45. Ibid.

46. Lori Long, *Surveys from Start to Finish* (Alexandria, Va.: American Society for Training and Development, 1986).

47. Scholtes, *The Team Handbook.*

48. Ibid.

49. Gregg D. Stocker, "How to Turn Concepts Into Action," *Quality Progress* 26, no. 1 (January 1993): 45–48.

50. Howard H. Bailie, "Organize Your Thinking with a Why–Why Diagram," *Quality Progress* 18, no. 12 (December 1985): 22–24.

51. Scholtes, *The Team Handbook.*

Recommended Reading

Brassard, Michael. *The Memory Jogger Plus+*. Methuen, Mass.: GOAL/ QPC, 1989.

Cleveland, William S. *The Elements of Graphing Data*. Monterey, Calif.: Wadsworth Advanced Books and Software, 1985.

De Bono, Edward. *Serious Creativity*. New York: HarperCollins, 1992.

Deming, W. Edwards. *Out of the Crisis*. Cambridge, Mass.: Massachusetts Institute of Technology, Center for Advanced Engineering Study, 1986.

Imai, Masaaki. *Kaizen: The Key to Japan's Competitive Success*. New York: Random House, 1986.

Ishikawa, Kaoru. *Guide to Quality Control*. Tokyo: Asian Productivity Organization, 1982.

Kepner-Tregoe. *Analytic Trouble Shooting*. Princeton, N.J.: Kepner-Tregoe, 1966.

McNees, William H., and Robert A. Klein. *Statistical Methods for the Process Industries*. Milwaukee, Wis.: ASQC Quality Press, 1991.

Scholtes, Peter. *The Team Handbook*. Madison, Wis.: Joiner Associates, 1988.

Tufte, Edward R. *The Visual Display of Quantitative Information*. Chesire, Conn.: Graphics Press, 1983.

Tukey, John W. *Exploratory Data Analysis.* Reading, Mass.: Addison-Wesley, 1977.

Wheeler, Donald, and David Chambers. *Understanding Statistical Process Control.* Knoxville, Tenn.: Keith Press, 1986.

Index